THE BRINGER OF LIFE

A Cosmic History of the Divine Feminine

Hayley A. Ramsey

Foreword by Scott F. Wolter

Adventures Unlimited Press

Acknowledgements

I would like to thank my family, Scott Wolter and
David Hatcher Childress and Adventures Unlimited Press.

THE BRINGER OF LIFE

A Cosmic History of the Divine Feminine

Hayley A. Ramsey

The Bringer of Life

by Hayley A. Ramsey

Copyright © 2023

All Rights Reserved

ISBN 978-1-948803-58-8

Published by:
Adventures Unlimited Press
One Adventure Place
Kempton, Illinois 60946 USA
auphq@frontiernet.net

www.AdventuresUnlimitedPress.com

Photos, unless otherwise noted, are by Hayley A. Ramsey

THE BRINGER OF LIFE

A Cosmic History of the Divine Feminine

TABLE OF CONTENTS

Foreword
by Scott F. Wolter

Every now and then, a soul comes into the world that just gets it. One of those souls appeared in 1999, a time when the world was becoming increasingly unstable and darkness was starting to set in. That soul had a challenging beginning, but thrived upon reaching adulthood. Before turning 20, this book was already on its way and has blossomed into the book in your hands as the author turns 23. Early on Hayley Ramsey was captivated by the mysteries of Knights Templar and their reverence of the ancient Goddess so many other Templar researchers never picked up on. It was one of the most tightly held secrets within the order and as anyone who has been initiated with knowledge of the ancient mysteries knows, the best place to hide something is in plain sight. It began in the early twelfth Century when the charismatic leader of the Cistercian order, Bernard de Clairvaux, who also wrote the charter for the Poor Knights of the Temple of Jerusalem, later known as the Knights Templar.

Bernard had a fascination with the Virgin Mary to the point where the Catholic authorities became uncomfortable. His miracle is the Blessed Virgin nursing her child on one breast, with her other exposed breast squirting mother's milk into Bernard's mouth. No wonder the Church at the time was a bit squeamish, but they would have lost their minds if they knew Bernard's truth. The Virgin was simply a metaphor for his true belief in the ancient Mother Goddess who represented one half of the dualistic aspect of Deity that was meant to be honored and respected on an equal level with the Male aspect. The Church would have considered this the ultimate heresy that took two centuries for them to finally figure out. The Inquisition made exaggerated claims of heresy that justified the arrest of hundreds of knights, dozens being tortured and eventually burned at the stake. Was the eradication of the Templars really all about money and perceived heretical acts? Or was the Goddess one of the untold truths behind the suppression of the Templars in 1307 the Church had pushed into the shadows for over 700 years. But like all dirty little secrets people try to hide, sooner or later they come out into the light. Ramsey will also address the age-old question within Masonic circles where a consensus has still not reached; did the medieval Knights Templar evolve into modern Freemasonry? Along with this is the other elephant in the room, if the answer is yes, then was the Templars veiled adoration of the Goddess also brought into the lodge. The answer to these questions will likely come as a surprise.

Who is the Goddess and why was she so revered in ancient times? Is Goddess veneration still around and if so, where can she be found today? Ramsey does a deep dive into the history of cultures who revered the Goddess and what her journey has been over the past five millennia. What makes this work so important is the timing of examining the role of the Goddess in ancient times to the present. The world is currently going through unprecedented challenging times, be it horrific racism, misogyny, political division and COVID-19 pandemic to the war in Ukraine that has brought humanity to the brink of Word War III. Is it merely coincidence these tragedies have reached unprecedented levels or is there more to the story?

Some like me would say yes, and point to a scientific reason that also incorporates mystical prophecy that is tied directly to a little known astronomical phenomenon known as the Precession of the Equinoxes. Precession is a 26,000 year-long cycle of the movement of the zodiacal belt of the twelve primary constellations that encircle the earth. Astronomer priests throughout millennia have tracked precession marking its movement on the morning of the spring equinox annually with each constellation spending approximately 2170 years as the primary constellation in the eastern sky for its "Great Month." Because of the earth's slight wobble as it rotates, the movement of the zodiacal belt slowly progresses as does the history of humanity when considered in association.

Events such as the building of the Sphinx in Egypt, which originally had the head of a lion that faces due east staring at the constellation of Leo at the time it was constructed, geologists now say was over 10,000 years ago. During the change of the age of

Taurus the Bull to Aries the Ram, we saw the change from the old religion of Polytheistic Dualism in Egypt to the new religion of Monotheistic Dualism roughly 3,500 years ago. The attempt by Pharaoh Akhenaten to implement the change in religion is symbolized by the images of him holding the Shepherd's crook, which herds the rams and sheep of Aries, and the flail which herds the bulls and Taurus the Bull crossed on his chest.

The next change in the ages of precession was when Aries gave way to Pisces the Fish roughly 2,000 years ago. This change corresponded with arguably one of the influential and important moments in history, when John the Baptist, dressed in a sheep's wool, holding a Shepherd's crook with a lamb in his arms or at his feet, all symbols of Aries the Ram, initiated (baptized if Roman Christian) Jesus who became the "Fisher King" or new king in the new age of Pisces the fish. Precession has brought us to the present when the constellation of Pisces has descended below the horizon and a new constellation is about to take its place.

This change in age alone is a significant event, but this time marks not only the end of a great month, but also the end of the "Great Year" of the 26,000 cycle. What we all are living through now is one of the most profound moments in human history and the world is largely oblivious to it. Mystics say this transition to the new age of the new year will begin with great challenges and difficulties to humanity we are in the middle of at this very moment. The prophecies also say that if we are able to overcome these challenges, the future indeed looks bright. However, to get through the challenges we now face it is important to know the truth about where we have already been.

This book is part of the education of the masses that is vital to our very survival as a species. The curious will be encouraged to learn the new Great Year begins with the constellation of Aquarius, the feminine water-bearer which brings life, just like the Goddess has always done throughout time. Who better to bring the light of the Goddess than a true heavenly gift at the beginning of the Age of Aquarius? That gift is Hayley Ramsey and her wonderful and important work in this book.

Chapter 1
The Cosmic Womb

What are we? And truly, who are we? What are we made of? These are all questions the majority of mankind ponders at some point in life. Quite simply we are the Universe. We are carefully composed of all the elements that make stars. How crazy is that? This is a quite simple way of putting it—but frankly it is not simple at all. The Universe is complicated, intricate, and incomprehensibly magnificent. There are no boundaries, no limits, and it is capable of nearly anything and everything.

The basic and main elements that make up the human body consist of Hydrogen, Oxygen, Carbon, Iron, Nickel, and many more. According to Dr. Judith Ries at University of Texas at Austin, nearly 100 tons of cosmic dust falls to the Earth every day. That is approximately 40,000 tons a year. Now much like the stars, our bodies are shedding particles and regenerating them constantly. This is similar to the way our bodies produce chemical elements constantly. But how old are these materials in our bodies that were once exploding stars?

Who is ultimately birthing life? Who has always birthed life? To answer that question, with our modern-day knowledge, it has always been females. In cases when life has come about another way it typically was by way of technology and not nature. In nature we find consistency and symmetry. For as long as nature has been observed, the female has always been the mother and she still is today.

If the female has always been the bringer of life, who is to say our Universe was not created by a feminine Creator, or Creatress? By considering this we are looking at the most ancient and prevalent traces of creation. Man cannot create life on his own. However, there are cases when females can reproduce on their own, asexually. When females reproduce solely on their own, this is known as "parthenogenesis." Genesis literally means origin, while it is no coincidence that *parthenos* is the Greek word for virgin. Could women at one point in human history conceive by parthenogenesis? If so, what changed and when?

Parthenogenesis currently is seen occurring in lower plants and invertebrate animals like rotifers, aphids, ants, wasps, and bees, but rarely among higher vertebrates. It is thought that over 2,000 species can reproduce through parthenogenesis in today's world. Is this just simply an adaptive trait? Or is this how it was originally? All human embryos start off as female in the womb, afterall.

As far as we know, the Big Bang was the beginning of existence as we know it. Imagine absolute silence so silent that it was loud. Then *bam*! A large boom echoes around us as cosmic energy collapses and then explodes and expands, but never stops expanding. This Big Bang never really ended. This expansion, or birth, that began 14 billion years ago is still expanding today. This expansion will continue to accelerate forever—and the only thing we can attribute it to is an energy form that we do not really know or understand. This is referred to as dark energy.

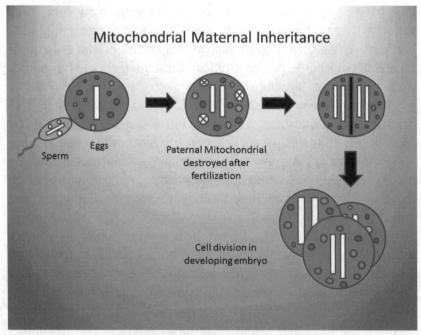

Mitochondrial Maternal Inheritance DNA diagram.

We cannot see it, hear it, touch it, but we do know it is there. Is this truly the reason for the Big Bang? Probably. Do we know why, what, or how? No. Scientists have come to believe that dark matter is what black holes are partially made from. Black holes could very well represent the Big Bang but on a smaller scale, showing the expansion of the universe within one energetic sphere. We still do not really understand what a black hole is—there have been movies made about it, such as *Interstellar,* speculating, trying to make sense of the vast cosmic mysteries that we have yet to understand. Do these black holes span different dimensions? What *are* they? Could they hold the keys to understanding the Big Bang and therefore creation? In 1971 Stephen Hawking proposed that black holes had formed in the very chaotic beginning of the Big Bang. If this were the case, black holes would have existed well before the first stars began to brighten up the cosmos.

Some might even wonder if this dark energy is "God," "Goddess," or some kind of divine creation energy. Goddess would seem to be appropriate because birth or creation energy would have a feminine feel to it, correct? She is often associated with *darkness* after all. Could this "dark energy" really be the cosmic thing that surrounds us, fills us with spiritual or religious energy when things work out in our favor? The energy that hears and sometimes answers our prayers? The only thing I have heard this attributed to is God, or something divine. This would make sense because we cannot hear, touch, or see a physical God/Goddess, so why couldn't our divine creator be an energy of some sort? Afterall, we are all an energy force in constant motion.

If we consider that female organisms are the only gender known to birth life whether its sexual, asexual, or parthenogenetic, it would be biologically probable and possible that the energy that essentially "birthed" the cosmos might be a feminine energy. This may be proven or disproven someday in our Universal future. However, if it is proven, can you imagine what this means spiritually *and* scientifically? This would take cosmic evolution to a whole new level. As well as our perception of life and creation. Could this even have something to do with our ancestors' perception of Earth being feminine and the Sun always being masculine?

There is obviously a difference in energy emitted from males and females. If we could put numbers behind these energies, could we define what masculine and what feminine energy is? There has to be a balance between opposites, cosmic dualism (which we will discuss later on) if you will. Throw out every personal belief, every opinion, and let's explore this ideological theory with fresh eyes.

When most stars die, they explode and emit intense light energy. This chemical reaction produces all of the elements necessary for organic material to be created—and then life to eventually develop. Perhaps the ideas that our ancestors had about stars being masculine (solar deities) were in fact not so far-fetched. This would imply that space is feminine and dark, perhaps even one large womb for starlight (the masculine) and chemical energies to inhabit, and then eventually create life.

In saying this, I would like to propose a theory that it seems the ancients were well aware of. What I would like to propose is this: *The Cosmic Womb Theory.* What does this mean? Exactly what it sounds like! The Big Bang was started by something, this dark energy, and what if it were determined to be a feminine energy? Then the expansion of the Universe is really just an expansion of a giant womb (the feminine), where stars (the masculine) can explode and fill the cosmos with its potentially life creating material, and then bam, create life! We made it here somehow, right? Just by being in the right conditions, at exactly the right time…

The Cosmic Womb Theory shows that the sacred union of two opposites started a long time ago. The Universe birthed Herself, and then created stars (putting it simply), so that in turn these two forces could create organic material to create life. For human reproduction, a masculine and a feminine force is also needed. Literally, we are children of the cosmos. Special, right? This is a means of cosmic reproduction absolutely necessary for us to be here, or for any life for that matter!

When a star goes supernova, it can end in two ways. It can continuously contract into a ball of neutrons until it becomes a compact white dwarf. When it stops emitting light, it becomes known as a black dwarf. The alternative ending to a supernova is simple and not so simple at the same time: a black hole. A black hole is made from dark matter, something else we really cannot see or detect aside from its gravity. Could these black holes be made of the same dark energy that could possibly be feminine? What do black holes really do aside from suck in anything and everything in their wake? Do they actually take all of the matter they attract and recycle it into the cosmic womb for a type of cosmic rebirth?

There are many ancient cultures that believed and taught this, one being Vedic philosophy. They call the source of creation *Hiraṇyagarbha,* which is Sanskrit for "golden womb" or even "universal womb." It is considered the source of the Universe's birth and creation, and even referred to as the soul of the universe. The Hiraṇyagarbha Sūkta, the supreme god of gods, was said to have floated around in the darkness of the universal womb for a year or so. While he is referred to as the god of gods, he is born from the great universal womb, implying a connection to a feminine presence... perhaps Shakti?

The Universe around us is just waiting patiently for us to explore Her, discover Her secrets, and ultimately understand where we came from. The ancients seemed to have a pretty good idea.

"She is the Universal Womb. She is before everything." —The Secret Book of John

1.1 Shakti

The Hindu cosmic creation story is attributed to *Shakti.* This is the primordial cosmic energy, the energy that spurred the Universe into ecstatic motion. This energy is not only creative, but destructive, and the ultimate energy Source of the cosmos. Shakti is sometimes referred to as the *creatrix* and is known as "Adi Shakti" or "Adi Para Shakti." Adi Shakti is the primordial inconceivable energy, the supreme being they would call God— except that Shakti is in fact, considered the *divine feminine; she* is God-dess, seen as mother and creator goddess. She is considered infinite, *Anaadi,* with no end and no beginning. Instead Shakti is simply forever, *Nitya.* Perhaps Jesus himself embodied the Shakti energy, and even taught it. Could this be why he called himself the *alpha and omega,* the *beginning and end?* We will dive into this concept more in Chapter 11.3.

What is important here, is that other ancient cultures attributed the unseen God energy to the Goddess, much as I propose in the beginning of this chapter. If Shakti is the primordial cosmic creation energy, then She could be what dark energy, dark matter, and black holes are made of, right?

One of the oldest representations of Shakti in India is in the form of a triangular shaped stone, dating back 10,000 years. The stone is most commonly known as the Baghor Stone, an Upper Paleolithic archaeological artifact discovered near the village of Medhauli in the Sidhi District of Madhya Pradesh, India, in the Son River Valley. The stone, which has been interpreted as a goddess cult object, was discovered near the base of the Kaimur Escarpment at Baghor I during the first excavations in 1980. The site was occupied between 9,000 BC and 8,000 BC. The artifact was found sitting in the center of what appeared to be an altar, which was likely used for ritualistic purposes.

Other names for Shakti include *Amma,* which tends to sound a lot like "Ma" or "Mama." One form of Shakti's name I find most interesting is *Mariamman.* In this context, Amman actually means "mother" and "Mari" means rain/water. (See Chapter 16.1 for more on the goddess etymology.)

Shakti's masculine counterpart is Shiva, but Shiva came after Shakti. This is also reminiscent of the gnostic creation story.[1] Therefore Shiva is the son and consort of Shakti. Shiva also embodies the beginning and end, creator and destroyer aspect. Shiva's worship has always been secondary to Shakti's reverence, as he is just a secondary part of Her.

The *Shaktisangama Tantra* says, "Woman is the creator of the universe, the universe is Her form; woman is the foundation of the world, She is the true form of the body. In woman is the form of all things, of all that lives and moves in the world. There is no jewel rarer than woman, no condition superior to that of a woman."

Hindu teachings explain that every woman is the goddess incarnate; that every woman who walks upon this planet has Shakti within her. Simply put: that creation energy that birthed the

---

[1] See Chapter 9.7 The Ophites & Gnostic Creation

cosmos is living within each woman and is waiting to be tapped into.

Kundalini is born from *Shakti*. Kundalini is an energy that is said to be within all humans, a dormant energy that is longing to be awakened. Kundalini literally translates to "coiled snake." The spine and the seven chakras were often equated with a snake. Kundalini is the divine feminine energy of Shakti, the formless aspect of the goddess, that rests at the base of the spine, the root chakra. Kundalini is to be awakened by tantric practice which then leads to spiritual liberation. This can be achieved through yoga, mantra, and tantra—or tantric sex.

In tantric traditions Kundalini is "the innate intelligence of embodied Consciousness." Kunda is a noun that means "bowl," "water-pot," or "vessel." These are shapes and objects often associated with the female womb, the goddess, fittingly. Kunda is also the name of a serpent deity found in the Mahabharata. This is one of the age-old associations of the goddess and the serpent.

The first time that *kundalini* appears to be mentioned is in an eighth century text, *Tantrasadbhāva-tantra*. However, there are other earlier tantras that talk about the concept of the movement of the *Shakti energy* in an upward channel from the base of the spine. Professor David Gordon White, an Indologist, points out that this divine feminine energy is also referred to as *bhogavati*. This word means both "coiled" *and* "enjoyment." The goddess has always been associated with pleasure, but this brings both the physical pleasure as well as the spiritual bliss, or transcendence, found in *moksha*. Moksha is the ultimate escape of the matrix, if you will. Within moksha the Seeker is able to escape the cycle of life and death, achieve enlightenment, spiritual immortality, and attain knowledge of their One True Self. This sounds a little like the monopoly that the Roman Catholic Church has on *salvation* now doesn't it?

Moksha is considered the bliss of Shiva's creativity, but also of his union with Shakti. Moksha is seen to be achieved when Shiva and the goddess Shakti enter Divine Union with each other. This Divine Union between them is one of tantric lovemaking, giving and receiving the Kundalini between each other.

Kundalini is often said to be a "cosmic energy" that originates at the base of the spine and rises all the way up to the crown chakra similar to prana. The yogi Gopi Krishna believed that, "As the ancient writers have said, it is the vital force or prana which is spread over both the macrocosm, the entire Universe, and the microcosm, the human body... The atom is contained in both of these. Prana is life-energy responsible for the phenomena of terrestrial life and for life on other planets in the universe. Prana in its universal aspect is immaterial. But in the human body, Prana creates a fine biochemical substance which works in the whole organism and is the main agent of activity in the nervous system and in the brain. The brain is alive only because of Prana." In Hindu tradition, Prana is the energy that is within all things, originating from the Sun, or even larger cosmic bodies.

The American professor and mythologist Joseph Campbell explained Kundalini as, "the figure of a coiled female serpent—a serpent goddess not of 'gross' but 'subtle' substance—which is to be thought of as residing in a torpid, slumbering state in a subtle center, the first of the seven, near the base of the spine: the aim of the yoga then being to rouse this serpent, lift her head, and bring her up a subtle nerve or channel of the spine to the so-called 'thousand-petaled lotus' (Sahasrara) at the crown of the head... She, rising from the lowest to the highest lotus center will pass through and wake the five between, and with each waking, the psychology and personality of the practitioner will be altogether and fundamentally transformed."

What we can conclude is that the Hindu people had a very expansive concept of the divine feminine, the cosmic creation energies that we are still baffled by today in modern physics, and the way of awakening those energies within our own bodies for spiritual enlightenment. If the Kundalini is within all of us, does this mean that we all have the ability of achieving union with the goddess?

1.2 Biological Maternal Inheritance

What if someone told you that you only inherit mitochondria from your mother? Could it be true? The answer is a startling... yes! Even more startling, no one truly understands why paternal mitochondrial DNA is just wiped completely off the record. Our cells are saying, *that is not the important stuff. This is!*

So what are mitochondria? According to the U.S. Library of Medicine, mitochondria are, "structures within cells that convert the energy from food into a form that cells can use. Each cell contains hundreds to thousands of mitochondria, which are located in the fluid that surrounds the nucleus (the cytoplasm)... mitochondria also have a small amount of their own DNA... In humans, mitochondrial DNA spans about 16,500 DNA building blocks (base pairs), representing a small fraction of the total DNA in cells."

How amazing is it that the most important DNA we have that feeds other cells, that tells other cells how to behave, how to convert energy, how to survive essentially, is passed from mother to child? What a seemingly strange thing. Could this imply we had to come from one original woman, and not a man? Many questions are raised. Another being, why is the male's mtDNA eliminated as if it does not matter? At the beginning of our ancestry, was male mtDNA irrelevant? Were females able to reproduce on their own? Or perhaps this was an adaptive mechanism that evolved over time due to a lack of males. Do we have female ancestors that were capable of parthenogenesis? Modern science still cannot answer that question. Maybe someday these questions can be answered, and more importantly point to bigger truths. Does everything point to a cosmic mother? Be it energy or physical?

1.3 The Genetic Eve

We are all familiar with the name Eve, the biblical mother of all who screwed it up for humanity. More on that Eve later. For now we will dive into the one woman that science says all homo sapiens have descended from. Who is this Eve, and how long ago did she exist?

Now that we have a better understanding of mitochondrial DNA, it will make it much easier to explore the genetic past leading back to our ancestral mother. Deep in all of our mitochondrial DNA, all of us have a common female ancestor known today to DNA experts as *mitochondrial Eve.* How did this come to pass? No, Eve was never the first human, but rather the only human that all modern-day humans ever descended from. This happened sometime in genetic history where women of other lineages failed to produce offspring. Therefore, no other mitochondrial lineages continued to exist within DNA.

Mitochondrial Eve existed somewhere between 100,000-200,000 years ago. We know that modern humans, homo sapiens, originated in Africa about 300,000 years ago due to a change in climate according to the Smithsonian Institute.[2] It was likely in the next 100,000 years that our common ancestor existed.

There are so many questions to be answered about this one common ancestor of ours. Why do we not know who her mother was and so on and so forth? Was she the first in her own lineage to have evolved into a *Homo sapiens*? Who was it that was our ancestral father in that same sense, our Adam? We do not know since male mitochondrial DNA is not passed down. You have to wonder, was there ever a time when male mtDNA *was* passed down? If so, when did it stop?

Ultimately, all humans that exist today are all related back to this one woman about 200,000 years ago. That is about 7 billion people currently living, that are all descended from one woman, not to mention all those that have lived and existed from then until now. What a genetic legacy. Imagine how different the world and evolution could have been if there had been other female lineages that also existed beyond our mtEve?

[2] *"Homo sapiens."* The Smithsonian Institution's Human Origins Program, 22 Jan. 2021, https://humanorigins.si.edu/evidence/human-fossils/species/homo-sapiens.

Chapter 2
The Goddess and Creation

Our home planet, Earth, is the only planet we are aware of that contains thriving life. Our "Mother" planet has been worshiped since the dawn of intelligent life on Earth. Going back before men and women were here to worship her, our planet took a really long time to become what she is today. A long time ago, cosmic debris was pulled into Earth's place in the solar system by the Sun's gravity.

The Sun then heated this debris as it rotated much like the Earth still does today. As it rotated it picked up more and more debris, being heated by the Sun, until it became so hot and compact it cooled into the rocky ball that evolved later to host life. Of course this process took millions and millions of years.

The way the Sun's rays penetrated the cosmic debris and gravitationally pulled it into the perfect place it is in today is perhaps one of the most beautiful and poetic happenings in our Universal history. Because of the Sun's gravity, light and heat energy, the Sun captured our Earth right into place so she could turn into a planet that could host life. Then to imagine we are here billions of years later is extraordinary. The Universe seemed to know what she was doing all along.

Now eventually two elements seem to run into each other at just the right time. This is the most important love story in the history of life. Two lonely elements collide to form an unbreakable bond that becomes cosmically constant where life is now possible. Hydrogen and Carbon join together becoming the first organic material known as Hydrocarbon. This is a sensational occurrence! Once again, we really do not know who, how, or what caused this to happen right when it did, but it created the building blocks for life as we know it today. If it were not for the romantic collision between these two elements, organic material may never have been created, therefore, we would never have existed. Flash forward.

The time is 300,000 years before the present, when our Neanderthal ancestors were roaming the Earth, approximately 100,000 years before modern *Homo sapiens* emerged. According to the literary work "Death Rituals, Social Order and the Archaeology of Immortality in the Ancient World" by Joao Zilhao and edited by Colin Renfrew, University of Cambridge, Michael J. Boyd, University of Cambridge, Iain Morley, University of Oxford, the Neanderthals actually began burying their dead around this time! This is significant on so many levels. This means they had a spiritual awareness and buried the dead in the womb of Mother Earth because they believed the dead could be "born again." Have we ever stopped to wonder why mankind has always buried the dead in the earth? Did we ever consider that this was done out of spiritual belief and not out of convenience?

Or perhaps these early hominids did not have this complex thought process; however, most creatures do not do anything without purpose. The first evidence of religious rituals were certainly centered around nature (Earth, Moon, and Sun). These people lived in a time where all they had was nature, and they seemed very in tune and connected to it. To be in tune with not only what happens on Earth, but also in the heavens (outer space) is amazing. They tracked celestial bodies, they harnessed this energy, and they clearly knew its significance! This was not just a Stone Age concept. As above, so below.

In fact, ancient native Americans practiced this same reverence for the heavens, as did most cultures—and even Central and South American people! More recently so did the Knights Templar, in their architecture; be it underground chambers or cathedrals, they were all built with knowledge of celestial events. Interestingly enough they still honor the goddess or divine feminine just as much, if not more, than the masculine.

The ancients all around the world are known for worshiping the Mother Goddess (Earth) and living fairly peacefully. Women were sacred in society. Because, after all, they connected with the divine realm when conceiving and brought life to the Earthly realm when giving birth. When you truly consider how incredible a woman's ability to grow a child inside her body and birth it is, I think anyone would find it quite sacred and beautiful.

24

Later on the ancient people of North America adopted this reverence for Mother Earth, and even had many ceremonies to worship her and connect with her. They treated their women with respect, just like they did their Mother. The land was their church, altar, and paradise.

To our ancestors, war was not an everyday topic, and for the most part people lived in harmony. They lived in love, knowing the miracle of life was surrounding them as their women cared and nurtured the children and sick people around them. Men were not more important than women and vice versa. They appreciated that they did need each other to successfully raise children, that women were immaculate goddesses able to bring forth life from their bodies. Now of course there was war, and there was disharmony, but not to the degree there is in our first world society.

Life was simpler without material objects, without the Internet, pornography, media, and television. There were not "ideas" or "standards" as to how a body should look. Everything was much more sacred. Women's bodies were sacred. Their motherly spirit was sacred. When humans can learn to live in peace with one another life and love can be a beautiful thing.

Perhaps we began burying our dead hundreds of thousands of years ago because our ancestors realized we are all related. In the Lakota language, they say "Mitakuye oyasin," *all of my relatives/relations,* meaning we are all related in a very deep way. We are made of the same elements that Earth is, and Earth is made out of cosmic debris. Maybe we are returned to the Earth in death to prepare us for our return to the ever expanding Universe, to maybe be part of a star again someday, or maybe a new planet that will form billions of years from now. Either way, we will be born again cosmically into something fantastic.

2.1 Sky Woman & Turtle Island

A great story has been passed down through many generations about the creation of Turtle Island, or North America as we know it today. This creation story typically involved a woman, a Sky Woman, who fell to Earth and thus human life on Earth began. This story is traditional to the Potawatomi people, but on a larger scale, related to many Iroquois tribal creation stories. In a book by

The Bringer of Life

Robin Wall Kimmerer, known as *Braiding Sweetgrass: Indigenous Wisdom, Scientific Knowledge, and the Wisdom of Plants,* she tells the story of Sky Woman and Turtle Island. It goes like this:

In winter, when the green earth lies resting beneath a blanket of snow, this is the time for storytelling. The storytellers begin by calling upon those who came before who passed the stories down to us, for we are only messengers.

In the beginning, there was the Skyworld.

She fell like a maple seed, pirouetting on an autumn breeze. A column of light streamed from a hole in the Skyworld, marking her path where only darkness had been before. It took her a long time to fall

In fear, or maybe hope, she clutched a bundle tightly in her hand. Hurtling downward, she saw only dark water below. But in that emptiness there were many eyes gazing up at the sudden shaft of light. They saw there a small object, a mere dust mote in the beam. As it grew closer, they could see that it was a woman, arms outstretched, long black hair billowing behind as she spiraled toward them.

The geese nodded at one another and rose together from the water in a wave of goose music. She felt the beat of their wings as they flew beneath to break her fall. Far from the only home she'd ever known, she caught her breath at the warm embrace of soft feathers as they gently carried her downward. And so it began.

The geese could not hold the woman above the water for much longer, so they called a council to decide what to do. Resting on their wings, she saw them all gather; loons, otters, swans, beavers, fish of all kinds. A great turtle floated in their midst and offered his back for her to rest upon. Gratefully, she stepped from the goose wings onto the dome of his shell. The others understood that she needed land for her home and discussed how they might serve her need.

The deep divers among them had heard of mud at the bottom of the water, and agreed to go find some.

Loon dove first, but the distance was too far and after a long while he surfaced with nothing to show for his efforts.

26

One by one, the other animals offered to help—Otter, Beaver, Sturgeon—but the depth, the darkness, and the pressures were too great for even the strongest of swimmers. They returned gasping for air with their heads ringing.

Some did not return at all.

Soon only little Muskrat was left, the weakest diver of all. He volunteered to go while the others looked on doubtfully. His small legs flailed as he worked his way downward and he was gone a very long time.

They waited and waited for him to return, fearing the worst for their relative, and before long, a stream of bubbles rose with the small, limp body of the muskrat.

He had given his life to aid this helpless human. But then the others noticed that his paw was tightly clenched and, when they opened it, there was a small handful of mud. Turtle said, "here, put it on my back and I will hold it."

Skywoman bent and spread the mud with her hands across the shell of the turtle. Moved by the extraordinary gifts of the animals, she sang in thanksgiving and then began to dance, her feet caressing the earth. The land grew and grew as she danced her thanks, from the dab of mud on Turtle's back until the whole world was made. Not by Skywoman alone, but from the alchemy of all the animals' gifts coupled with her deep gratitude. Together they formed what we know today as Turtle Island, our home. Like any good guest, Skywoman had not come empty-handed. The bundle was still clutched in her hand.

When she toppled from the hole in the Skyworld she had reached out to grab onto the Tree of Life that grew there. In her grasp were branches—fruits and seed and all kinds of plants. These she scattered onto the new ground and carefully tended each one until the world turned from brown to green. Sunlight streamed through the hole from the Skyworld, allowing the seeds to flourish. Wild grasses, flowers, trees, and medicines spread everywhere. And now that the animals had plenty to eat, many came to live with her on Turtle Island too.

2.2 The Cailleach & Scotland

In ancient Scottish tradition, there was one major Mother Goddess figure, and she was known as the *Cailleach* (pronounced cauli-och). She is also sometimes known as the Cailleach Bheurra (pronounced bure-uh). The word bheurra is a Scottish Gaelic word referring to the sharp cold. Could this be where the word "brrr" comes from, a word we say when cold? The Cailleach in Gaelic literally means "veiled one." I find this intriguing in many aspects, but most importantly because in all esoteric traditions we often find names that refer to the goddess as being "veiled." The Cailleach is also known as the old hag and is often associated with the crone aspect of the triple goddess. Typical of the crone, She is most commonly associated with the winter season, and is sometimes even referred to as the Queen of Winter. The word *cailleach* is also said to be the origin for the Scottish lowland word "carline" which refers to a charmer/witch.

The Cailleach is said to rule over the months between Samhain, October 31, (pronounced sow-een) and Beltane, May 1. According to Scottish legend, She predates even the Celtic people. A Highland folktale even said, "from the long eternity of the world." There are many different tales of goddesses from around the world that resonate with the Cailleach. For example, the Hindu goddess known as Kali is considered the supreme deity above all in Indian tradition, and is the ultimate manifestation of the cosmic creation force, Shakti. The names are very similar linguistically, yet the traditions stem from different sides of the world. This could indicate that there were Indian immigrants appearing in Great Britain, or that the ancient Gaelic people were travelling to places like India. Also like Kali, the Cailleach is said to possess not only creative abilities, but destructive ones as well.

The Cailleach is credited with creating the land, by wading through the water, dropping boulders and stones, creating the hills and mountains of Scotland. There is even a mountain on the Isle of Skye named after her, Ben Na Caillich. There is another mountain that is deeply connected to stories of Her creation, and that is Ben Cruachan, located just near Loch Awe. According to legend, there was a well on the summit of Ben Cruachan. It was this well that the Cailleach drew her water from. The well was covered by a heavy stone slab, which it was essential to replace by sunset or the water contained inside the well would spill out and flood the world. One evening, She removed the stone slab to draw her water and lay down for a wee rest. Exhausted, She fell into a deep sleep and as soon as the sun dipped below the horizon, water began streaming down the mountainside. The roar of the water woke the Cailleach, but not before many streams and waterfalls down the mountainside were created.

There is also a house named for her, the House of the Cailleach or Taigh na Cailleach. This is located at the head of Glen Lyon, which fittingly is near Glen Cailleach. This seemingly unremarkable old house is dedicated to the goddess and likely has been for thousands of years. Still to this day, a ritual in Her honor takes place twice a year.

Beltane, which takes place on May 1, also known as May Day, is the Celtic festival that marks the beginning of summer. At this time the stones that seal the entrance of Taigh Na Cailleach are removed, the roof is freshly thatched, and a family of stones resembling people—the Cailleach, the Bodach (old man), and the Nighean (daughter) are all brought outside, where they watch over the land throughout the summer months. At Samhain, which celebrates the coming of winter, the stones are placed back inside the house before it is once again sealed up. Another Samhain tradition connected to the Cailleach stems from Corryvreckan, the world's third largest whirlpool, which is located north of the Isle of Jura. It is said that She comes here to wash Her great plaid. However, the Cailleach removes her plaid now clean and white. She then uses it to cover Scotland in a blanket of snow. All winter long, She wanders about, striking the ground and trees with her staff to keep any life from springing forth.

The Cailleach has often been considered the goddess of horned animals, but also of deer. Another name She has been called by is Cailleach Mhor Nam Fiadh (the great old woman of the deer). It is said that in old Highland tradition, Gaelic prayers were said to Her before stag hunts. If prayers to Her were not said before a hunt, then it would not yield a successful result.

Other names She has been known by are Cailleach Nollaig (the Christmas old wife) which had a Christmas Eve tradition associated with Her, but also Woman of Stones. Many stone circles and cairns have been erected in dedication to Her.

Descriptions of the Cailleach's appearance have always made her out to be an ugly old woman, who was wearing an apron and had a creel strapped to Her back. Usually She was carrying either a wand or staff that had magical powers. This staff or wand was probably made out of blackthorn. Because this was often what witches made their walking sticks out of, later on this was used when burning witches at the pyre. Charming.

2.3 The Goddess in the Beginning

Human beings are the only mammals that are spiritually conscious. The question is, at what point in our vast evolution did that begin? When did humans start experiencing emotional connection? Scientists contend that the ancient species of human *Homo erectus,* who lived about two million years ago, were caring for the elderly people and not leaving them behind as previous species did. As simplistic as it sounds, this is the foundation for the first spiritual evolution. It would be this action that would lead to the very first and most primitive form of religion: ancestor worship.

Sometime between 335,000–236,000 years ago, the species *Homo naledi* began to bury their dead in caves. Why did people bury their people in tombs, or even in the ground, for that matter? One could argue that for thousands of years, caves have been used for initiation into mystery traditions. Caves were always a place where one went to seek hidden knowledge, be it a monk or an initiate of an esoteric group like the Knights Templar. Caves were equated with the womb of the goddess, and after one completed their spiritual quest or initiation, they would emerge "reborn" from the womb of the Earth. Humans knew that the Earth was a life-giving entity, water flows through streams and rivers like the veins of the planet, plants grow from her bosom, animals feed from the plants, and us from these animals. To equate Her with the archetypal mother would not be so far fetched, considering that these people's lives depended upon the Earth, nature, and Her cycles. Their view would have been that they belonged to the Earth, because that is all they know. Therefore if they had come from the Earth, isn't that where they should return to upon death? This correlates perfectly with the concept of a lively fertile goddess and the goddess of the underworld.

A cave in France contains a stone circle that is 176,000 years old, likely the oldest stone circle to have been discovered to date. Bruniquel Cave[1] appears to have been inhabited by the Neanderthal, and served as an important spiritual location. What makes this stone circle unique is what it is built from. Four hundred stalactites were used to create this monument. The questions remain, what was the purpose of the stone circle? Did it serve as a calendar, like so many other stone circles that came later? Or was it something else entirely? It is hard to say considering the next oldest stone circle did not appear until 12,000 years ago at Gobekli Tepe in Turkey—nearly 164,000 years later—and was built by *Homo sapiens* and not Neanderthals.

Reverence for the universal mother figure likely developed with human emotional intelligence, which we cannot exactly pinpoint in evolutionary history. I would personally hypothesize that it began when people began burying the dead and practicing mortuary rituals, which was likely around the *Homo naledi* era (335,000-236,000). Around this time, people quite possibly could have begun having what we would consider emotional connections. Prior to this era, our ancestors were focused solely on survival. When people begin to bury their dead instead of just leaving them out in the elements, it is likely because they have stopped leading such a nomadic lifestyle and settled a certain area. With more structure, stability, and time that would have been spent traveling—people began to turn inwards.

Kissing appears to be an act committed by emotionally intelligent parties, and for a long time there was no evidence to tell us when the first kiss occurred. Ancient hominin species were absolutely engaging in sexual activity as reproduction was occurring, but when they began associating emotion or kissing with the act is unknown. In 2017 a Neanderthal tooth was discovered

[1] Drake, Nadia. "Neanderthals Built Mysterious Stone Circles." Science, National Geographic, 3 May 2021, https://www.nationalgeographic.com/science/article/neanderthals-caves-rings-building-francearchaeology#:~:text=Sealed%20since%20the%20Pleistocene%2C%20Bruniquel, other%20extinct%20megafauna%20just%20inside.

in Spain which contained a specific bacteria which humans still have in their mouths today that is associated with gum disease. The interesting aspect is that it was an early human who was kissing a Neanderthal, showing this was likely the beginning of interconnectedness between early humans and Neanderthals. Regarding the discovery, anthropologist Laura Weyrich of Pennsylvania State University said, "If you're swapping spit between species, there's kissing going on, or at least food sharing, which would suggest that these interactions were much friendlier and much more intimate than anybody ever possibly imagined."

That begs the question, when in evolutionary history did people begin kissing? To this day, scientists still cannot provide any explanation for why humans are inclined to kiss. Sheri Kirshenbaum proposes that humans kiss to exchange sensory information and gain insight into the energy, health, and vitality of the other party. Humans are the only species that kiss during sex, or even associate kissing with the act. There is something to be said for that; does a kiss convey a certain type of consciousness or awareness between two emotionally intelligent people?

The earliest goddess figurine emerged approximately 40,000 years ago in Europe. There were potentially earlier goddess figurines over 100,000 years old, but an ongoing dispute remains; they are basic in appearance, and lack the specific detail that the younger ones have. We must wonder, when did an understanding of the goddess emerge? With burial rituals?

Modern humans have many features that prove unique to our species. For example, human women's vaginal canal is tilted at such an angle to indicate that our bodies were built for face to face sexual intercourse, whereas no other species copulates this way. All other species tend to engage in intercourse from behind. Why is it that humans were meant to experience sex face to face? Looking into another's face promotes a certain type of intimacy that cannot be experienced when it is done in a different position like all other animals. Why then, are women built this way? What in evolution caused us women to evolve in a way that our sexual organs were built to share emotional intimacy and connection with our sexual partner? Over the course of the last 10,000 years it appears that ritual lovemaking occurred around the world in different traditions, and that it could bring a source of power, enlightenment, or even God, into the two engaging parties.

Very few other mammals engage in sexual activity outside of mating season. Humans tend to engage in sexual activity for recreational purposes on a regular basis. Sex began as a necessary biological act in order to reproduce, however it evolved into a much more complex desire. Yes, modern people have intimate relations when the physical urge arises, but it is also an act done out of love and emotional desire; something purely unique to modern humans, *Homo sapiens*.

Women's bodies are incredible all in themselves. They are able to conceive and carry a child for nine months and then feed the child from their very breast. During pregnancy, hormones are obviously constantly changing, and one of the adaptive hormonal changes is hair growth. Pregnant women's hair grows twice as fast and twice as long for up to 12 months after birth. Why? When holding the baby against the mother's breast, it is a natural instinct for the baby to take a fistful of hair as a comfort and safety mechanism.

Another unique attribute to the female body is an organ that exists solely to experience pleasure: the clitoris. Men unfortunately do not have a pleasure organ that exists just to experience pleasure. Women are biologically built to experience sexual pleasure for the purpose of pleasure in *addition* to experiencing sex for the sake of reproduction. Could this be the reason that many cultures associated the goddess with lust, euphoria, and indulgent behavior?

Ancient cultures must have seen women bearing children, bleeding monthly without dying, and thought how incredible that was for hundreds of thousands of years. This could very well be the reason that women became revered in so many different societies around the world within the last several thousand years. Being able to bleed so much monthly without dying would have been seen as an indication of immortality.

There was a time when ancient civilizations were predominantly matriarchal and matrilineal, and that time lasted up until about 3000 BC. Many anthropologists and archaeologists suggest that women reigned supreme because of the lack of understanding of the relationship between sex and pregnancy. If the father was not known, matrilineal descent this make much more sense. With the shift to a patriarchal and patrilineal society came the concept of ownership of woman and child. This is when the culture and the spirit of the goddess began to be suppressed. This is when shame was bestowed upon the feminine, and women were silenced. The ways of the goddess began to fade and a new society based around a masculine deity began. Where did She go? Where can we find her now?

Chapter 3
Ancient Holidays of
the Goddess

What is Paganism? Is it "Satanism"? In today's world there is a large misunderstanding of what it means to be Pagan. According to the New Oxford American Dictionary, Paganism is; "a religion other than one of the main world religions, specifically a non Christian or pre-Christian religion." Paganism can be a lot of things. These "Pagans" occupied Eur-Asia for many thousands of years, and began building monuments and megalithic structures as long as 20,000 years ago.

Contrary to popular belief, being "Pagan" does not insinuate one is promoting or practicing anything evil. Pagan is something *all* of our ancestors were prior to the human invention of Christianity (and other modern religions) sometime in the first century AD. In contrast, Judaism is nearly in full swing by 2000 BC, or 4000 years ago. Not many know that Jewish traditions are so ancient.

Now this being said, the ancients that occupied the planet all obviously had a deep reverence for the Mother Earth and the celestial bodies in the Universe. To them, Earth represented Mother [Goddess] and the Sun represented Father [God]. Now if this Cosmic Womb Theory that I proposed in the first chapter were to actually ring true, it would be baffling that the ancients really understood this concept and attempted to harness energy by building massive stone monuments to align with the heavens. If this were to be fact, why is this theory not prevalent today? Easy, the Roman Catholic Church. But that is for another chapter.

Growing up in church, we are all taught that the Pagans, Druids, Wiccans, and any other religion with multiple deities are bad, evil, Satanic, or whatever else the church wants to make them out to be, solely because they are not Christians. In fact, Pagan people seemed to live much more peacefully thousands of years ago before Christianity came to be; this religion has been the reason for many thousands of deaths.

With the lack of materialism in ancient times, the people connected with everything on a much deeper level. We cannot and will not seem to give up the ways we were taught growing up, and because of this stubbornness we do not feel comfortable challenging religion, history, and philosophy. Sadly, people are afraid of what they do not know or understand.

With this old Mother Earth spirituality they had a deep appreciation for all who could bear children. The ancients rejoiced when one of their women received her first menstruation because this brought her closer with "Goddess" or Mother Earth. Typically, their menstruation cycles aligned with the moon cycles. For some, this was a week of self-reflection, purging of bad energy, and cleansing of the body, mind, and spirit.

Now, the women could be like Earth and bear children, and this was the ultimate goal: motherhood. This is where the number thirteen comes into play. It is not an unlucky number. In fact, it is the goddess number, and for a good reason. Thirteen is the number of menstrual cycles women have every year. Female cycles are on a 28-day cycle, just like the Moon.

While the ancient people of our past worshiped many gods and goddesses, the feminine deities seem to be the most popular. Even in today's world, ancient Pagan gods and goddesses can be seen in Christianity and other holidays/religions around us.

3.1 Goddess Holidays

O Christmas tree… except it actually started out as a Pagan winter solstice tradition. Did no one realize this song is about tree/nature/Mother Earth worship? Not actually a Christian holiday tradition. And as a matter of fact, there is a passage in the Bible that so much as forbids the decorating of a tree.

In the King James Bible, Jeremiah, Chapter 10:2-5, it says, "Thus saith the Lord, Learn not the way of the heathen, and be not dismayed at the signs of heaven; for the heathen are dismayed at them. For the customs of the people are vain: for one cutteth a tree out of the forest, the work of the hands of the workman, with the axe. They deck it with silver and with gold; they fasten it with nails and with hammers, that it move not. They are upright as the palm tree, but speak not: they must needs be borne, because they cannot go. Be not afraid of them; for they cannot do evil, neither also is it in them to do good."

Why do Christians today decorate evergreen trees with silver and gold and lights? The tradition began thousands of years ago. Also, the tradition of putting a five-pointed star on the top began with the Pagans.

The five-pointed star has been an ancient symbol going back thousands of years that represented Venus. The pentacle has been perceived in the modern era as being a sign of devil worship, while in reality its true meaning is anything but. Over the course of eight Earth years (which is exactly 13 Venus years), Venus makes the pattern of the pentacle in the heavens as you track Her. So why is it that the ancient Pagans put a star symbolizing Venus on top of their tree? Venus has always been revered as the Queen of Heaven, consort of the Sun, the King. Venus is the third brightest object in our sky after the Sun and Moon.

Our ancient ancestors began preparations for the sacred holiday known as Winter Solstice. This is the day that the Sun begins its journey back to Earth, longer days will return and forget the harsh winter weather.

3.2 Frigga & Winter Solstice

The Norse goddess Frigga, also known as Freya, was responsible for spinning the wheel of fate. The word "yule" comes from the Norse word "jul" meaning wheel. In Norse mythology Frigga sat at the wheel spinning every individual's fate—the wheel being symbolic of the cycle of (eternal) life. Essentially she is responsible for creating the destiny of all mankind. In the tarot deck the Major Arcana card "Wheel of Fortune" is likely based on Frigga's wheel of fate.

Another tradition stemming from this goddess is the hanging of the Christmas wreath. The wreath was a symbol of Frigga's spinning wheel.

The first night of the Winter Solstice celebration was known as Mother Night. This was the longest night of the year because Frigga was working hard to birth the Sun (Baldur) to bring light again. Then of course, the Sun is born again and can bring warmth and life on December 21.

3.3 Other Cultures and Winter Solstice
- Egyptian goddess Isis gave birth to Horus on December 21
- Japanese Sun goddess Amaterasu was born December 21
- Rhea gave birth to Saturn December 21
- Maya/Aztec creator god Quetzalcoatl/Kukulkan was born December 21
- Saint Lucia, also known as the goddess of light from Sweden to Italy, is honored with festivals of candles to help us make it through darkness during solstice
- The birth of Hindu goddess of knowledge and Queen of Heaven, Saraswati, is celebrated during Yuletide
- In the Hopi culture, the supernatural beings called Kachinas return to Earth during this time

3.4 Festival of Isis
January 9 is thought to be the celebration of Egypt's mother goddess, Isis. This celebration may have to do with the story of her bringing back her husband, Osiris, from the dead, and giving him life again. Elvis Presley's birthday is interestingly on January 8, and he was often seen wearing an ankh necklace, and even posed much like the winged Isis, but in his cape.

3.5 Tu B'shevat & Asherah
January 17-18, this is an ancient Hebrew-Canaanite "Festival of the Trees." On this day, the ancients would plant new seeds. The first mention of Tu B'shevat appears in a Jewish text, the *Mishnah*, in about 200 A.D. There is a link to a "Tree of Life" and the creation of mankind. Originally, this festival honored the Canaanite goddess Asherah. Asherah was often associated with trees and was seen as the "Mother Goddess" not only by the ancient Canaanites/Phoenicians. Interestingly enough, she is even mentioned in the Hebrew Bible. Potentially she is seen as Yahweh or El's wife. While many did not believe Yahweh had a wife, this makes a lot of sense, and we will get more into this in a later chapter.
3.6 Easter

Elvis kneeling in the Isis Position.

Easter is known as a Christian holiday, but is it really? Probably not, based on historical evidence. Easter is allegedly named after the goddess Eostre or Ostara. According to the English Monk Bede (7th-8th century), the former Pagans called April the "Eosturmonap" or the "Month of Eostre/Easter." Just like you thought, this goddess is a goddess of fertility, dawn, and light. It was at this time there was once again lots of feasting, celebrating spring, birth, and life/motherhood.

The earliest account of Eostre goes back to 788 B.C. and she is referenced then as Eastragena, a matron goddess. It is likely she was worshiped in the triplet, the Maid, Mother, and Crone (wise old woman). The German word for Easter is Oster, coming from Ostaria.

Of course the association with eggs has to do with birth and life. The infamous Easter Bunny was originally a hare, and was associated with spring because of the animal's intense mating routines. Hares are also capable of conceiving another fetus while pregnant, which of course was a beautiful thing to our ancestors.

Interestingly enough, according to an article of Swiss Club

of South Wales written by Martin Frutiger, "The practice of decorating eggshells as part of spring rituals is ancient, with decorated, engraved ostrich eggs found in Africa which are 60,000 years old. In the pre-dynastic period of Egypt and the early cultures of Mesopotamia and Crete, eggs were associated with death and rebirth, as well as with kingship. Decorated ostrich eggs, and representations of ostrich eggs in gold and silver, were commonly placed in graves of the ancient Sumerians and Egyptians as early as 5,000 years ago…"

This goddess is naturally associated with the spring equinox that occurs on March 21. This of course was an ancient celebration honoring the goddess Ostara, and was called the Ostara Sabbat, which is still observed by Wiccans and other Pagans today.

3.7 Festival of Veneralia

This festival of "Venus" first occurred on April 1, 220 BC in Rome. This festival revolved around a cult worshiping the feminine, "Venus Verticordia" or "Venus, the changer of hearts." This seems to be the original "Valentines Day." This was a day where the statue was taken down to the men's baths, bathed by women, and then decorated with jewelry and flowers. On this day, men and women would pray and seek help in their love and sex lives. In 114 BC, Venus was given her own temple.

3.8 Navratri, Hindu Festival of the Great Goddess

Navrati is a Hindu festival that is largely celebrated in India that takes place at the end of September just after the autumn equinox. This is an ancient practice that celebrates the triumph of good over evil. This festival lasts nine nights; interesting that it is nine because three is the cubic root of nine, the goddess number (not to mention the goddess is worshiped in the triplet, and nine months of pregnancy). The festival is dedicated to the glorification of the divine feminine, Shakti, the Mother Goddess. She is worshiped also in nine different ways.

Chapter 4
The Goddess in Stone

A topic of many curious conversations are these massive mega-lithic structures. When we think of large megalithic sites we always imagine Stonehenge. Stonehenge is just the tip of the megalithic iceberg—they are literally everywhere. They were built as calendars, or monuments to summer and winter solstice, spring and fall equinox, and to other celestial events.

4.1 Dolmen des Pierres Plates, France

While there are thousands of dolmens and stone chambers all over the UK, Europe, and Asia only a few that we know of can be tied to the Mother Goddess symbol. There was one site in particular that fascinated me. This site is known as Dolmen des Pierres Plates in Brittany, France. Built by the ocean, this is a unique spot that is unfortunately prone to flooding, so who knows how much has been washed away over the thousands of years since it was in use.

While this site tends to flood quite easily due to its close proximity to the ocean, on this particular September day we found it dry enough to enter. There are a few different "rooms" you see as you enter the dwelling.

One of the many symbols inside this structure that seemed the most significant appeared to have a boomerang shape. It appeared to me that it represented the Mother Goddess. This shape would represent the woman in the birth giving position with her knees up, which coincidentally makes the shape of the letter "M."

In taking this interpretation a step further, my own personal interpretation of the pairs of circles inside the shape is quite simple. I have failed to find anyone else's opinion or interpretation of the symbols inside the prominent Mother shape, so thus far it is the only interpretation I can consider.

It appears to me that those carved circles represent the three sets of internal organs that come in pairs inside the female body. These

The cave-like entrance to the Dolmen des Pierres Plates.

organs would be the ovaries, kidneys, and lungs. Perhaps these organs were meant to be symbolic of something deeper. If you stand with your back facing the inscribed rock, you will inevitably see a light chamber, which was obviously there on purpose. We just so happened to be there around the time of the fall equinox close to sunset.

I noticed how the light was shining to illuminate that particular

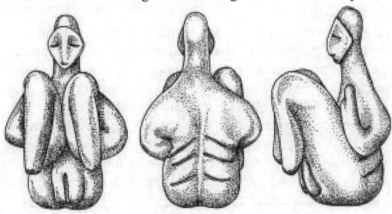

Ancient figure in birth giving position.

42

stone and only that stone, and how as it set it began at the top of the stone and set at the bottom. The moving rays of the setting sun seemed to tell a story. I watched in curiosity.

I could not quite figure it out at first. All afternoon, this curiosity grew and grew, and I tried to imagine what the inscription might mean. Later on at the hotel the idea hit me. When I thought of the process in reverse it all made sense. In the morning, as the Sun was rising, the light pouring in through the light chamber would light up the bottom of the carved stone. The last pair of organs to be illuminated would be the ovaries, indicating the beginning of life, or

The Story of Life Stone at the Dolmen des Pierres Plates.

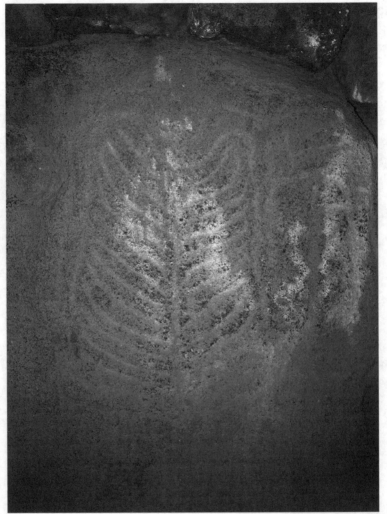

The Mentrual-Lunar Calendar, Dolmen des Pierres Plates.

the beginning, birth. The first set of organs to be illuminated would be the lungs In this story being told, this should mean that one should return to the womb, or even Mother Earth's womb in order to be born again. As the Sun continues to set, next the kidneys would be illuminated. While the kidneys seem a little odd, I would assume that these would be showing us a cleansing stage, purification, or even enlightenment, ending with the womb and upright legs in the birth giving position.

When we look at this same stone as the Sun sets, it tells us a similar story. However this time it starts with birth, the ovaries light up first, then the kidneys, and lastly, the lungs. After the "last breath" per se, the Sun has totally set and leaves the dolman in complete darkness. Beautiful symbolism and archaeoastronomical engineering for such a "primitive" people.

Another interesting carving inside this same dolmen is outlined with a similar shape, but differs significantly. It seems to have 12 or 13 horizontal strokes, depending on if you count the bottom out laying line. Could this be a lunar calendar since it has about 13 lines and there are 13 lunar cycles in a year? There is a reason the number 13 has always been associated with Goddess, and that is because in ancient times, women's menstrual cycles usually went hand in hand with the lunar cycle. So, in addition to perhaps being a lunar calendar, could this be a menstrual calendar? With the other carved shapes pointing to the feminine worship, this would make sense.

Of course there are many other sites around the world that have incredible celestial alignments with magnificent engineering feats, but not all of them have to do with the divine feminine worship.

In a later chapter, it will be made obvious that the Knights Templar, who orchestrated the building of many cathedrals in medieval times, used this sacred feminine shape as inspiration for their architecture.

4.2 Newgrange, Ireland

The first thing that will stand out to you about the picture of the front of Newgrange is the big symbol that contains three spirals all connected together. That would be what is known as a "triskele." This ancient shape represents two different aspects of Goddess. One aspect is the three trimesters of pregnancy. The second aspect is the triple Goddess. There are three parts that make up the great goddess. We have the first phase, "Maiden," who is obviously the young part of the trio. She is innocent and has not yet had children. The second phase is "Mother," a woman who is a little older and wiser than the Maiden, and has had children. The final phase is "Crone," the wise old woman.

A site is that seems to lean in that direction would happen to be Newgrange in County Meath, Ireland. Across the lintel stone, we see eight X's. In forensic geologist Scott Wolter's book, *Akhenaten to the Founding Fathers: The Mysteries of the Hooked X*, he and

Alan Butler determine this is a Venus temple. There are multiple reasons why the number eight is associated with Venus, but we will discuss that in a later chapter. The X's are symbols that represent union—union between male and female, the top V representing the womb or the feminine V, and the upside down V representing the phallus. This is a symbol used all throughout the ancient world.

Could the chamber at Newgrange really be representing a woman's reproductive organs? The inside of the chamber is shaped like a crucifix, and on solstice when the sunlight pours into the chamber, it barely touches the back wall. This leaves the two sides to the cru-

The entrance to Newgrange.

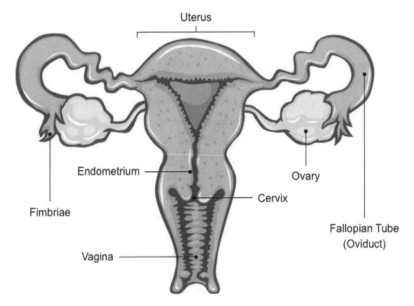

Female reproductive system diagram.

cifix untouched. However in those two sides, there are large bowls that could have been used for any number of things. Some archaeologists suggest they were used for placing the remains of the dead, but could it be possible that there were baptisms and such rituals occurring here instead? A ritual that symbolizes rebirth from Mother Earth's womb? If you look at the diagram showing the woman's reproductive organs, you can see where a crucifix may be found. Now apply this to the chamber at Newgrange! If you were walking into this chamber, you would be essentially entering the womb.

The ancients realized how sacred was the union that connected two people to create new life, and really emphasized that through inscriptions and buildings. The X symbol is found all over Ireland, from Newgrange to the Hill of Tara.

Unfortunately, at the Hill of Tara, the chamber is blocked off so you cannot go inside. However, peeking through the bars, you can still manage to see the symbols inscribed on the inside. There are X's and many spirals and other inscriptions as well. Perhaps these X's were placed inside the dolmen-like chamber to indicate that chamber was a physical representation of that union.

The chamber at the Hill of Tara is built facing east so that on a special day the light will fill up the chamber, much like at Newgrange, the solar deity representing the masculine and the structure representing the divine feminine, Mother Earth's womb.

4.3 The Cross & The Ankh

After considering that perhaps the ancient people (here thousands of years before Christ) used the shape of the crucifix to represent the female reproductive organs, it made me think some more. Well, where were the first crucifixes worn and viewed as having holy and sacred qualities? It is in fact very well known that the place in question happens to be Egypt. The ankh seems to date as far back as approximately 3100 B.C., during the Early Dynastic Period in Egypt which lasted until about 2613 B.C. This means the first ankhs came into the picture over 5,000 years ago!

According to Newgrange's official website, the chambers were constructed to align with Winter Solstice sunrise 5,200 years ago. This means this site in Ireland was built in the shape of a cross, or the women's reproductive system, three hundred years *before* the emergence of the "ankh" in Egypt. Could the "loop" on the top of the ankh be a newer interpretation of the female womb? Perhaps the Egyptians had a better understanding of the female anatomy at this point?

This is an interesting concept. The first crucifixes that were worn and venerated are actually known as the Egyptian ankh. This is pretty interesting. Ankh, in Egyptian, literally translates to "breath of life." The ankh actually seems to look more like the internal female reproductive organs with the rounded top (uterus) than a normal crucifix.

With this in mind, it is sort of ironic that people were crucified on a cross, because essentially they are being killed on a physical representation of the womb, which to me indicates right there a sense of rebirth is coming. Is there more to this than just coincidence? Is it possible we have many Christians around the world wearing a cross around their neck thinking it

An Egyptian Ankh.

48

is symbolic of Christ's crucifiction when it really is a symbol of the goddess and the female's sacred reproductive organs?

While there are many different theories as to what the "ankh" might actually represent, I will name justva couple. Egyptologist E.A. Wallis Budge (1857-1934) proposed that it was in fact, the *tjet* or the "knot of Isis" representing her belt buckle that was symbolic of the female genitalia.

A scholar by the name of Adele Nozedar believes that it is a union symbol of the masculine and feminine. He says that, "The volume of meaning that can be squeezed from such a simple symbol is awe-inspiring. The ankh represents the male and female genitalia, the sun coming over the horizon, and the union of heaven and earth."

Whatever the meaning it held to the Egyptians, it was significant. In many art depictions, it was always the gods and goddesses depicted holding the ankh, or giving it to somebody. It seemed to have an ancient attachment to Isis originally, but later on, it is said to be associated with Anubis as well.

4.4 Gavrinis, France

Another interesting site in Brittany, France, on an island in the Gulf of Morbihan, is Gavrinis. This site was allegedly called a passage tomb, which seems to be the go to explanation for sites archaeologists cannot explain. However, Dr. Terence Meaden says Gavrinis was designed not for burying the dead but to conduct sacred rituals. Many archaeologists say that the carvings are depicting the Mother Goddess. The carving on the right side appears to have some type of calendar, probably lunar if we are dealing with the goddess, that runs down the right side of the stone.

In *The Civilization of the Goddess*, UCLA archaeology professor Marija Gimbutas says that these arcs are actually meant to be vulvas. Much like Newgrange, the chamber faces southeast so that the Sun can rise and fill the chamber with light on the morning of Winter Solstice.

Unfortunately, when I visited, the guide here was insistent on these alignments being "coincidental" and obviously was not familiar with the patterns of many ancient civilizations. I have encountered this at many different ancient sites, and it is a shame. The astronomical alignments at archaeological sites only enhance the

Gavrinis Passage Tomb Vulva Stones (Photo by Joachim Jahnke).

intrigue, in my opinion. The penetration of the chamber represents the divine union between the god in the heavens and the earth goddess, an ancient and sacred dualism.

4.5 The Goddess Stone & Sacrificial Table, America's Stonehenge, New Hampshire USA

An incredible archaeological complex lies situated in the countryside of Salem, New Hampshire, known as America's Stonehenge, known previously as Mystery Hill. I visited for the first time in May of 2019 after emailing back and forth with the owner of the site, Dennis Stone, who has dedicated his whole life to researching not only his own site, but other megalithic sites throughout the world. I was stunned to find out that America's Stonehenge was inhabited as early as 4000 years ago (2000 BC) which we know due to carbon 14 dating that has taken place at the site. That being said, we know there have been people drawn to this area for quite some time. There is an abundance of standing stones, stone chambers, astronomical alignments, serpent effigy walls, foreign inscriptions, and even a sacrificial table. Ancient inscriptions in Celtic Ogham (used between 300 AD and 900 AD), Punic/Phoenician (800 BC—600 AD), and Libyan (300 BC to 300 AD) have all been found around this particular property. Essentially this site appeared to be a site used by many different cultures over the years. There are many intriguing aspects of America's Stonehenge, but the one feature that I cannot take my mind off of is what we deemed the "Goddess Stone."

Knowing I have a particular interest in the sacred feminine and ancient goddess worship, Dennis took me to an area a little ways away from the main complex where this stone could be found. He had mentioned it to me over email in the weeks before my visit,

The Goddess Stone at America's Stonehenge.

51

Sacrificial Table at America's Stonehenge.

and I was so excited to see the stone in person. The stone appears to have the side-view image of a pregnant woman carved into it. All of the ancient inscriptions were carved by goddess-worshiping people. Was this carved by pre-Columbian voyagers thousands of years ago? The other possibility is that it was carved by Native Americans who see women as the backbone of society, and of course revere the goddess in the form of Mother Earth.

Another controversial artifact can be found here nestled into the center of the archaeological complex known as the *Sacrificial Table*. The table itself is a large granite slab that weighs 4.5 tons and is 9 feet long. At the top of the table which is near another stone chamber known as the *Oracle Chamber*[1] the table is 5.48 feet (2 megalithic yards) while it is considerably narrower at the bottom being 6.8 feet wide (2.5 megalithic yards).

---

[1] The *Oracle Chamber* is a man made chamber which allows for sound to echo loudly out beneath the *Sacrificial Table*, perhaps utilized by a shaman or priest/priestess who would speak as the host to a god or goddess during ritual birth and/or death.

Along the perimeter of the table are curious grooves that appear to run out of a groove angled downwards at the front of the table. At the base of the table just below this groove, a cut out in the rock can be found where it is believed that a basin once sat to collect the draining fluid. We know in ancient times blood was collected for ritual purposes whether it be from menstrual bleeding or sacrificial ceremonies. With the ancients revering water as a life source, they knew that fluid surrounded the baby in the womb, thus amniotic fluid would likely have been considered sacred.

Was this table used for human sacrifice? Possibly. There was another possibility that came to my mind upon seeing it. What if it were used for ritual *birthing?* Was there even any evidence to support it? I was curious about the amount of fluid involved in childbirth. Women usually lose about half a quart, or 500 milliliters of blood following a normal childbirth. This amount can nearly double (1 quart or 1,000 milliliters) during a cesarean birth. At full term (40 weeks) there is nearly 600 milliliters of amniotic fluid that surrounds the baby, which is the same fluid that begins to gush when a mother's water breaks upon going into labor. Between the blood loss and amniotic fluid, there is a potential for the total loss of 1,100-1,600 milliliters of fluid.

For comparison, this could be up to more than two bottles of wine! This is a significant amount of fluid that would certainly be getting in the way during the childbirth process. These grooves would assist in channeling the fluid out of the way while the doctor or medicine person could tend to the mother and child during the labor and birthing process.

Upon proposing my theory to Dennis, he pointed out that the NEARA (New England Antiquities Research Association) was founded by his father, Robert E. Stone in the basement of his house alongside family in 1964. This is an on-

Mt. Mineral Carving.

The author at the Illumination Chamber, America's Stonehenge (Photo Mark Hood).

going organization that documents and examines archaeological sites across New England. Dennis's father subsequently created the logo for NEARA, which is an odd looking symbol to anyone who doesn't know what they are looking at. This symbol appears to be a human sitting with their knees up as if in the birth giving position. At the neck you see what looks like maybe a necklace or a long cut. This logo for NEARA appears to have been inspired by a carving found in Massachusetts at Mt. Mineral, a place with a spring said to have powerful healing waters. The mineral waters there likely became a sacred place to the ancient people who inhabited the area, and maybe even those who built America's Stonehenge.

Dennis's father, Robert, painted this beautiful scene of the stone with the carving that he decided to use for the NEARA logo. The carving on the stone shows that same figure sitting with knees up, a line around the neck area, and inside of a shape that appears to be identical to the shape of the Sacrificial Table. At the bottom left of the carving is a circular carving. Could this be the basin at the foot of the table that is depicted? Why would they depict this scene of the Table near a spring approximately 65.5 miles away from the Table at America's Stonehenge?

Sacred springs have long been associated with the divine feminine, whether it be an ancient goddess or the Christian personification of the Mother Goddess: Mary. Water being the element that fills the womb is clearly associated with birth, rebirth and purification—this is why we practice baptism as a form of purification, dedicating one's life to their god. Someone at some point in history, found an important relationship between the Table at America's Stonehenge and the sacred springs at Mt. Mineral and carved the curious image still there today. Did it have to do with childbirth? Was it a point of pilgrimage for pregnant women? What were the traditions that tied it to the Table?

Ancient cultures around the world have always had traditions of an audience witnessing a divine and/or royal birth; from ancient Egypt to Victorian Britain. Even think about the most iconic story of childbirth—Mary giving birth to baby Jesus in the stable. The three wisemen come to see Jesus. In ancient Egypt, there were birth houses known as *mammisis*[2] where royal births would be observed.

These birth houses were temples of childbirth essentially, and usually depicted scenes of a divine nativity in relation to the local holy triad. These birth houses depicting the scene of childbirth were found in the Late Period (664 BC-332 BC), Ptolemaic (305 BC-30 BC) and Roman temple complexes. The divine triad would have been something like Isis (mother), Osiris (father), and Horus (child). In each area of Egypt the gods used in the triad varied, but the tradition of a holy trinity began hundreds of years before the birth of the historical Jesus.

With that knowledge in mind, many ancient cultures including Egypt, saw the king as the divine incarnation of their chief god—thus acting as holy man and leader for the people. This tradition was observed and found all around the world. Could the table have served dualistic purposes: a place to witness the birth of the heir to the tribal or royal throne, while also a place to witness ritual death?

4.6 The Illumination Chamber, America's Stonehenge

While visiting America's Stonehenge, just before viewing the Goddess Stone, Dennis showed me a stone chamber that had previously had no documented astronomical alignments. As I tend to do when I see a stone chamber, I crawled in. I was surprised to see that in the back of the chamber there appeared to be a roughly

---

[2] *UCLA Encyclopedia of Egyptology*

Just before full illumination, Spring Equinox (Photo Dennis Stone).

egg-shaped white stone incorporated into the building of the wall. Immediately I was reminded of the Newport Tower (mentioned in Chapter 13) that was only a few hours away in Rhode Island. The stone in this chamber clearly was not worked on to the degree that the egg-shaped stone at Newport Tower was, but in many cases the ancient people picked up natural stones that resembled something sacred. In this case they saw the white stone that was nearly the shape of an egg, an oval, or more specifically the yoni, all symbols of the goddess. (See the diagram in 13.6)

The age of this chamber very likely predates the Newport Tower. (See 13.4 for more on the Newport Tower.). Knowing there were people inhabiting the site as early as 2000 BC we can hypothesize it was in an earlier era, serving as something of a ceremonial site. With all of the different ancient inscriptions, it is clear that this site drew a number of different people and different cultures in.

Knowing that Newport Tower has a winter solstice alignment that illuminates a white egg-shaped stone, possibilities began running through my mind. Was there a potential solar alignment here? If so, what day? What time? It had to be sunrise, I thought, considering the opening of the cave was more eastern orientated.

Having my iPhone on hand, I pulled up the Sunseeker App, that would be able to tell me exactly when and where the Sun would set in relation to my location, on certain days of the year. Sure enough, it appeared there was a chance it could have been built to capture the penetrating rays of the Sun on the morning of March 21, the spring equinox, and likely around 9 am like Newgrange and Newport Tower. Excited, I scurried out of the chamber to tell Dennis

Partial illumination, Spring Equinox (Photo Dennis Stone).

my hypothesis. He too was intrigued, and promised to let me know what happened the following March.

On the morning of the spring equinox, I woke up early and eagerly awaited Dennis's message. This was my first time ever *potentially* finding a previously unknown astronomical alignment, so I was really hoping my hypothesis would be proven true. Finally around 7:45 am, Dennis alerted me that it appeared the Sun was rising and illuminating the inside of the chamber. The shape of the illumination looked like a sharply pointed finger reaching upwards. It became obvious then that the entrance to the chamber had been built to cast this exact shape of light. Why? It was precisely the *exact* same shape of the egg-shaped keystone. Giddy with excitement, this confirmed that this was an intentional feature of the chamber! Finally, Dennis sent a photo of the chamber at 7:55 am Eastern Time; the stone was fully illuminated. I was over the moon, pun intended, at this discovery. Dennis then deemed this the *Hayley Chamber.*

The only issue I had was why it wasn't 8:55, closer to 9 am. Firstly, if this site was built prior to the creation of the world's time zones by Sir Sanford Fleming in 1878, then Eastern Time could not have been considered in the construction of the chamber. While contemplating this with Dennis, he mentioned that not too far away the Atlantic Standard Time Zone begins, which would be an hour ahead, therefore illumination would be reached at 8:55 instead of 7:55. Once again, the ancient people wouldn't have used a time zone and would have built based on their own observations. With this in mind, we can hypothesize that they intended the alignment to occur at 9 am.

4.7 The Gate of the Goddess, Bulgaria

Near the Sredna Gora mountains lies a beautiful megalithic site known as the "Gate of the Goddess." Archaeologists say it was constructed between 1800 and 1600 BC. This window was built in the shape of a V, or the feminine triangle, and it was certainly done so on purpose. The entire monument resembles female genitalia, with the rounded stone on top representing the clitoris. In addition to this, it has an astronomical alignment! Only on the morning of Summer Solstice, as the Sun rises, the light shines directly through the window, showing the union of male and female, heaven and earth.

The Gate of t he Goddess, Bulgaria.

In this beautiful photo by Filipov Ivo, you can see the Sun on the morning of the solstice.

The big question here though, is why did they build so many structures in reverence to this union, or to the divine feminine? Were they purely monuments? Or did they have the ability to harness certain energies at specific times of the year? Were they able to harness some type of life giving, goddess energy?

4.8 Carnac, France

In Carnac, France, lie the famous Carnac alignments. The Carnac alignments extend quite a ways, all the way into the ocean even. These people felt the need to quarry and drag *thousands* of standing stones into place. Why? We really do not know. But there are many different sets of standing stones all over Europe. One alignment in the Carnac area in particular seems to have a different feel to it. Built in a rectangle, it embodies the Pythagorean triangle, a whole two of them.

One of the stones here is said to have healing properties. While looking at it from a step back, it immediately becomes clear what it is supposed to look like. A vagina. I asked our friend and Carnac expert, Howard Crowhurst, "Um, Howard, is this stone supposed to look like…" and he interrupted with a grin.

59

"Yes, it is. Now if you come and stand with your back right here…" he led me to the stone and I leaned back against it. I was skeptical. I did begin to feel an unexpected kind of sensation. What I felt was an energy that seemed to buzz into my own body. Howard continued on telling me that resting here was supposed to help the healing process, be it a mental or physical ailment.

That being said, I believe it has to tie back to that belief that Mother Goddess is all loving, all healing, and all accepting. Mothers are known to be nurturing, caretakers of all, and it seems to me the ancients knew this and portrayed it in a way everyone would understand. The female genitalia.

4.9 Sheela Na Gigs

Sheela na gigs, figures of nude women exposing their vaginas, are often found on churches as well. While they are notorious for being found in Ireland, they are also present in Great Britain, Spain and France. It was believed that their presence would scare evil spirits away. Sheela na gigs are often associated with the Celtic goddess, the old hag, the Cailleach. Mircea Eliade, in her book, *The Encyclopedia of Religion* associates the sheela na gig with the ancient hag goddess that granted kingship to the worthy. Many men would refuse Her advances as *She* was old and ugly, but one man did take her to bed. It was after their sexual encounter that She was transformed into a young and beautiful maiden who bestowed royalty upon him and they ruled together as King and Queen.

The sheela na gig figures could have been inspired by a practice called "anasyrma." Anasyrma literally meant, "exposing the genitals." This was primarily a Greek practice that was done in rituals, in humor, and also as a protection mechanism against evil spirits. Mockery was seen as a way to keep evil entities and misfortune at bay. This practice in Greece dates back as early as the 4th-5th centuries BC.

Notice how the vagina of the sheela na gig is an exact oval, the vesica piscis. They are odd looking indeed, but you have to wonder if part of their root in culture was the protective aspect of the goddess. In medieval Christianity it was always Mary who was invoked for protection. This tradition of calling upon "mother" for protection would be instinctual, likely since the dawn of humanity. Who do we

Kilpeck Sheela Na Gig, England.

look to for safety and security, if not our own mother?

4.10 The Venus Figurines

A site in central Turkey, Çatalhöyük, astonished archaeologists with the amount of goddess figurines found. Many goddess figurines have been found here. This site itself was settled by farmers around 7500 BC. Those that previously occupied the area were likely nomads. Nearly 1500 years later, in 6000 BC, the inhabitants of the area carved goddess idols.

The particular figurine, known as the "Seated Woman" was found in the corner of a room near an altar. Anthropologists and archaeologists suggest that this figurine was used in rituals. The figurine can be found at the Museum of Anatolian Civilizations in Ankara, Turkey. Archaeologist James Mellaart, who discovered the figurine in 1961, proclaimed that the settlement was a matriarchy.

Willendorf, Austria produced another Venus figurine. This

61

"Sitting Woman" Venus figurine from Çatalhöyük, Turkey.

one was much older than the Seated Woman. The Willendorf Venus was discovered in 1908 by a worker named Johann Veran during excavations led by archaeologists Josef Szombathy, Hugo Obermaier, and Josef Bayer at a Paleolithic site. The stone it was carved from was oolitic limestone, a stone that is not native to the area in which it was found. This Venus figurine is between 25,000-30,000 years old, meaning that whoever had the idol carried it here from wherever it was carved. One of the closer sources for the oolite could have been just on the other side of the Alps in northern Italy, near Lake Garda.

The stone figure had been found with a red paint-like substance covering it, probably in connection to the female menstrual cycle. There are many examples around the world of goddesses being called the "red goddess" or the "blood goddess." In some instances, such as in India, the figurines and/or artifacts were covered in red ochre to represent the menstruating goddess.

Dating to 35,000-40,000 years ago, during the early Aurignacian, at the very beginning of the Upper Paleolithic, the oldest Venus figurine was carved, the Venus of Hohle Fels. It was discovered in a cave called Hohle Fels near Schelklingen, Germany in 2008 by an archaeological team led by anthropologist Nicholas J. Conard of Universität Tübingen Abteilung Ältere Urgeschichte und Quartärökologie. This was quite an exciting discovery, as it beat the other earliest Venus figurine by nearly 5,000-15,000 years.

The Venus of Willendorf statuette.

The Bringer of Life

This figure was not carved from stone, but from mammoth ivory, making it a rather unique Venus figurine. It is believed that because the head has a perforated protrusion, it was meant to be worn as an amulet.

Nicholas J. Conrad with regard to his discovery said, "This figure is about sex, reproduction... it is an extremely powerful depiction of the essence of being female." Why were all of the Venus figurines depicted as such large females? This is likely because having large hips and breasts indicated that a woman was healthy and strong, and would make a good mother. As food was not an easily obtainable luxury as it is today, to see a large woman, or any human, likely indicated that they were well fed and therefore full of strength. Women were always seen to be full of strength, even to the most primitive people, for She could conceive of life in Her very womb and carry life within Her belly for nine months, then deliver an entire human into this world.

A total of 200 of these Venus figurines have been found all over Europe and the Middle East.. There are two other Venus figurines that could potentially be older than even the Venus of Hohle Fels, but remain controversial. These are the Venus of Berekhat Ram (230,000-280,000 years old) and the Venus of Tan-Tan (300,000 to 500,000 years old.) These artifacts are far more primitive art, and it is not clear if they were both meant to be made to appear to be female. They are not nearly as distinct as the other mentioned Venus figurines. That doesn't exclude the possibility that people were revering the sacred feminine at this time and even earlier.

If the Venus of Hohle Fels was indeed meant to be worn as an amulet, who wore it? Was it women who were trying to become pregnant, was it pregnant women who were seeking a healthy pregnancy, did the Venus figurines represent the Great Mother Goddess? Could this indicate that people 40,000 years ago were spiritually aware and revering a higher deity? Could this be the earliest known form of ancient goddess worship? When spirituality and ritual began to emerge, was it the goddess they first revered above all else?

Chapter 5
The Goddess in the Old World

There is a pattern we see in ancient mythology surrounding the goddess all around the world: the consort who is depicted as her son and lover. This son/lover is also almost always killed or sacrificed, so the goddess must then mourn his death. In Egyptian tradition we find that Osiris and Horus are nearly one and the same in this way. You will also see in later chapters that this same tradition follows in the Gnostic Chritian creation story.

5.1 Mediterranean Goddesses
Cybele, Phrygian Mother of the Gods

Worship of the goddess Cybele began in Asia Minor, more specifically in Phrygia, around the 8th century BC. Some argue that her cult existed even earlier, and that this cult of Cybele evolved from Çatalhöyük. Her cult spread to nearby Greek colonies and then into mainland Greece sometime in the 5th century BC at a temple in Athens. She later appeared in Rome during the Second Punic War (218 -201 BC). In Rome she became known as Magna Mater ("Great Mother"). In Minoa she became heavily associated with the goddess Rhea. Her consort was said to be Attis, who was not in fact a deity, but a priestly youth in Phrygia. Similarly to Jesus being known as a "shepherd," Attis was known as shepherd as well. In reality, the representative of Cybele in the temple would have been a high priestess—who really may have taken a young shepherd as her ritual lover. People within the temple also had duties, and tending the flock may have literally been a job of someone within the priesthood. Perhaps Attis was the title bestowed to the Chief Priest of Cybele. In the 2nd century, the King of Pergamum wrote many letters to the Shrine of Cybele at Pessinos. It is in these letters that the king addresses the Chief Priest of Her Shrine as Attis. In these temples it is likely that there were sacred sexual marriage rites (hieros gamos) that took place on certain occasions between the High Priestess acting as Cybele, and the Chief Priest, Attis the shepherd. Cybele is also commonly depicted with her companion, the lion. This could be due to the close proximity of the constellation Virgo who is preceeded by Leo, the lion.

5.2 The Sumerian Goddesses

While many of the goddesses are the same entity with slightly different stories and names, the importance of the goddess was not just spiritual. The feminine was revered within society as well. This was observed within the royal lineage in Assyrian society. The right to kingship passed not through the paternal lineage, but through the maternal line. The daughter of Sargon, Enheduanna, became chief priestess also known as the "moon minister" to the Most High.

Nammu

Throughout the world, ancient cultures' creation stories abound. In Sumer, their creation story can be attributed to Nammu. There is a dualistic composition to her character. The first part depicts her as the goddess creator and she is said to give birth to the cosmos. This side of her represents femininity, beauty, and motherhood. It was said in ancient Sumerian tradition that the cosmos was created from the primeval waters (similar to Egyptian tradition), and these primeval waters were the body of Nammu. She gave birth to the cosmic mountain, An-Ki, who created Enlil, god of air, who then separated his parents into two different beings. The masculine air god was An, and the feminine earth goddess became Ki.

Later on, as society began to shift from a predominantly female run society, the story of Marduk wove its way into the ancestral stories. In this story, Nammu is a havoc wreaking serpent dragon who is slain by Marduk. After her death, it is said he constructed heaven and Earth from Her body. The idea of Mother Earth is quite relevant here. The Earth deity has always been feminine. Could these stories be the origins of the serpent in Genesis?

It is interesting that an African people not too terribly far from Sumeria, venerated the nommo. These people are known as the Dogon, and are believed to be descended from Egyptian lineage. The Dogon live in Mali, West Africa. Their ancient astronomy

The "Burney Relief" of a Babylonian Goddess, circa 1800 BC.

lore dates back to 3200 BC. The "nommo," which is very similar linguistically to the name of the goddess Nammu, allegedly were demi-god like creatures who were fish-like men. These fish-men have been visiting the Dogon people for thousands of years, and claim to come from a planet in the Sirius star system. Could there be a connection between the goddess who came from the primeval waters, Nammu, and these purported beings from elsewhere in the cosmos?

The Bringer of Life

Tiamat

The Babylonian counterpart of Nammu, Tiamat, came later. She became best known in the Enuma Elish Epic. Like Nammu, She is the goddess of the primeval sea, and is seen as salt water while her consort, Apsu, was the fresh water. Their son, god of the waters, became angry and killed Apsu. Tiamat, angry and grieving, set out with a team of serpents to avenge his death. Marduk then killed her, and like the story of Nammu, Tiamat becomes the sky and the Earth. The blood from her serpent son, Kingu, was then used to create humanity. Could this be the origin of the English word, *king?*

Inanna

This goddess was depicted as having wings! Similar to Isis, the only Egyptian winged goddess... could there be a connection? Not only was Inanna/Ishtar winged, but she also usually was shown to have bird-like feet and was surrounded and guarded by owls. To these ancient cultures, typically owls were not good omens, they were called "depression birds of the night." However it appears to Inanna the owls were her protectors, her guardians, and perhaps spirit guides as well. There is an interesting connection to owls in Egypt and the sacred feminine—hold tight!

Inanna was the goddess of sex and desire, but also of war and combat. She was not your typical housewife! In fact she appeared to be a rather intimidating and strong goddess. So much so, that soldiers and military leaders would actually go pray in her temple before going to battle or before making any major decisions. Inanna's temple was also considered a sacred place for pregnant Assyrian queens. Upon giving birth, the queens would rest, and their newborn babies would feed from the breast of Inanna's priestess.

Inanna (remember she is Ishtar) also was strongly associated with the planet Venus, *the Goddess in the heavens.* In the Babylonian Library of Ashurbanipal lies an ancient document pertaining to Venus, dating to approximately 1600 BC. This document talks about the effects on Earth due to Venus over a 21-year cycle. They called Venus the planet "Nindaranna." Not too different from Inanna. The Assyrians identified Venus as "Ishtar."

Ishtar

While Ishtar and Inanna were two separate entities, they eventually merged into one and the same. The consort of Ishtar was also her son, a shepherd named Tammuz, and goes hand in hand with the idea of the dying son/lover which we observe with Cybele, and later in the story of Jesus. Ishtar became known as the goddess of the morning and evening star, Venus, just like Inanna.

Nisaba

Nisaba is known as the scribe of the gods and the keeper of knowledge—both mortal and divine. Nisaba is the daughter of Anu (the god of the sky) and Uras (Earth goddess). She could be the equivalent to Saraswati, the Hindu goddess of knowledge.

5.3 The Egyptian Goddesses
Isis

Isis is the Greek name for the Mother Goddess the Egyptians knew as Au-set. Au-set literally translates as "throne." She is known for being the wife and sister of the god Osiris. She was adored by all the people more so than any other god or goddess.

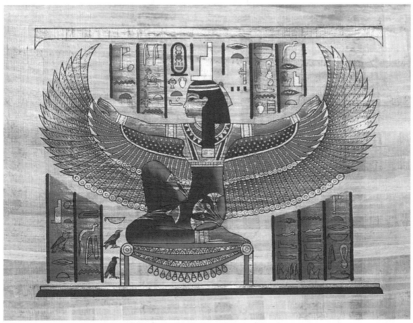

Papyrus depicting Isis in black.

69

Her role in culture was as the all loving mother known for taking in orphan children as her own, and taking care of everyone. She was a very powerful healer and sorceress as well. Au-set is the "Queen of Heaven."

Isis and Osiris were purportedly real people who ruled Egypt before the time of the Pharaohs. In early depictions of Isis you see an empty throne as Her headdress. This is likely because descent in Egypt was indeed matrilineal, therefore it was She who determined the next ruler, not the Pharaoh. Isis became the archetypal wife, queen, and mother. She came to be called "mother and wife of all Pharaohs." This is very similar to gnostic creation stories as well as many other traditions. (See 9.7)

Isis, for many worldwide, stood for the Universal Mother Goddess. Her cults spread far and wide out of Egypt, and even to France and other parts of Europe. Because she represents the Universal Mother Goddess, one of her traditional colors is black. To the Egyptians and members of her cult, black represented the color of the primordial Universe. Black was the color of the Universe, or perhaps the gigantic *cosmic womb* I propose in Chapter 1, that is vast, dark, and empty before She, the Universe/dark energy, creates the explosion of light known as the Big Bang.

In some cases she is depicted in a white dress, or with white garments or accessories. The white would represent purity, light,

A depiction of Isis on the wall of Seti I, Valley of the Kings, circa 1279 BC.

70

Papyrus depicting Osiris judging the architect Kha and his wife, circa 1295 BC.

and love, transcendence. A papyrus shows a depiction of Isis wearing a green and red gown, which is interesting because these are the colors that Mary Magdalene most often wears in biblical art. To the Egyptians green meant many things. They called the afterlife the "Field of Reeds" or even the "Field of Malachite." Green is the color of Osiris's skin, because it stands for life, for spiritual resurrection, or as Christianity knows it: *eternal life.* For Isis to be shown wearing green shows her ability to create life, or to renew it. Green is also the color of the eye of Horus. Isis was a magician, working very much with the living but also the dead in the underworld. Red was the color of fire, chaos, life-force energy, blood, and death. The opposite of green. Isis's wearing of the green and red likely shows her ability to work with both realms: the living and the dead.

There is also a very strong connection between Isis and the Virgin Mary, mother of Jesus Christ. Even Isis was deemed "virgin mother" and probably for many reasons, one reason being that she allegedly conceived Horus by standing over Osiris's dead body, therefore an "immaculate conception."

The concept of "virgin" obviously has changed over the last few thousand years. It used to mean "young unmarried woman" or even to go as far as to say "independent woman, not owned by any man." The title "Virgin" seemed to be given to any woman who

71

Isis and Horus to Mary and Jesus.

was deemed royalty or had committed a humble and loving act. For example, the Virgin Mary was not a virgin as we understand the term.

Practically speaking, science has never witnessed an "immaculate conception" so until someone can prove otherwise, if a woman becomes with child, it is because she has gone to bed with a man. It takes two parties to procreate. Regardless of who the biological father of the child was (which was probably Joseph), Mary did give birth to a historically significant man, Jesus, who later becomes known as the Christ, *the anointed*. Perhaps the story was wound to fit the Pagan narratives to make their conversion easier, or maybe Jesus and his family were attempting to allegorically recreate the story of the slain shepherd who is resurrected by the goddess. Osiris was depicted with a crook and flail, showing that he was a shepherd of his flock, of his people, just as Ishar and Tammuz, Persephone and Adonis, and even Jesus and Mary Magdalene. Jesus was referred to as the "good shepherd" in John 10:11: "I am the good shepherd. The good shepherd lays down his life for the sheep." Mary Magdalene's name could even mean "watchtower" as it is associated with a tower. Was Mary the "watchtower" over the shepherd's flock?

In ancient Egyptian culture, Isis and Horus were always depicted in art in very much the same way baby Jesus and Mary are. Horus was the "sun god" while Jesus, centuries after his death, became known as the "son of God." There are interesting parallels here. The "wafer" can be traced back to ancient Egypt, where they likely ate them in ritual, the round wafer representing the Egyptian Sun disk, the solar deity, as the body of Osiris. By consuming the body of Osiris, they would embody the god. The idea of a "sun god" being born in December and resurrected around springtime throughout other ancient cultures and religions is universal.

One of the strong symbols of Isis is the vulture. In some instances we see her wearing the vulture over her head. To the ancient Egyptians, the vulture was the bird of the pharaoh. The vulture represented the eternal Mother Goddess as they believed the bird became pregnant and could lay eggs by parthenogenesis, or without male intervention. Isis spreads her wings and takes to the sky like a vulture after her consort is killed.

We see the son-lover concept here. Osiris, husband of Isis, is killed in battle when fighting his evil brother Set/Seth. Set kills his brother and cuts him into 14 pieces and spreads them across Egypt. Then Isis weeps, and flies across Egypt to locate all of the parts of Osiris. Once she puts them back together, she stands above him and miraculously conceives. Thus, Horus is born of a "virgin" conception. Horus and Osiris are often seen as one and the same here.

There is another element to Isis that is rather mysterious. We see many depictions of Isis, and later Hathor, and many other elements of the Egyptian goddess depicted with horns. Many scholars have said the appearance of horns on Isis, Hathor, and the other goddesses is just showing the assimilation of Hathor and the other goddesses, as they all become one.

A fascinating case is presented by Christopher Knight and Robert Lomas in their book, *The Book of Hiram.* One of the subjects they discuss is the astrological connection between the horns we see on the Egyptian Goddess and the planet that is known as the Goddess in the Heavens, Venus. How are the two even connected?

The ancient peoples' spirituality all has to do with nature: we also know that they depended upon the cycles of nature to be able to plan crops, shelter, and movement based on the season. They also looked to Venus. As She prepared for Her descent into the

Underworld She would have been an Evening Star, and upon Her resurrection you would see Her as a Morning Star, thus restarting the cycle. If you were to track Venus every day over the course of this cycle from Earth, you would be seeing the pattern of Venus high in the sky in the west, then how she slowly dips down below the horizon in the middle of the cycle (representing the Goddess in the Underworld or in darkness). She who is veiled, and then rises again in the eastern sky. This pattern very closely resembles the horns we see depicted on the head of Isis as well as the other goddesses.

A depiction of Horned Isis.

Nekhbet

Nekhbet is yet another enigmatic goddess of the Egyptian past. She was popular in predynastic Egypt, meaning before 3100 BC. Nekhbet was considered a creator goddess and was dually associated with another goddess, Wadjet. Later they merge. Interestingly, Nekhbet is the most strongly tied to the vulture and the serpent! She is known as the "vulture goddess." She was a royal protector of all children and expectant mothers.

Specifically, it appears she was most revered around the town of Nekheb. In the Pyramid Texts from the Fifth Dynasty, they say that Nekhbet is "Father of Fathers, Mother of Mothers, (She) who has existed from the beginning, and is Creator of this World." She was represented on the King Nemes headdress as a serpent or vulture. From the Fourth Dynasty on, she is represented as a vulture which represented the "great and royal wife."

Nekhbet and her counterpart Wadjet are represented as two serpents on the royal headdress. Nekhbet and Wadjet were the protectors of royal women in the Eighteenth Dynasty.

As well as being related to Isis (Au-set) by the vulture connection, she may have a stronger connection to her than we thought. Nekhbet and Isis are the only winged goddesses in Egyptian history, and both seem to have a relationship to Horus, the Sun God. In the story of Isis, Osiris and Horus, there is an interesting tale that relates almost all Egyptian goddesses with Isis. Nekhbet's part in this story occurs when Isis must find all of the dismembered parts of her husband's body that the evil brother of Osiris (Set) has hidden. It is at this point perhaps Isis assumes the vulture status of Nekhbet and flies over the ground, seeking the pieces of her beloved.

Another nickname Nekhbet assumes is the "pharaoh's nurse." This ties her to yet *another* goddess…

Hathor

The cow headed goddess is called Hathor. She is associated also with Horus, and in fact, her name means "domain of Horus" or "temple of Horus" according to an article on Ancient History Encyclopedia by Joshua J. Mark. She is also known for being the daughter of the Sun god, Ra. According to the scholar Geraldine Pinch, "Hathor was the golden goddess who helped women to give

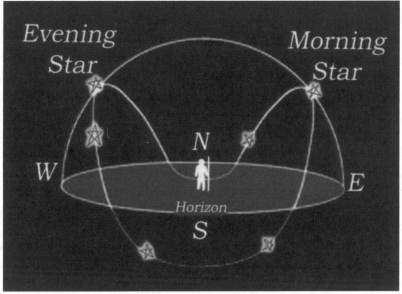

A diagram of the Horns of Venus.

75

birth, the dead to be reborn, and the cosmos to be renewed. This complex deity could function as the mother, consort, and daughter of the creator god. Many lesser goddesses came to be regarded as "names" of Hathor in Her contrasting benevolent and destructive aspects. She was most commonly shown as a beautiful woman wearing a red solar disk between a pair of cow's horns."

It is said that Isis absorbed many of *Hathor*'s characteristics. So did Hathor come before Isis? We know the first worship of Hathor began in Dendera in around 3000 BC under the name of *Mistress of Dendera*. It was by 2700 BC that She was worshiped as Hathor, and Her popularity spread. Isis (Au-set) begins being referenced in the Pyramid Texts (c. 2350–c. 2100 BC). So, was Hathor the original Isis? Isis was the creatress of the Universe, ruler of the skies, and the Mother of all, specifically relating to the Milky Way above. She presumably is also a form of Hathor, because Hathor is said to be the mother or wife of Horus as well. The original Mother Goddess. This "part" of Isis as Hathor is essential to the raising of Horus. Isis becomes like the "cow goddess" by breastfeeding Horus her milk.

One cannot ignore the fact that this cow goddess likely had been a personification of the Milky Way, spread across the night sky. The Milky Way was seen as the milk that came from the udders of the heavenly cow. In this sense Hathor was closely linked to Nut/Nun, the cosmic deities.

Sekhmet

A goddess embodies many qualities, several of which we have seen through the other Egyptian goddesses. The one quality, the one goddess we have yet to meet is the warrior goddess, the protector. A fierce warrior, a goddess of healing, the lioness, She is known as Sekhmet. While she is known for being the goddess of war and destruction, she is also known for her healing abilities. She is also known as the daughter of Ra, and is strongly associated with fire. As is Isis. In the Jumilhac papyrus, Isis is said to have magically become "Her mother Sekhmet" by her own will.

This "Isis Enigma" is essentially telling us that Isis takes whatever form is necessary to accomplish her Mother Goddess tasks, such as protecting her children, be it her actual children or children of the Earth, and leading them into battle watching over to heal them (Sekhmet), or nursing her children with milk (Hathor), or turning into a vulture to search for the lost parts of her brother and husband, Osiris (Nekhbet).

5.4 The Phoenician-Canaanite & Biblical Goddesses

Astarte, also known as Ashtaroth and the Queen of Heaven, was worshiped primarily by the Canaanites who frequently burned offerings and poured libations for Her. Her name meant "star" or sometimes "light from the East" because of Her association with the planet Venus, the Morning Star. She was typically seen as the goddess of love, sex, and war. Her worship began sometime in the first millennium BC. She was also worshiped in Egypt, Ugarit, and amongst the Hittites.

In Jeremiah 44, he speaks to the people of idolatry, and tells them to quit worshiping false idols. The women say in response, "We will not listen to the message you have spoken to us in the

The Tanit Stele, British Museum.

The Tanit Stele, Carthage, Bardo National Museum.

Jesus Son of Joseph Ossuary, Israel Museum, Jerusalem.

name of the Lord! We will certainly do everything we said we would: We will burn incense to the Queen of Heaven and will pour out drink offerings to Her just as we and our ancestors, our kings and our officials did in the towns of Judah and in the streets of Jerusalem."

King Solomon was said to have built a temple to Her near Jerusalem. Later it was removed during Josiah's reform. She was the wife of the supreme god, Baal. Astarte was one and the same as Ishtar and later Isis.

Asherah, sometimes called Elat, was the consort of the creator god called El, Yahweh, and sometimes Baal. Asherah was worshiped in Syria and Palestine and known as "She Who Walks On the Sea." This is an important designation, as the Christian equivalent of the goddess, Mary Magdalene, has many associations with the sea, especially in southern France. Asherah had a strong connection to trees, and was often represented by the "*asherim* trees." This is mentioned in the Bible over 30 times. These sacred trees or

The constellation Virgo.

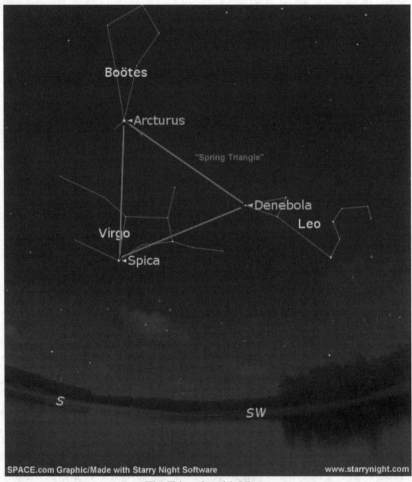

The Triangle with Virgo.

poles were usually used in ancient Israelite ritual, and were erected usually next to a statue of Baal. The tree in essence represented the idea of the "Tree of Life" which appeared to be a universal belief around the world.

She is called the "creatress of the gods" in ancient texts found at Ugarit from the late Bronze Age (1550–1200 BC). Her husband at Ugarit is El, who is the "creator." Second millennium inscriptions refer to Her as the "Lady of the Serpent."

5.5 Tanit the Moon Goddess & the Flower of Life

Her name is also spelled Tinith or Tinnit—but they all refer to the same goddess. She is one of the oldest goddesses of all time, worshiped as the wife of Amon/Amen *and* Baal as well as some of the other goddesses whom you have read about. Tanit was the main goddess of Carthage—an area now in Tunisia, North Africa. Carthage was allegedly founded in 813 BC by the Phoenician Queen Elissa (aka Dido). Tanit was very often depicted in a triangular form, which could very well be where we get the restroom symbol for women today. The triangle is a

The Seal of Solomon.

very ancient and very basic symbol of the goddess. It represents the pubic triangle, the womb, and also the Nile Delta. The water and the land were feminine aspects associated with the Mother-Earth Goddess.

In the first stele showing Tanit (p. 77), *She* is shown wearing what looks like a crescent moon, or even the crescent of Venus, on Her head. Her arms are bent upwards, which later in history became the symbol of distress for a Freemason to recognize another Freemason in distress, interestingly. Many depictions and steles of Tanit show Her with Her arms in this position.

With regard to the origin of the distinct triangular shape that represents Tanit, Scott Wolter shared an intriguing theory with me. He proposed that Tanit's shape came from the constellation Virgo, which appears to show two arms up much in the same way. During the springtime, Virgo appears in the midst of three stars that form an equilateral triangle: Arcturus, Spica, and Denebola. Is this the origin of the Tanit symbol? If so, is the constellation Virgo the origin for the Masonic symbol of distress?

The second stele (p. 78) shows the Flower of Life above Her, an ancient symbol that dates to as early as 6000 BC in the Temple of Osiris in Abydos, Egypt. The Flower of Life has six petals, and could very possibly represent the Morning Star, Venus. This likely indicates Tanit's association not only with the Moon, but with Venus. The same symbol was later seen on 1st century Jewish ossuaries, or bone boxes. The Talpiot Tomb, supposedly the Jesus family tomb, contains many ossuaries. (See 11.3 for more on the Talpiot Tomb).

The Flower of Life could be associated with what later became the "Star of David" which also was a six pointed star. If you draw an outline around the flower, it becomes abundantly clear in its connection to the Seal of Solomon. In this way, the symbol has two triangles, the upward masculine triangles, and the downward facing feminine triangle. It is the dualistic union of opposites: male and female, heaven and earth, etc.

Several Knights Templar grave slabs also contain this symbol. In December of 2021, I was visiting the St. Magnus Cathedral in Orkney where the oldest gravestone was a Templar gravestone. On the slab is a Templar sword and the Flower of Life symbol.

A Templar grave stone at the St. Magnus Church in the Orkney Islands.

Chapter 6
The Goddess in Arabia

6.1 Al-Lat/Elat

She was referenced in a text as early as the 5th century BC by Herodotus. He identifies her as *Ailat,* the equivalent of the Greek Aphrodite. Her name translates to "Goddess" as Allah translates to "God." It is noted that she, in all her forms around the Middle East, is associated with the planetary body Venus, known as the Queen of Heaven. Al-Lat is known as Asherah or Astarte (the biblical goddess we discussed in the last chapter) in the land of Canaan but also as Elat. Under Greco-Roman influence she is associated with Athena, and the Roman equivalent of Minevera. This goddess, Al-Lat, was known as Lat and Latan in South Arabia as well as Northern Arabia, as told by inscriptions of Her name found there. In Eastern Arabia she was known as Taymallat.

In Ta'if, where she was called ar-Rabba ("The Lady"), she was venerated in the form of a cubic granite rock. Her shrine was decorated with ornaments of gold and onyx. This same shrine was also worshiped as Al-Uzza by the Quraysh, and guarded by the tribe Banū Thaqīf. The land surrounding Her temple was so sacred no animal could be hunted and no man's blood could be shed.

It is interesting to note that the lion is a very important symbol of this aspect of Goddess. The cult of this specific goddess spans from Syria to Iraq, to Arabia, parts of Iran, Yemen borders, and was worshiped by many different groups and cultures, just as Isis's cult spread far and wide from Egypt to Europe. Throughout the Middle East, Goddess was always associated with harvests, corn, and agricultural affairs. She fulfilled the aspect of Mother Goddess by providing crops and food for the people.

6.2 Qedarites & Al-Lat Goddess Worship

The Qedarites are an ancient nomadic Arabic tribe that has been described as the most organized of the Northern Arabian tribes. The Qedarite Kingdom reached its peak in the 6th century BC and controlled much of Arabia. The bible tells us that the Qedarites descend from the second son of Ishmael, who is seen to be the ancestral forefather of Islam. They are mentioned in the Bible's books of Genesis (25:13) and 1 Chronicles (1:29), where they are also frequently talked about as a tribe. However there is no archaeological evidence to give us a clue as to when the tribe of the Qedarites ceased to actually exist as a culture and as a people. We do know we see a lack of evidence beginning in the 2nd century AD. The Qedarites were known allies of the nearby Nabataeans. It is assumed the Qedarites were probably absorbed into the Nabataeans over time, but there is not enough archaeological evidence to determine what really happened. The possibility also stands that this group left the area for a new land or new place to call their kingdom.

One must note that after the first documented king of the Qedarite Kingdom, Gindibu, whose reign lasted from 870-850 BC, there are solely queens ruling the Qedarite Kingdom. Not with a king consort, but solo queens.

Based on the archaeological record, we know that before most cultures became patriarchal over time, but thousands of years ago began as matriarchal cultures. Men revered women as the bringers of life, and this was likely because a lot of ancient people did not understand the connection between sex and pregnancy. We do know that in the Qedarite kingdom, even when the time came in 676 BC that queens stopped ruling and kings took over, they still revered Her, Al-Lat. We know this because of a silver bowl found at Tell Maskhuta in the eastern Nile Delta in lower Egypt, that was dated to the 5th century BC. The inscription names a man as "Qainū son of Gashmu," with the vessel described as an "offering to han-'Ilāt (Al-Lat)."

Al-Lat, Al-Uzza and Manat

These three goddesses seemed to be worshiped in the triple. Gerald R. Hawting, a British historian and Islamicist, states that scholars have seen these three goddesses associated with cults devoted to the heavenly body of Venus. This worship of Goddess in reverence to Venus was observed in Syria, Mesopotamia and

84

A depicition of the Three Daughters of Allah.

the Sinai Peninsula. The three goddesses as a trio were known as the "three daughters of Allah" in the Koran.

Al-Uzza has mostly been worshiped as a fertility goddess, and the youngest of the trio. Her name means "most mighty." Al-Uzza had a sanctuary in a valley on the road from Mecca, the sanctuary having three acacia trees into which She was said to descend. Her worship seems to have originated in the south of ancient Arabia, Sheba/Saba (present day Yemen). The Greeks viewed Her as their Ourania ("The Heavenly") as well as Caelistis, a Moon Goddess and the Roman name for the Carthaginian Tanit goddess. Herodotus himself stated that the supreme Goddess of the Arabs was Ourania, whom he says was called Alilat. It would make sense that potentially Goddesses went by different names in different regions, but perhaps they are one and the same.

She is often identified with Isis. As I mentioned earlier, in a similar fashion, Al-Lat's cult was spread far and wide just like the cult of Isis. Al-Uzza is mostly known for being the goddess of the Nabataens, who lived close to the Qedarites. She was invoked by sailors on ocean voyages for protection. In the city of Petra, in

A depicition of Al-Uzza.

present day Jordan, Her veneration was plain and typical of the city's people. The Temple of the Winged Lions in Petra may be linked to Her worship. As we noted earlier, one of many of Al-Lat's symbols is the lion. However Al-Uzza's connection to the sea and voyages is typically represented by the dolphin. It is still interesting to note that the constellation Virgo, representing the maiden, is found right next to the constellation of Leo, the lion.

The consort of Al-Uzza is known as Hubal, the masculine deity of the ancient Arabians. He was primarily worshiped in Mecca and by the Quraysh people. In 624 at the Battle of Uhud, the Qurayshites' war cry was, "O people of Uzzā, people of Hubal!" Unfortunately in 630 AD, the temple dedicated to Her near Mecca was destroyed by Khalid ibn al-Walid, sent by Muhammad.

Manat's (the oldest of the three daughters) name derives from the word "mana" which means to determine fate respectively. The Jews in the bible survived on "manna" for 40 years in the desert. They claim it was a physical thing, but maybe it was actually called manna as it was a spiritual substance, a spiritual food and power that sustained them.

Manat played a slightly different role than our other two younger goddesses. She oversaw time, death, and fate and represented the old woman, the crone aspect of the goddess. Manat was the first daughter of Allah, according to religious texts.[1] She becomes the wife of Quzah, the Meccan god of storms, thunder, and the clouds. Manat's idol was of black marble, which is not surprising. In Egypt, and later Europe, there were many "Black Madonnas" worshiped as Goddess, and later on she became associated with Mary Magdalene and the Virgin Mary.

Because Manat oversaw the dead, time, and fate, she was often called upon to protect tombs, graves, and to curse those who disturbed them. One of the beliefs surrounding the elder sister goddess was that she would appear to the dying holding a chalice in her hand. Is it possible this was an early portrayal of the Holy Grail?

Since life could not come without death, and death without life, She was revered for her association with death. Al-Uzza was the maiden, she represented the young and innocent; Al-Lat was

---

[1] The Kitāb al-Aṣnām, or The Book of Idols

the mother (Goddess); and Manat was the crone, death. Therefore the waning moon is often associated with Manat, as the time of the living draws to an end as the waning moon moves toward darkness (new moon).

6.3 The Kaaba Stone

Within the Great Mosque of Mecca, a small black oval-shaped stone about seven inches in diameter can be found built into the eastern wall. This stone is known as the *Kaaba Stone*. According to Elsebeth Thomsen of the University of Copenhagen, the Kaaba Stone could very well be a glass fragment or impactite of a fragmented meteorite that fell approximately 6,000 years ago near

The Black Stone at the Kaaba in Mecca.

the Wabar impact craters, about 683.5 miles east of Mecca. The Islamic story of the stone tells that it fell from Jannah, or Paradise/ Heaven, shortly after Adam and Eve fell from Paradise, and Adam was tasked with building an altar to house the stone.

Muhammad was said to have first installed the Black Stone into the east wall of the Kaabah in 605 AD. His first revelation occurred five years later. Muhammad had blessed and kissed the stone, which made it a popular place of pilgrimage for the Islamic people. When they visit, if they are able, they are meant to kiss

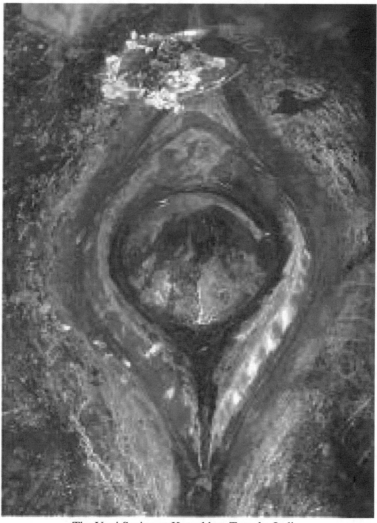

The Yoni Spring at Kamakhya Temple, India.

the stone and say the takbir, "God is greatest." This is said after completing the ritual seven circles around the Kaaba.

Before Islam existed, the stone was held sacred by the Pagan population. Many associated the Black Stone with Arabic goddesses and their fertility cults, specifically the goddess Al-Uzza. It isn't a surprise considering that the stone's shape is oval, the shape of the vagina, and in sacred geometry, the vesica piscis. (See diagram in 13.6) Surrounding the oval-shaped stone is a very yoni looking silver cover. This was added likely in the medieval era. We established earlier that the goddess was often associated with the color black as it was the color of the primordial waters of creation, a time before creation. The stone was placed in the eastern wall, which may be indicative of the connection to the goddess. Venus, as the Morning Star, can be found in the eastern sky before sunrise. The tradition of kissing the yoni shaped stone may be reminiscent of a much older ritual form of goddess worship.

Another yoni-shaped stone can be found in India at the Kamakhya Temple. This is one of the oldest temples associated with the Shakti traditions, dating back to the 8th century AD. It is known as the "locus of the goddess's own yoni." This is likely because of the natural spring that flows from the yoni-shaped stone. Every year when monsoon season begins, the natural spring turns red due to iron oxide and the priests use the red pigment to anoint the yoni stone. This is symbolic of the red goddess—the menstruating goddess, who is celebrated each June.

Is it possible the Islamic people associated this oval-shaped Kaaba Stone with the fall of "Eve" from Heaven, due to its shape, and because it literally fell from the skies? Was the kiss that Muhammad bestowed upon it something of an earlier form of goddess worship? The ancient people who revered the goddess certainly saw the connections to their own Arabic goddesses.

Chapter 7
Ancient Moon Time
& Native Stories

For thousands and thousands of years, mankind has looked to the night sky in awe and wonder. Our ancestors saw how the Moon changes during its cycle. Our ancestors kept track of the Moon phases, and they saw the effect the Moon has on the water. This is not new knowledge, the ancient people around the world all knew these things. And then they saw that women have a Moon too.

Every month, women have a menstrual cycle. Women's bodies operate on a twenty-eight day cycle, and have thirteen cycles every year. So does the Moon! If one chooses to observe a lunar calendar instead of the solar calendar (the calendar most of the world uses) they will see there are actually thirteen months in a year! Months of course derives from the word "Moons."

Every month, when the Moon time would come around for the women of the Earth, this would be a special time. This would be a time of inner purification, a time to reflect, prepare, and to harness the life-giving energy a woman has. In ancient America, native women probably went to a special cave to menstruate before they began building Moon lodges. I have heard from Lakota elders that "having your Moon is a ceremony all by itself." Around the world, there is evidence women used to spend time during Moon time in certain caves and bleed onto the ground. This was a sacred time of union with Mother Earth. A time to connect, release, and seek wisdom.

7.1 The Beginning of Moon Time

Nicholas Noble Wolf, a medicine man of the San Juan Pueblo in New Mexico, wrote in an article published in the Sacred Hoop magazine, Winter 2000/2001, "Most, if not all traditions of Native American spirituality hold Moon-time as a sacred time of purification during which women do not go into ceremony or use sacred objects such as pipes and feathers. Often people from Western culture see this as a disrespectful and negative stereotyping of a woman's menstrual cycle. We traditional people do not see it this way, as Moon-time is a place of honor and beauty." Noble Wolf goes on to tell a story about how women began to receive their Moon times. The story goes like this:

A long time ago, women did as they do now—they held the family, they held the power (life-force) for the family, they held the happiness and joy, they held the sorrow and disappointments. After time, the negative emotions and heartache that the women took upon themselves on behalf of their families would begin to weigh them down. The women would become sick and finally, could no longer take on the burdens of the family. Yet the nature to do so had been imbued into them by Creator.

One day, a woman was out in the forest, crying because the burden had become so great, when Raven heard her and asked, "Mother, why do you cry?"

The woman responded, "I love my family so very much. I hold my family in my heart and soul, but the pains of life have filled me up. I can no longer help my family. I can no longer take their burdens from them. I just don't know what to do."

Raven responded, "I understand the pain you feel, as I feel it also. I will go and ask Grandmother Ocean if she knows what to do." So Raven flew to the ocean and shared with Grandmother the plight of the women.

Grandmother Ocean answered, "If the women will come to me, I will wash their pain from them, but this won't help the ones who are far away. Let me ask my sister, Grandmother Moon, if she can help."

So Grandmother Ocean spoke to her sister of the women's plight. Grandmother Moon responded, "I am the power of the feminine. I will send into the women, my sisters, your waters carrying my power. Once every Moon cycle, you shall come into the women through me and purify them." And, she did this. So ever since then, every woman has a time each Moon cycle when she embodies the power of the Moon and flows the cleansing of the ocean. We call this the woman's time of the Moon, or Moon-time.

Next time you see a full Moon, you can look to her radiant beauty and know that Grandmother Moon helps keep everything in balance. The tides, the Moon times of all women, and so much more. She has always been a symbol of the sacred feminine, and she always will be.

Native Americans who lived on the plains, prairies, even forests, and down on the coast all seemed to build "Moon lodges" or "menstrual huts." These were lodges and huts built specially for the women having their Moon. The women would spend this week of Moon time with the other women having their Moon (women that spend time together tend to be on the same Moon cycle) and would typically occupy their time with arts and crafts, songs, prayer, and storytelling.

I attended Sun Dance (a Lakota ceremony) in the summer of 2019 and learned the importance of Moon time from my Lakota friends and family firsthand. If a woman has her Moon, she cannot be near a medicine man's ceremony, or touch food during the ceremony, because it is believed that women are so powerful at this time that they can affect the medicine man's ability to do spiritual work. The women could suck the energy and power right out of a man, it is believed. So if a woman makes a commitment to dance for the ceremony and she receives her Moon, she must leave the ceremony and perhaps choose to fulfill her commitment and dance somewhere else.

In the old days, around the world women would all gather during Moon time, because their cycles would synchronize, and they would spend it in either caves or lodges specifically for Moon time. Native Americans have called it a "Moon hut" or a "Moon lodge." Around the world some women would gather in caves, the womb of the Earth goddess, and offer their menstrual blood back to Mother. There is an ancient Hopi prophecy that states, "When the women give their blood back to the earth, men will come home from war and earth shall find peace."

The Bringer of Life

Within all women is the goddess waiting to be communed with. Within all women is unprecedented strength, love, and power. She is just waiting to be awakened once again.

Chapter 8
Return of White Buffalo
Calf Woman

For many thousands of years, there have been people living across North America, Central America, and South America. Twenty thousand years ago ancient people migrated across the Bering Land Bridge. There are thousands of years of history here! As people migrated here, and even possibly via an Atlantic route, they begin to leave their mark.

Like other ancient people, their world revolved around nature, much like the ancient Europeans on the other side of the globe at the same time. They lived in communities where survival in nature was the center of their life. They depended on Mother Earth to provide food, water, medicine, and shelter.

8.1 The Lakota & White Buffalo Calf Woman

Firstly, there are a few words you will hear quite frequently through the Lakota section. One of those is Wakan Tanka, which means "Great Mystery" or simply the divine mystery, God, or whatever you choose to call Him/Her. Then we have Tunkashila that can be taken to mean "Grandfather." However Tunkashila embodies all that of spirit and life. It is not just one. Rather it is both feminine and masculine. It is Grandfather, Grandmother, and so much more. In the story of the Chanunpa (sacred pipe), which White Buffalo Calf Woman brings to the Lakota people, the Chanunpa has both feminine and masculine characteristics. The offering to be smoked is put into the red pipestone. The red pipestone embodies all that of Mother Earth, the daughter of Her (women upon Earth), because women upon Earth bleed onto the Earth; it represents the cycles of life and fertility. The wooden stem we smoke from on the opposite end is the masculine. It is the tree, it is the outward growth of Mother Earth.

One of the ancient stories of the Lakota-Sioux people revolves around a woman. The Seven Rites that are practiced still to this day were brought to them by White Buffalo Calf Woman. Joseph Chasing Horse, Traditional Leader of the Lakota Nation, tells the story like this.

While two warriors were out hunting buffalo, a white buffalo calf suddenly appeared. As she approached them she changed into a beautiful young woman... which is how she came to be called the White Buffalo Calf Woman. One of the young warriors offended her with his lustful thoughts and White Buffalo Calf Woman asked him to approach.

As he stepped forward, a black cloud descended over him and when it dissipated all that was left of him was his bones. The other warrior fell to his knees and began to pray. The White Buffalo Calf Woman told him to return to his people, telling them she would appear to them in four days, bringing with her a sacred bundle.

And this she did, appearing to them as a white buffalo calf descending on a cloud. Stepping down, she rolled over on the ground, changing from white to black, then yellow, then red. When White Buffalo Calf Woman arose she was once again the beautiful woman, cradling the sacred bundle in her arms. Spending four days with the people, White Buffalo Calf Woman taught them sacred songs, dances, and ceremonies as well as the traditional ways. White Buffalo Calf Woman instructed them to be responsible caretakers of the land and to be always mindful that the children are the future of the people.

On the fourth day White Buffalo Calf Woman left in the same manner she had arrived, telling the people she was leaving the sacred bundle, the White Buffalo Calf Woman pipe, in their care. She promised to one day return for it and to bring harmony and spiritual balance to the world. White Buffalo Calf Woman prophesied that the birth of a white buffalo calf would be a sign that it was near the time of her return.

White Buffalo Calf Woman shows a major turning point in

native spirituality. It is said that before her, only Great Spirit was honored. She brought to them knowledge, wisdom, and the Seven Sacred Rites, and the peace pipe. According to legends, she says:

> In this bundle is a sacred pipe, which must always be treated in a holy way. No impure man or woman should ever see it. With this sacred pipe you will send your voices to Wakan Tanka, the Great Spirit, Creator of all, your Father and Grandfather. With this sacred pipe you will walk upon the Earth, which is your Grandmother and Mother. All your steps should be holy. The bowl of the pipe is red stone, which represents the earth. A buffalo calf is carved in the stone facing the center and symbolizes the four-legged creatures who live as brothers among you. The stem is wood and represents all growing things. Twelve feathers hang from where the stem fits the bowl, from the Spotted Eagle; these represent all the winged brothers who live among you."

> "All these things are joined to you who will smoke the pipe and send voices to Wakan Tanka. When you use this pipe to pray, you will pray for and with everything. The sacred pipe binds you to all your relatives, your grandfather and father, your grandmother and mother. The red stone represents the Mother Earth on which you will live. The Earth is red, and the two-leggeds who live upon it are also red. Wakan Tanka has given you a red road, a good and straight road to travel. And you must remember that all people who stand on this earth are sacred. From this day, the sacred pipe will stand on the red earth, and you will send your voices to Wakan Tanka. There are seven circles on the stone, which represent the seven rites in which you will use the pipe.

Ever since White Buffalo Calf Woman gifted the Lakota people with this sacred bundle, it has been passed on to a special keeper over the generations. Currently Chief Arvol Looking Horse is the keeper of the sacred bundle.

The seven rites are still practiced today. They are known as:

1. The Keeping of the Soul
2. Inipi: The Sweat Lodge Ceremony or Rite of Purification
3. Hanblecheyapi: Vision Quest
4. Wiwanyag Wachipi: The Sun Dance Ceremony
5. Hunkapi: Making Relatives
6. Ishnata Awicalowan: Preparing a Girl for Womanhood
7. Tapa Wanka Yap: Throwing the Ball

I will only dive into a few of these, but I highly recommend reading and learning about the other sacred rites. While seven is a universally significant number, I find it interesting that there are "Seven Gifts of the Holy Spirit." We know that the Holy Spirit is the sacred feminine within Christianity, and is represented by a *white dove* while She is represented by a *white buffalo* in Lakota tradition. These seven gifts are: wisdom, understanding, counsel, fortitude, knowledge, piety, and fear of God. There are also seven "sacraments" or *rites* that Jesus teaches in the bible. These are: Baptism, Confirmation, Eucharist, Reconciliation, Anointing of the Sick, Matrimony, and Holy Orders.

8.2 Inipi: Sweat Lodge Ceremony of Purification

The Sweat Lodge Ceremony is a ceremony that is typically done to begin something even greater. For example, it is done before the solstice and equinox celebrations still to this day, but also for any other ceremony occasion. Sweat Lodge is a lodge that is dome-shaped and covered in blankets. Inside the lodge there is a pit dug out to place rocks that have been heated by the fire outside the lodge. These rocks are referred to as the *grandfathers*. When everyone gathers inside the sweat lodge, water is poured over the hot rocks producing steam. Everyone begins to sweat.

Sometimes songs are sung, along with a drum, and the drum is meant to be the heartbeat of Mother Earth. The dome is symbolic of the womb, and one enters a sweat lodge to be "reborn" in a sense and to purify themselves. It is a very special time of prayer, healing, and sometimes very intense spiritual experiences. As everyone sweats, their sweat falls from their body to the Earth, connecting their bodies with Mother Earth as one.

Originally, women did not participate in Sweat Lodge because women experienced their own natural purification every month in the form of their "moon" or menstrual bleeding. Women would go to a "moon lodge" instead and bleed onto the ground. Men did not, and instead had to take part in Inipi, Sweat Lodge Ceremony. However, in more recent history that changed. Women now are mostly allowed to take part in this ceremony.

Sweat Lodge is a universal ceremony in the Americas, taking

The Altar and Umbilical Cord, June 2019.

place amongst many American tribes, especially middle American tribes. Whilst taking part in a sweat lodge at summer solstice in 2019 near Ohio's Serpent Mound, I found another part of this ceremony to be deeply rooted in the goddess. Outside the lodge was a line of rocks leading to a round circle of rocks. Inside the circle of rocks was an altar with a buffalo skull. When I asked Terri, the woman who was leading the sweat lodge, she explained to me that this line of stones was the "umbilical cord" of the lodge, of the womb of the earth, that ran to the altar. This line must not be crossed by anyone except the leader of the sweat lodge.

8.3 Wiwanyag Wachipi: The Sun Dance Ceremony

Sun dance honors Father, Grandfather, the Sun and Sky of course, but also our Mother Earth. There is a beautiful duality in this ceremony. This is a ceremony danced in honor of the Sun but also in honor of Mother Earth. Men dance for three days in a row to enter the spirit world. As they dance, they connect to Mother Earth and experience an enlightening spiritual experience in most cases, but for everyone it is different. Dancers continue to dance and fast, no food or water for three days. Sundance usually brings guidance, visions, and answers to its participants. In most cases in modern times women are welcome to dance as well but usually do not get pierced.

On the final day, some men will be pierced. The medicine man will come and pierce two holes in a man's chest, so that he may be tethered to the cottonwood tree in the middle of the arena. This tether is symbolic of the umbilical cord of Mother Earth. Men are pierced for several reasons, one being that they may try to experience some of the pain that their sisters do during childbirth. At the end of the ceremony, pierced dancers will lean back, and break free from the tether to the Tree of Life. This is their rebirth and return from the spirit world or the spiritual womb of Mother Earth.

8.4 Ishnata Awicalowan: Preparing a Girl for Womanhood

An event so special in a young woman's life that can now allow her to bring many more lives into this world—this is her first "moon." When a young woman has her first moon, she becomes able to be like Mother Earth and bear children. This celebration lasts four days. A medicine man will lead a ceremony in which she is purified as a woman now able to bring forth life from her body. Like in many ceremonies, a buffalo skull is the central object of the ceremony. Do not forget the sacred feminine connection to White Buffalo Calf Woman! After her purification, the entire community takes part in celebrations!

Different native cultures have different celebrations of the "Preparing a Girl for Womanhood Ceremony." But what is important is that almost every native culture *does* celebrate the transformation of girl to woman. From girl to goddess. Able to bring life. In the Apache traditions, this is Sunrise Ceremony, which has to do with a tradition about their divine feminine being, White Painted Woman. In Navajo traditions, this is known as Kinaalda. This celebration can be attributed to the "Changing Woman" or the first mother of mankind on Earth in Navajo creation stories. There are many different traditions of a goddess-like woman who brings gifts of wisdom, song, and knowledge. We will dive into the different cultures' perception of this feminine aspect of spirit.

8.5 Prophecy: Return of White Buffalo Calf Woman?

When did White Buffalo Calf Woman bring the sacred bundle? Where did she come from? Who was she after all? Was she a real person? These are relevant questions that many of us wonder when reading this story of the Lakota.

According to Lakota tradition, Chief Arvol Looking Horse who is now the keeper of the sacred bundle, was the 19th generation keeper of the bundle. To Lakota standards, one generation is equivalent to 100 years. So this would give us reason to approximate the appearance of White Buffalo Calf Woman about 2,000 years ago between 100 BC-100 AD. Although we cannot be one hundred percent sure, this is a good starting point.

Worldwide, what else was occurring at this time? In Central America, the end of the late pre-classic era (400 BC-250 AD) of the Maya is on the rise. Over on the other side of the world, the famous Cleopatra lives from 69 BC-30 BC, and one of the most prominent figures of history and religion is said to have been crucified, Jesus of Nazareth. Allegedly he had a wife, Mary

Magdalene, who was to continue the teachings of her husband, the teacher, and the sacred ideologies that he taught which would later be the basis for Templarism. Two hundred years earlier, the early sections of the Great Wall of China were being constructed.

Cultures around the world were continuing to advance, build, and thrive. So were the Native American people. Many tend to forget that they, too, played a significant role in our history. These people kindly helped the pilgrims when they landed on the coast. Yes there were many different tribes across the North American continent, but they all seemed to practice Mother Earth spirituality. Everything was a community effort. For everything we take from Mother Earth, there had to be something given to her, whether it be a tobacco offering, or a simple prayer of gratitude.

The Lakota people were so grateful for White Buffalo Calf Woman. They rejoiced in her appearance, and they begged her to stay. She insisted she must return to the place from which she came. However, she did say that she would one day return to Earth, to the people of Earth, when they were in need of her once more. Much like the prophecy of the "second coming of Christ," White Buffalo Calf Woman promises to come back and help restore balance, to bring her wisdom, teachings, and knowledge once more to the children of Mother Earth. Several actual white buffalo calves have made an appearance on the land. Has She returned? Or are we still anticipating Her return?

Chapter 9
The Bible and the Cover Up

Over the course of human history, mankind has known many different religions. The majority of the time that *Homo sapiens* have been practicing any type of spiritual or religious beliefs, may have been religious beliefs that had *nothing* to do with Christianity. Christianity only came about following the death of Jesus of Nazareth. The word "Christianity" came way after the death of Jesus. Let us get a few things clear. Jesus allegedly died on the cross between 30 and 36 AD. This is about two thousand years ago.

- Christ, a name applied to Jesus of Nazareth was more of a title given to Jesus later on in his life. Christ itself comes from the Greek word "christos" which means "the anointed one."
- Christianity and Catholicism are two separate and *different* ideas.
- Jesus of Nazareth, himself, was a practicing Jew.
- Jesus was a member of an esoteric sect of Judaism known as the Essene, who took vows of poverty and communality, preserved ancient knowledge and wisdom, and inspired modern Masonic orders.

The definition of "Christianity" according to Oxford Dictionary is, "the religion based on the person and teachings of Jesus of Nazareth, or its beliefs and practices."

The definition of "Catholicism" according to Oxford Dictionary is, "the faith, practice, and church order of the Roman Catholic Church." The Roman Catholic Church is not based purely on the teachings of Jesus, but true Christianity essentially, should be.

We cannot forget that mankind has been religious, spiritual, and have followed their own truths for *thousands* of years before the birth of Jesus of Nazareth.

9.1 The Beginning of the Christian God

The first well known and studied monotheistic religion is Judaism which is also the most ancient monotheistic religion as far as we know. What we know as Judaism today began in the Middle East about 4,000 years ago, in 2000 BC. Yet today a very interesting question floats around the minds of the religious scholars and philosophers: Are Yahweh and Elohim actually feminine in nature? Or are they truly only Father God as we have been taught?

Many bible verses refer to God as the "Lord of Hosts." In Hebrew this is "Yaweh Tseva'ot." The Hebrew word *tsava* translates as forces, which is a feminine noun! So these unseen forces are naturally feminine, adding a mysteriously feminine aspect to God. Perhaps this is the Holy Ghost, the Mother, the Bride of God— all embodied in the Creator. Or perhaps it is much more than that. Perhaps the Mother existed before the Father in ancient Hebrew tradition which would make sense based on other ancient beliefs and religions. While Yahweh is made feminine through the uses of a feminine noun, this could be literally looked at as not just God, but with the feminine energy, *Goddess.*

In the bible we see many feminine and masculine references to Elohim, so unlike today where God is seen as being solely masculine. Throughout religious history there has almost always been dualistic counterparts to the primary god. In ancient Egypt it was Isis and her consort, Osiris, in Canaan it was El and Elat, and to the Germanic tribes of Europe it was Odin and Frigg.

For thousands of years the feminine was worshiped right alongside the masculine! There was no separation.

9.2 The Goddess in The Bible, The Wife of God

What many people do not realize is that God was not always *"only"* God. He was the holy Father and husband of the holy Mother. Ancient texts from Ugarit (modern Syria) tell us that Asherah's/ Astarte/Elat/Elohim's consort was El and that she was the mother of over 70 gods and goddesses. She was worshiped throughout ancient Syria and Palestine and was often paired with the god of the Canaanites known as Baal, who assumed El's place. In the bible Yahweh and El are regarded as one and the same. Occasionally when paired with Baal she was known as Baalat. Archaeological evidence tells us that she was worshiped as the consort of Yahweh based on inscriptions found in southern Palestine.

Asherah is often associated with the seas and with serpents, potentially the inspiration for "Lilith" or the serpent in the Garden of Eden, being her consort's equal and ruling by his side. According to 2 Kings 23:7, Asherah was worshiped in the Jerusalem Temple alongside Yahweh as his wife. In this temple there were fertility rituals that took place between representatives of Asherah and Yahweh. This continued until the destruction of the Jerusalem Temple in 586 BC. It was at this time the Divine Mother began to be forced out of the temples in this region. If people were going to worship the feminine, they now had to do it secretly. Just because it was banned publicly did not mean people would not continue to practice their beliefs.

9.3 The Goddess and the Serpent

According to texts from the second century BC found at the Sinai, Asherah was referenced as "lady of the serpent." The serpent to many ancient cultures was a symbol of the goddess, rebirth, and fertility. For many reasons, the goddess has always been tied to the serpent all around the world. One of those reasons is that serpents appear to all be female: the only time you can tell the sex difference between a male and female is when mating occurs. An obvious reason the serpents are associated with rebirth is because of their ability to "rebirth" themselves and shed their old skins over and over throughout their lives.

A very well known man born Greek in 46 AD, and died Roman in 120, Plutarch, proposes that serpent goddess worship originated from the island of Crete. He argues that Crete means to create, and therefore is the basis of all mother goddess worship. Archaeological evidence does in fact tell us that Crete was the first place to worship the serpent goddess on a massive scale. The island of Crete has been inhabited for thousands of years, and its famous inhabitants, the Minoans, are a culture shrouded in mystery, but responsible for the rise of Classical Greece. Many scholars have been searching for answers, and one professor from the University of Washington, Dr. George Stamatoyannopoulos, says, "About 9,000 years ago there was an extensive migration of Neolithic humans from the regions of

Anatolia that today comprise parts of Turkey and the Middle East. At the same time, the first Neolithic inhabitants reached Crete.

"Our mitochondrial DNA analysis shows that the Minoans' strongest genetic relationships are with these Neolithic humans, as well as with ancient and modern Europeans.

"These results suggest the Minoan civilization arose 5,000 years ago in Crete from an ancestral Neolithic population that had arrived in the region about 4,000 years earlier. Our data suggest that the

Serpent Goddess idol, Crete.

Neolithic population that gave rise to the Minoans also migrated into Europe and gave rise to modern European peoples."

The peak of Minoan civilization lasted from 3000 B.C. to approximately 1100 BC. According to an article by Joseph Shaw, an excavation on the island of Crete yielded an artifact dated to the ninth century BC. It was a Phoenician shrine. The Phoenicians were an advanced seafaring people descending directly from the ancient biblical Canaanites and were notorious for their advanced seafaring skills that took them to Britain, around the continent of Africa, and all over the Mediterranean. While their city-states thrived from as early as 3,200 BC, it appears their maritime trading became extensive around 2750 BC. They were trading with the Minoans, colonizing new areas, trading in Egypt, Croatia, and all over the old world.

It would make sense that the Phoenicians would have brought their culture, their knowledge, and even their religious practices with them. According to the article mentioned above, they certainly did! So perhaps they brought their Mother Goddess, Asherah/Astarte, their Creatress and Queen of Heavens, with them. While their goddess was always associated with the serpent, the island of Crete became the center of serpent goddess worship. During excavations of Crete, Sir Arthur Evans uncovered several different serpent goddess figurines. Two of them date from 1600 BC.

Additionally, the serpent was associated with the *kundalini* and *Shakti* that we discussed in Chapter 1. The kundalini energy was said to coil at the base of the spine, and when tapped into, it would run up through all seven chakras like a serpent slithering up your spine. The kundalini energy was the manifestation of the Shakti energy, the divine feminine energy.

9.4 From Lilith to Eve

Everyone knows the story of Adam and Eve. Popular modern Christian teachings like to say that they were the first humans on Earth. However Jewish teachings tell a different story. In the book of Genesis, there is a story that is not made completely clear. Adam had a wife before Eve. Genesis 1:27 shows that a woman had been created by God, "So God created man in his own image, in the image of God created he him; male and female created he them." The text places Lilith's creation after God's words in Genesis 2:18

that "it is not good for man to be alone." Allegedly Lilith is created from earth and clay just the same Adam is, and the two are created equal. It is not until Genesis 2:22 that Eve is created from Adam's rib. So what happened in between these two women?

An early Hebrew narrative known as *The Alphabet of Ben Sira* tells of Lilith and her relationship with Adam. It tells us a story like this:

> After God created Adam, who was alone, He said, "It is not good for man to be alone." He then created a woman for Adam, from the earth, as He had created Adam himself, and called her Lilith. Adam and Lilith immediately began to fight. She said, "I will not lie below," and he said, "I will not lie beneath you, but only on top. For you are fit only to be in the bottom position, while I am to be the superior one." Lilith responded, "We are equal to each other inasmuch as we were both created from the earth." But they would not listen to one another. When Lilith saw this, she pronounced the Ineffable Name and flew away into the air.
>
> Adam stood in prayer before his Creator: "Sovereign of the universe!' he said, 'the woman you gave me has run away." At once, the Holy One, blessed be He, sent these three angels Senoy, Sansenoy, and Semangelof, to bring her back. Said the Holy One to Adam, "If she agrees to come back, what is made is good. If not, she must permit one hundred of her children to die every day." The angels left God and pursued Lilith, whom they overtook in the midst of the sea, in the mighty waters wherein the Egyptians were destined to drown. They told her God's word, but she did not wish to return. The angels said, "We shall drown you in the sea." [The angels don't seem very nice, or is that just me?]

Lilith then tells the angels to bugger off essentially, but in the written tale Lilith allegedly says that she basically has to kill babies. Why? Likely because our ancient patriarchal society wants to literally demonize any woman that disobeyed her husband. Shocking? Not at all. Lilith was offended that her own husband did not want her to enjoy sexual intercourse and let her be on top, and left the man. Who could blame her right? I guess Eve was content with being on the bottom all the time. In any case, why would the church leaders omit this story? Was it perhaps because they were worried that it might inspire women to some Lilith-like behavior?

Lilith leaves him because he will not treat her as an equal. It is at that time she is cursed. These legends of Lilith have wandered the Earth for over four thousand years according to ancient texts and the archaeological record. One popular reference to Lilith goes back to 2000 BC in the ancient epic of Gilgamesh.

Many associate Lilith with the goddesses Ishtar and Inanna, as being their handmaiden or holy temple prostitute in Babylonian and Sumerian traditions. In many ancient cultures there was a Sun or male deity that had dominion over all other gods. Right by his side was his queen and consort. It was typical in temples, on certain days in Mesopotamia and Egypt, to have consort union or sexual rites practiced by priests and priestesses in representing both the sacred feminine and the sacred masculine.

So if Lilith really was a priestess of the great goddess, she had a place of honor, representing the Divine Mother herself. Legends have it that Mary Magdalene was a priestess of Isis, and of course the church tried to make her out to be a prostitute. Sounds a lot like Lilith, doesn't it? Going back to the dawn of spirituality, the sexual union was considered so sacred, perhaps because it was believed nirvana, or paradise, could only be achieved through woman, and during sacred union.

However one cannot help but wonder, why did Lilith have such a special place in history? If she was a priestess of the goddess, why is she the only priestess throughout thousands of years of temple prostitutes, that had such a giant impact on history? Many are familiar with her because she was a woman that demanded equality. During sex, during daily life, and any other aspect of her life she demanded her husband treat her as his equal. So why was she smeared to be some kind of child-eating demon?

Is it because religion has always attempted to slander free thinking women's names with horrendous titles? It is interesting how over the course of thousands of years women who were forthright, honest, and brave were somehow all made to seem evil. Is this just by chance? Or have certain men in certain religions feared women and the power they possess?

Biblically we know that women of the era were not submitting to this new idea of a single masculine deity, obeying their husbands, and following a new religion. These women followed the ways of their ancestors and worshiped the Goddess. As we have ssen, in the book of Jeremiah, written around 626 BC-587 BC, chapter 44, verses 16-19, they say, "We will not listen to the message you have spoken to us in the name of the Lord! We will certainly do everything we said we would: We will burn incense to the Queen of Heaven and will pour out drink offerings to her just as we and our ancestors, our kings and our officials did in the towns of Judah and in the streets of Jerusalem. At that time we had plenty of food and were well off and suffered no harm. But ever since we stopped burning incense to the Queen of Heaven and pouring out drink offerings to her, we have had nothing and have been perishing by sword and famine." The women added, "When we burned incense to the Queen of Heaven and poured out drink offerings to her, did not our husbands know that we were making cakes impressed with her image and pouring out drink offerings to her?"

These women are declaring that when they abandoned their worship of the Goddess, all began going badly. They are also declaring to Jeremiah that their husbands were aware of their worship of the Queen of Heaven. The husbands probably too participated in this "idolatry," likely because as they were raised around a goddess-worshiping matriarchal society. Judging from the behavior of Lilith, I would say that this is the kind of upbringing she had, in a matriarchal goddess-worshiping society where women were put on a pedestal and treated as sacred. Adam clearly was not from the same society.

9.5 The Fruit of the Goddess

Is it surprising that the tale we all know from Genesis, Adam and Eve, is also about a woman getting into trouble? How dare Eve eat from the Tree of Life? She bites into the Fruit of Knowledge, and becomes aware of their sexuality. This story was likely crafted by Levite priests, because they feared their followers being tempted not by knowledge per se, but by the old religion of the goddess. The followers of the goddess religion led a completely different lifestyle. Sex was sacred, used as a means of spiritual enlightenment within ceremony, and women were viewed as wise and the embodiment of

Goddess Herself.

So what fruit was it exactly, that Eve allegedly ate from the Tree of Life? Today, many associate the fruit with the apple, but the fruit was more than likely a fig, of the fig tree. It was in fact fig leaves that Adam and Eve used to cover themselves. The fig was one of the first plants that humans seriously cultivated and grew. Figs dating back 11,000 years ago have been found by archaeologists near Jericho in the Jordan Valley. The figs have been dated to 9400-9200 BC. This means that people were cultivating the fig before they began growing barley and wheat, which came 1000 years later. This fruit must have been *very* important to them.

In fact, the Mother Goddess of Mesopotamia, Ishtar, was strongly associated with the fig tree. She is even depicted as taking shape as a fig tree. The fig tree came to represent sexuality, which is likely why Levite priests used it in the story of Adam and Eve. The people back then understood the story was indeed about trying to make the old goddess religion out to be evil and sinful because it encouraged sacred sex. Therefore the Tree of Life represented the knowledge of sexuality and the goddess religion.

Egyptian tradition tells us that the fig was also a symbol of the cow goddess, Hathor. The Pharaohs of Egypt were said to drink the milk of Hathor, similar to the Mesopotamian kings drinking from the milk of Ishtar. A third goddess of the old world that is associated with the fig is the Arabian goddess Al-Uzza that we discussed in an earlier chapter. It is important to note that the fig tree contains a milk-like sap that was used as a topical medicine. The fig tree had many medicinal properties, and healing has always been associated with Mother (Goddess) figures. It was also believed that eating figs helped make male sperm more fertile. The fig also has hallucinogenic properties which may have been the reason why it was associated with "knowledge" and spiritual awakening which made it perfect to use within the well concocted story of Adam and Eve.

Demeter gave a fig to Dionysus as a gift in Greek mythology. The connection to the goddess is in nearly every ancient tradition out there. This means that the fig tree was likely known by most people in the biblical times as symbol of the goddess. Even the Buddhists viewed the fig tree as a sacred symbol. It represented enlightenment because it was said that Buddha himself reached enlightenment beneath a fig tree.

The bible makes a few references to the fig. In the Book of Deuteronomy the fig is mentioned as one of the Seven Species (Deuteronomy 8:7-8) when describing the land of Canaan; "For the Lord your God is bringing you into a good land—a land with brooks, streams, and deep springs gushing out into the valleys and hills; a land with wheat and barley, vines and fig trees, pomegranates, olive oil and honey." Interestingly, the pomegranate also has goddess connections. It was a symbol of Aphrodite and fertility.

The fig is mentioned again in Micah 4:4, "each man under the fruit of his vine and under the fruit of his fig tree." It was common to sit and meditate or pray beneath such trees. This phrase was written in the context of describing a peaceful era to come.

We now see the significance of the fig in ancient times, and why it was seen as a symbol of sin to the Levite priests.

9.6 Eve

The name "Eve" in Hebrew has been believed to have a few different meanings: "to live," "to breathe" or "mother of life." Funny enough, the name Eve comes from a root word meaning snake, which is even more evidence that this story was made up. Adam is a name that roughly translates to meaning "son of the red earth" since he was made from the dirt. The story of Adam and Eve is most likely just an allegory, a story that was put together to shame women into being good husband-obeying housewives.

The serpent that tempts Eve becomes a symbol that today many consider the equivalent of Satan. However, this was not the case at the time it was written. The serpent is clearly a reference to goddess worship. The mother goddess of old has long been known as the "serpent mother goddess." In ancient Egypt, it represented Wisdom, which has always been feminine, and was found on the crown of the Pharaoh for thousands of years.

Another belief that has stemmed from this most likely made up story is that women must bear pain during childbirth because of Eve's sin. Firstly, was there ever a time that childbirth *did not* hurt? Every animal that gives birth as humans do also bears pain, and that cannot also be Eve's fault. The Levite priests were just looking for any way to scare women into behaving. The truth is, childbirth has always hurt, and grumpy old men decided to put a monopoly on that and use it to their advantage. That's all.

In Genesis, it is said that Eve came from Adam's own rib, but according to an online article by Dr. Nicholas J. Schaser[1] she came from his *side* and therefore can be considered his "other half." Dr. Schaser contends that this is obvious when you look at the Hebrew word "tsela" that is used. It does not mean rib. It is used many times in the bible, but is never used to mean rib except, allegedly, in Genesis. The Hebrew word has always meant side. This is likely an allegory to the fact that woman is man's other half, his complement. Taken this way, this may make Eve Adam's equal. Almost. Until she is blamed for the fall of humanity and all that.

I propose that if it did in fact mean what has long been believed, that she did come from Adam's rib, that it likely was a reference to the fact that they were related, or of the same tribe. Eve seems to be a bit less testy than Lilith was, but it was clear that the latter was of a different society where women were treated as equals, if not on a pedestal. Eve was likely representing a new age in which women respected and obeyed their husbands. After Lilith left Adam, she was cursed by God for her bad behavior and made into a demon-like figure for disobeying Adam. Eve still gets into trouble and is to blame for the fall of humanity, but never leaves Adam. She represents a woman likely raised in Adam's own society and religion, unlike Lilith.

9.7 The Ophites & Gnostic Creation

The word Ophite derives from the Greek word ophis, meaning serpent. The Ophites were a gnostic Christian sect, (gnostic meaning to know) that existed in the Roman Empire in the 2nd century AD. One of their most important characteristics was their belief in *dualism.* Dualism ultimately highlights a spiritual importance in cosmic opposites such as: good and evil, dark and light, male and female, heaven and hell, etc. The Ophites were the even more ancient Greek version of the medieval French gnostic sect, the *Cathars.* They, like the Cathars, believed the god Jehovah, from the Old Testament, was the Demiurge or subordinate god that

[1] Dr. Nicholas J. Schaser, et al. "Did Eve Come from Adam's 'Rib'?" Israel Bible Weekly, 11 May 2021, https://weekly.israelbiblecenter.com/eve-come-adams-rib/.

created the material world. He represented materialism, greed, and suppression. So who did the gnostics consider the benevolent God? They believed in a Supreme Being who was purely spiritual without any ties to this physical world that the Demiurge had created.

The serpent was particularly important to gnostic sects, and still is today. The serpent was a liberator of mankind that represents the unknown spiritual Wisdom and knowledge that had been withheld by the Demiurge in the book of Genesis. The Serpent in the Garden of Eden encourages Eve to eat the apple to receive the knowledge that is being hidden, kept, *veiled,* and suppressed by the Demiurge, so that she can now understand the difference between good and evil. And so she does, and the material god is enraged.

The gnostic people believed that Christ was the spirit that filled the man Jesus with the saving gnosis, or knowledge. In some gnostic traditions, the serpent is actually representing the Christos, or known more popularly as the spirit Christ, that fills Jesus. According to the same gnostic traditions, the Divine Mother Sophia was the mother of Jehovah, the God of the Material world, and when she shared Her divine Wisdom with her son, he wanted to keep this secret and not share it with his material world. Therefore the Christos comes and brings his sacred knowledge to Adam and Eve. In the book of Proverbs 3:19, Sophia-Wisdom is considered co-creator with God, the Demiurge. "By Wisdom the Lord laid the earth's foundations, by understanding he set the heavens in place."

Sophia is talked about quite a bit in the Bible. Even in Ecclesiasticus 1:1, it says that, "All Wisdom comes from the Lord, She is with him forever." Then only a couple verses later, in Ecclesiasticus 1:4-6, in reference to the creation, it says, "Wisdom hath been created before all things, and the understanding of prudence from everlasting. The word of God most high is the fountain of Wisdom; and Her ways are everlasting commandments. To whom hath the root of Wisdom been revealed, or who hath known Her wise counsels?"

Sophia is said to be the Mother and the Bride of Christos, the Supreme Being, the true God—not the Demiurge. This could be the basis for the worship of Isis being the Mother and the queen-consort of her son, Horus. This also alludes to the importance of two different women named Mary in Jesus's life. We have the Virgin Mary, who conceives by the Holy Spirit, or the Divine Mother,

114

The Immaculate Conception by Giovanni Battista Tiepolo, c. 1769.

Sophia. The Holy Spirit fills her womb, her son Jesus, with Christos. Jesus's wife and consort is also Mary—but Mary Magdalene. She is known for her nurturing, loving, and caring spirit. She embodies the Divine Mother, Sophia. She and the Virgin Mary are full of the same Wisdom and knowledge.

Sophia and the serpent are one and the same, while the serpent has represented the Mother Goddess since the dawn of time. The serpent knows the secrets of mortality, how to shed its own skin and become new, and symbolically represents this sacred spiritual Wisdom and knowledge. In fact, there are many incredible pieces of art that depict the Virgin Mary standing on top of a serpent on top of the world. The one on the previous page is *The Immaculate Conception* by Giovanni Battista Tiepolo, 1767-1769, and is now at a museum in Spain.

Mary stands on top of the world because she is the Queen of Heaven, She embodies all that is and was and will be, She embodies the spirit of the Divine Feminine, Sophia. Her feet are placed where they are to symbolize Her position. As with most esoteric art, there is one relevant phrase, "As above so below."

We will start with below here. We see the Virgin Mary standing on top of the Earth, more specifically she stands with her right foodton the Serpent. Most will say the serpent represents Satan. But he does not! He represents the Virgin Mary's son, Jesus, as well as Sophia's son, Christos, embodied on Earth. Sophia/Virgin Mary stands with one foot on top of him because she is his Mother, but the other foot stands beside him on the Earth because She is his wife, his consort, and his equal—this is the part that represents Mary Magdalene, wife of Jesus, also embodying Sophia. The Serpent here has an apple in its mouth, the forbidden fruit, or the sacred knowledge the Christos has. To the left of the apple we see a rose—a symbol that is known to represent blood, a bloodline, or a lineage of the Christos and Sophia on Earth, or of Jesus and Mary Magdalene.

Above, we see the dove hovering over the crown of Sophia/Mary. The crown represents her sacred divinity, and we can count nine stars. The nine stars we see more than likely represent pregnancy and birth, since a woman's gestation lasts nine months. The dove is a symbol of love, peace, and works as a messenger to deliver these ideas. The dove is Sophia and Christos as one, above all else, where the masculine and feminine can join together in the cosmic realm.

Chapter 10
Woman, Man's Way
to Salvation

Why is it that men and women found salvation for thousands of years before the coming of the alleged Christ? Not to mention, Jesus came from a woman, the Virgin Mary who becomes known as the "Queen of Heaven." The church insists we can only find salvation through Jesus Christ. However, people were finding salvation through other holy rituals for thousands of years. The other popular route to heaven was woman—she could bring a man to salvation through sacred sex.

Sex today is ridiculously advertised through anything and everything on the media, so how are we supposed to understand it can truly be a sacred thing? Our ancestors believed so strongly in this sacred union between the female and the male that they claimed to find salvation that way. Many different cultures, rituals, and all involve sex.

In May Sinclair's book, *Infamous Eve: A History,* Sinclair tells us about a sex ritual that the Cathars practiced, but even earlier, originated from India. She says, "The Agape Love Feast, an adaptation of an Indian Tantric rite requiring sexual union and eating of either or both the semen and menstrual blood after it had been offered to the Father... continued to be practiced in western Europe by early Christian sects."

The ancient people used menstrual blood all around the world, seeing its sacredness, where the modern people of today shy from anything menses related. The ancient Egyptians used the bleeding woman's blood for magic and ritual, as well as skincare. They believed it would help with sagging breasts and scarring. Menstrual blood was considered to be rejuvenating. As the spring planting ritual began, the Greeks would have ceremonies that involved spreading menstrual blood mixed with wine over the field in a kind of sympathetic magic meant to increase the fertility of the soil.

There is a people known as the Bauls whose religion is made up of influences from Hinduism, Islam, Buddhism, and Tantra. The Bauls are found all over Bengali India and Bangladesh. What makes the Bauls unique is their reverence for menstrual blood. They are a very joyous and musical community, often wandering in a nomadic fashion. The Bauls see men as being incomplete, as they do not bleed monthly like women do. Naturally when a girl's first period comes, it is an occasion to celebrate in this community. They take the menstrual blood and mix it with cow's milk, camphor, coconut milk and palm sugar, which is then enjoyed as a celebratory drink by close friends and family.

Dr. Kristin Hanssen interviewed a Baul woman, Tara, in 2002. She recalled her experience of drinking her own menstrual blood with friends and family and said that everyone seemed to feel that, "Powers of memory and concentration were enhanced, their skin acquired a brilliant glow, their voices grew melodious, and their entire beings were infused with happiness, serenity, and love."

10.1 Goddess, Agape

Agape was an ancient Greek Goddess, sister to Aphrodite, and a goddess who allegedly chose to never marry. She did not like the way she saw Zeus treat Hera, and decided she would never bow to any man, according to legend. She was the true goddess of intimacy and sex. However, "agape" today is known to mean or represent simply "love." She is quite a difficult goddess to track down, or prove she was really worshipped. All that I have been able to find on her is subject to speculation and is legend that has been passed down through the ages. But all legends tend to begin with a kernel of truth, right?

So if Agape really were worshipped, she would have been popular sometime around 500 BC-500 AD, give or take. In the beginning of the new age, it appears she is represented in a trinity: maiden, mother, and crone. This is traditionally the way goddesses come to be worshipped on a world-wide scale, as it represents the three stages of womanhood, and also the three trimesters of pregnancy. Three is an especially sacred number to the Divine

Feminine. The names applied to this goddess in the triple form go as follows: Agape, Chionio, and Irene.

However, there is another aspect to this legend of worship of Agape in the triple form. There is an interesting story about three Christian women by these names who became known as saints for their martyrdom. This is likely where and why the names and worship for Agape in the triple form come from, or perhaps it was the opposite. Maybe Christians made up this story in another attempt to be able to worship this Pagan goddess, Divine Feminine, in their church. This is not the first nor will it be the last. The church certainly put the Blessed Virgin Mary on a pedestal.

10.2 Christian Martyrs or Goddess?

Over time, it becomes difficult to distinguish what is myth and what is fact. Did these Christian martyrs inspire the Greco-Roman worship of Agape? Or was it the other way around? Here is the story about the three Christian martyrs: Agape, Chionio, and Irene.

In 304 AD, the Roman governor of Macedonia was a man named Dulcitius during the reign of the emperor Diocletian. He is most well known for his role in the persecution of the three Christian women in Thessalonika. The story goes that the three women were brought before Dulcitius because they refused to eat food that been a sacrificial offering to the gods in ritual. When the women were asked why they disobeyed and did not eat the offering, Chionio allegedly responded, "I believe in the living God, and for that reason did not obey your orders."

Dulcitius is said to have given Chionio and Agape a rather harsh sentence that put two of the three women to death; "I condemn Agape and Chionia to be burned alive, for having out of malice and obstinacy acted in contradiction to the divine edicts of our lords the emperors and Cæsars, and who at present profess the rash and false religion of Christians, which all pious persons abhor." Curiously, only the younger two of the three women are sentenced to death but all three were brought before the governor. This does not really make much sense.

After Chionia and Agape were burned at the stake, Dulcitius found that Irene had kept Christian books in violation of existing law. He examined her again, and she declared that when the decrees against Christians had been published, she and several other Christians fled to the mountains. She would not give up the names of all the others who had fled with her, and claimed only the other people knew the location of these Christian scripts. Dulcitius then ordered Irene to be stripped and exposed in a brothel. This was done, and no one harmed Irene while at the brothel. The governor then gave Irene a second chance to abide by the laws, which she refused. Dulcitius then sentenced her to be burned at the stake as well. Four other individuals were tried with the sisters: Agatho, Casia, Philippa, and Eutychia. Of these, one woman was remanded as she was pregnant. The fates of the other three are unknown, which is interesting as they are associated. The names are all important.

The name Agatho, which was originally a Greek boy's name, is now popularly known as a girls name, *Agatha*. The prefix, Agath, according to the Merriam-Webster dictionary, means good. I continued to look up the other names' meanings. The name Casia is a girl's name that derives from the biblical name *Ketziah*. Ketziah is the name of one of Job's three daughters interestingly, mentioned in the book of Job. Cassia itself is actually a spice tree. Supposedly the name Ketziah or Cassia is now known to represent feminine equality since Job only had three daughters and they all received his inheritance.

Philippa is the feminine version of Phillip and typically is known to mean "lover of horses." The prefix or word philean means "to love." The second part of the word—hippos—refers to the horse.

The name Eutychia is even more exciting because this is the name of the Greek goddess of happiness and good fortune. In Roman mythology her equivalent is Felicitas. She is mentioned in the bible as well, as one of the four daughters of Philip the Evangelist according to Eusebius. Even more interesting is that these four daughters, including Eutychia, were all said to be prophetesses.

While I am not quite sure how it all ties together yet, it appears these names are more symbolic in the story of Agape and her two other sisters. However Agape, being known as the goddess of sexual love, comes to have a certain ritual named after her in

The Last Supper, Leonardo da Vinci, 1495 and 1497.

gnostic teachings, "The Agape Love Feast" which was mentioned earlier.

10.3 The Last "Love Feast"

It is no secret that the Jewish sect that Jesus belonged to, the Essenes, took part in the Agape Love Feast. According to Christian standard, the Agape Love Feast was traditionally a meal of bread and wine, or *the bread, the body and the wine, the blood of Christ.* It almost sounds like this is an adaptation from the original Agape Love Feast, which involved the drinking of the menstrual blood and semen after it had been offered to the gods. At the Last Supper, Jesus tells his disciples to eat the bread as it is his body, and drink the wine as it is his blood. In the ancient ritual of the Agape Love Feast, following this ritual was a sexual union between man and woman.

According to Christian teachings, there were only twelve disciples present at the Last Supper, the Passover meal. These twelve disciples of course are all male. Now, why is this significant? This makes for 13 people present at the feast. Thirteen of course is a number that is very significant in connection to the Grail, the Templars, and the Divine Feminine. It is not really in any way connected to man, so why specifically twelve disciples and Jesus? Very quickly we will have a small lesson about the importance of 13.

- 13 moon cycles in a year
- Women have 13 menstrual cycles in a year

• The planet Venus, known as the "Goddess in the Heavens" makes a perfectly precise five-pointed star over the course of eight Earth years, and on Venus, this is 13 Venus years!

A five-pointed star.

The five-pointed stars you know and see everywhere are ancient depictions of Venus. They have always represented Her. Now they are everywhere! Also… the inside of the star is a pentagon. What else is a pentagon? But that is for a later chapter…

Back to the Last Supper! Thirteen attendees, including Jesus. Now Passover was typically a family affair, and it always included women. The wife of the rabbi always held a special position. So where are the wives of the disciples in the Bible? And more specifically, where is Jesus's wife, Mary Magdalene? Of course in the painting by Leonardo da Vinci, there is a very soft, female character next to Jesus, who is supposed to be John, but has quite feminine features. Da Vinci himself was allegedly part of a Templar order, so why would he paint such a feminine figure if it was supposed to be a man?

There is no doubt he was capable of making John look more like a man. Although John is described to have subtle and soft features, when it comes to art, there was a specific technique artists employed when painting women. To make a woman appear much softer, the artist would paint them with an angle, tilting their head, and so forth and so on. So what is the deal? Is this the Magdalene next to Jesus, or simply an overly feminine John? And if this is the case, then who is this woman on the right leaning towards Jesus wearing the same colored robes? Could this be the Virgin Mary, pointing toward her heart? And what about when the alleged Mary Magdalene is moved to the other side of Jesus? Coincidence? Perhaps, but perhaps da Vinci purposely did this to convey a message he would be outwardly condemned for if he announced it verbally and publically.

The Last Supper, Mary switches sides.

Back to the Agape Love Feast, could this have truly been celebrating a union between Mary Magdalene and Jesus? A marriage, or a result of their union, a child? Perhaps they were not engaging in the gruesome acts of the ancient Love Feast, but perhaps it had been adopted and adapted based off of this ancient ritual, and the bread and wine Jesus asks his disciples to eat and drink is symbolic of the holy bloodline that should descend from him. Perhaps this is an initiation to a group that would protect his children, and all that sprang forth from his vine, from then on. And perhaps that bloodline was able to live on through Mary Magdalene's body, her chalice, her womb, and so Jesus's followers continued to find salvation through his wife, Mary, as she carried Jesus's blood within her womb and beyond. The bloodline of Kings would always be continued via the route of women who gave birth to the royal descendents of King Jesus and Queen Mary. Salvation would now come from the body of women, as it always has and always will.

Today the Agape Love Feast lives on in church potlucks, and the traditional "Sunday dinner."

10.4 The Ancient Tantric Rite

This ancient secret rite is known as *Kula-yaga*. The word "kula" means "power of the Supreme Lord" and represents consciousness and embodiment of this consciousness. This practice is written about in a book called "Tantrāloka" (translates into "To Throw Light on Tantra") by a Hindu man named Abhinavagupta who lived from 950 AD to 1016 AD. In this book, he makes clear that it is only for those that are advanced in their spiritual journeys.

The ritual begins with self spiritual purification. One must close their eyes and imagine their body burning from the feet to the head to burn away the image of self, so that all is left is just your awareness of consciousness. Next, from head to feet, one must now imagine the divine light of the Goddess shining from them radiantly and full of beautiful and pure energy. Beyond that, a sexual union occurs between male and female, and then a mingling of sexual "fluids of bliss" are to fill a chalice offered to the gods and goddesses, and then it is to be consumed.

It is hard to say how far back this tradition goes, but considering there were probably different variations, we can guess a thousand years at least before the time of Abhinavagupta. Many different societies and cultures believed spiritual salvation was found through the goddess, so when and why exactly did that change? Was it just the arrival of Jesus Christ? Or was this concept just a coverup by the church?

Chapter 11
The Forgotten Christ Bride

"And the companion of the Savior was Mary Magdalene.
He loved her more than all the disciples, and used to kiss her
often on her mouth."
The Gospel of Philip (63:33-36)

The idea that Jesus took a bride has been such a controversial and shocking claim. But why? Why is it so shocking to believe that a man married a woman? Jesus is historically and religiously a very important man, but a man nonetheless. I have heard so many argue, bicker, and get quite defensive over the celibacy of Jesus. So many believe that he could not have been capable of divine miracles and have been a father, but why could he not be both?

The evidence for whether Jesus did or did not marry is rather scarce. However, we do know that Jesus's status as rabbi would have made marriage a requirement. Traditionally the teacher would have passed on his duty as rabbi to his son… Why would Jesus not marry in this case? It would have been a taboo thing for him not to based on his Jewish faith. They believed it a duty to "go forth and multiply." (Genesis 1:28)

11.1 The Creation of the "Prostitute" Magdalene

Mary Magdalene, a Saint, a prostitute, and perhaps the wife of Jesus the Christ—who is this enigmatic woman? The belief of Magdalene being a prostitute began in 591 when Pope Gregory I made it clear that if she were anointing his feet, she must be a promiscuous woman as anointing and touching one's feet was a rather intimate act. Maybe she was engaging with an intimate act with Jesus because she was his wife? Pope Paul VI announced in 1969 that this was a wrongful statement made by Pope Gregory I, and that Mary was not in fact a prostitute.

She was far from a prostitute. Mary Magdalene was a woman who is believed to be from a town called Magdala which is 120 miles north of Jerusalem right on the sea of Galilee. Magdala supposedly comes from the Hebrew word "migdal" meaning tower. The full name of this place in biblical times was "Magdala Tarichaea." Tarichaea means "salted fish." Therefore, it is *Tower of Salted Fish* or just simply *Tower of Fish.* Obviously fishing played a large role in the seaside village. Let us not forget, Jesus is often called the "fisher of men" and in Grail lore, "Fisher King." A certain Jewish text is known to talk about the sinful nature of this town, Magdala. This text is "Lamentations Raba" and tells how God judged and destroyed this place because of its fornication. Perhaps this was the first way this sexual stigma became attached to Mary Magdalene. She carried the name of a town known for its destruction by God himself.

It must be considered that there are other towns with similar names, such as in Egypt there was a town called Magdolum, as well as an Ethiopian town called Magdala. Could this alternate place of origin give credence to Magdalene being an Egyptian princess or priestess of Isis? Mary Magdalene was most commonly depicted in red/orange and green. Why is this? Could it be because of the Egyptian meaning of the colors green and red, life force and death? Mary Magdalene embodied both of these qualities, as she taught by the side of Jesus, and saw him resurrected. Isis was once depicted in the same colors. (See 5.3)

And those "seven demons" cast out of her? According to Laurence Gardner's book, *The Illustrated Bloodline of the Holy Grail,* "Prior to marriage, Marys were under the authority of the Chief Scribe who, in Mary Magdalene's time, was Judas Sicariote. The Chief Scribe was also the Demon Priest Number 7, and the 'seven demon priests' were established as a formal opposition group to those priests who were the 'seven lights of the Menorah.' It was their duty to supervise the community's female priestesses, just like the Devil's Advocate, who probes the background of potential candidates for canonization in the Roman Catholic Church today. Upon her marriage, Mary Magdalene was naturally released from this arrangement. Hence, 'the seven demons went out of her' and she was permitted sexual activity…" So was this

Giampietrino, Saint Mary Magdalene, 1521, Portland Art Museum.

the explanation for the "seven demons" exorcised out of her? Was it really her just being released from an agreement as Gardner states? Unfortunately at this time we do not have enough evidence to prove Gardner's above statements.

We must also consider that Jesus was the one to first have the *seven demons* or *demons*. In Mark 3:20-34 it says, "And the multitude cometh together again, so that they could not so much as eat bread. And when his friends heard of it, they went out to lay hold on him; for they said, He is beside himself. And the scribes which came down from Jerusalem said, He hath Beelzebub, and by the prince of the devils casteth he out devils...because they said, He hath an unclean spirit. There came then his brethren and his mother, and, standing without, sent unto him, calling him. And the multitude sat about him, and they said unto him, Behold, thy mother and thy brethren without seek for thee. And he answered them, saying, 'Who is my mother, or my brethren?' And he looked round about on them which sat about him, and said, 'Behold my mother and my brethren!'"

What exactly are the demons that went out of Jesus? Whatever this reference was, was it symbolic for something else? Were Jesus and Mary Magdalene going through the same ritual? This goes to show that Mary Magdalene was not any more *unclean* or *sinful* than Jesus was. This also proves that Jesus was never perfect and without sin. He was an equal to everyone else, he was *Son of Man.* Therefore we have to wonder, was this cleansing of *seven demons* something of Essene or Nazarene ritual? Was this some type of initiation?

Seven is obviously an important number, as the Earth was created in seven days, we have the seven sacraments, seven chakras, the seven deadly sins, and above in the heavens we have the Seven Sisters, the Pleiades. Is it possible this could have been in reference to the seven deadly sins? The *Secret Book of John* was purportedly one and the same as the *Book of Love* that the Cathars taught from. The *Book of Love* says that seven demons rule over our physical body: Zathoth, Armas, Kalila, Iabel, Sabaoth, Cain, and Abel. There were also seven demons that presided over the energetic body: Michael, Ouriel, Asmenedas, Saphasatoel, Aarmouriam, Richram, and Amiorps. Is it possible *these* were the seven demons that Jesus and Mary had cast out of themselves? The evil and sin that already lived within us? To expel the demons would figuratively allow space for the Holy Spirit to fill, and therefore achieve perfection and/or purity.

To attain *earthly perfection* as it is likely that both Jesus and Mary Magdalene did, you would have to purify yourself of all sin, just as the Cathar *Parfait* or *Perfecti.* The Perfecti obtained a level of purity and perfection because they had come to a state where the Holy Spirit could dwell within them, therefore releasing them from the earthly suffering and allowing them to become *perfect* by union with the Holy Spirit. In later Cathar tradition this was done in a ritual called the *consolamentum*. Would it be so impossible to wonder if it was not a ritual degree that Jesus was administering to Mary? Catharism itself is traditionally believed to be the result of the direct influence of Jesus and Mary Magdalene's teachings. The Cathars taught from the *Book of Love*.

In the *Secret Book of John* in relation to purity and perfection the Lord says, "Be not afraid. I am with you always. I am the Father. The Mother. The Son. I am the incorruptible Purity."

11.2 Sophia the Holy Spirit

"She is the Universal Womb. She is before everything. She is: Mother-Father, First Man, the *Holy Spirit*." —**The Secret Book of John**

Who was Sophia? Who was She to Jesus of Nazareth, the Christ? Sophia is the Mother or Goddess of Wisdom, in Gnostic tradition. She *is* the Holy Spirit in the Holy Trinity. Therefore we have the Father, the Son, and the Holy [Mother] Spirit. Because Jesus was believed to be the "Christos" of Gnostic teaching, therefore his consort must have been "Sophia" who was represented by Mary Magdalene. For example, we know that it was Mary Magdalene who saw Jesus first after the *crucifixion*. He passes on the duty of continuing his teachings to Mary Magdalene. Acts 1:1-2 says, "In my former book, Theophilus, I wrote about all that Jesus began to do and to teach until the day he was taken up to heaven, after giving instructions through the Holy Spirit to the apostles he had chosen." The Holy Spirit is obviously a veiled reference to Mary Magdalene, who baptized with her oils, and Acts says he has given instructions *through* the Holy Spirit to the apostles. Mary Magdalene is instructed by Jesus to continue on his traditions, and the apostles are offended that it was She who he called upon, a woman, and not them. The only time we ever see Jesus in the Bible giving instructions to anyone that are meant to be passed on to the disciples is during his post-resurrection meeting with Mary Magdalene.

Just later in the same chapter of Acts, Jesus says, "For John baptized with water, but in a few days you will be baptized with the Holy Spirit." We know Mary Magdalene used oil to baptize.

In more traditional Christian churches still today, people are baptized with the oil Catechumens as it is said to have purifying and protective properties like sage. Acts 10:38 says, "...how God *anointed* Jesus of Nazareth with the Holy Spirit and with power, who went about doing good and healing all who were oppressed by the devil, for God was with Him." Anointment is always done with oils, and we see Jesus anointed twice in the Bible, by none other than Mary Magdalene herself. Once again in Luke 4:18, Jesus says, "The Spirit of the Lord is upon Me, because He has anointed Me to preach the gospel to the poor. He has sent Me to heal the brokenhearted, to preach deliverance to the captives and recovery of sight to the blind, to set at liberty those who are oppressed."

Jesus has made it very clear in the scripture that baptism no longer shall be done with water, but *with* the Holy Spirit. The oil is found throughout the Bible as a symbol of the Holy Ghost. Mary Magdalene Herself embodies the Holy Spirit, so it is no surprise that She is called as such and uses the oils for baptism. The anointment of Jesus with the oils is reminiscent of the of the Bridal Chamber in the Song of Solomon, at the time of the marriage consummation between Solomon and his Shulamite bride. It also parallels ancient Egyptian and Mesopotamian marriage traditions between pharaoh and queen in which *messeh* was used,: the oil of crocodile fat, to anoint the king. It is also worth mentioning that the High Priest of Jerusalem was called "the anointed" or in Hebrew, Messiah. Christ[os] is the Greek translation of Messiah. Jesus became High Priest when he "ascended into Heaven." The Holy of Holies within the Tabernacle was considered Heaven, and only the High Priest could enter. Not only was it facing east, but Venus rises in the east as the Morning Star with the Sun, and the Holy of Holies was also called the *bridal chamber*.

We know this because it says in the Gospel of Philip, "There were three buildings specifically for sacrifice in Jerusalem. The one facing the west was called 'The Holy.' Another facing the south was called 'The Holy of the Holy.' The third facing east was called 'The Holy of the Holies,' where the high priest enters. Baptism is the 'Holy' building. Redemption is the Holy of the Holy. The Holy of the Holies is the Bridal Chamber. Baptism includes the resurrection and the redemption; the redemption takes place in the Bridal Chamber."

Coming back around full circle, the Holy Spirit, Wisdom, and Sophia are all one and the same.

Constantine the Great actually dedicated a church to *Divine Wisdom,* which came to be known as the Hagia Sophia. Later in 538, Justinian I rebuilt and consecrated the church. Dating to the late 6th century is a hagiographical tradition that claims *the* Saint Sophia had three daughters: Faith, Hope, and Charity. The early Roman Martyrology dedicated a feast day to these saintly daughters of Sophia, August 1, which happens to be 10 days *after* the Feast Day of Mary Magdalene: July 22. August 1 in particular is what is called a cross quarter day which occurs between two major solar events. In this case, it falls between the summer solstice and the autumn equinox. Therefore it is one of eight Pagan sabbats of the year. In Celtic mythology, this day is known as Lammas/ Lughnasad.

There are many different tales of Sophia, and of the origins of the Gnostic teachings. I have found a Gnostic site that probably tells the best and most detailed version of Gnostic creation myth, including the importance of the Demiurge (or material realm God of the Bible), the Christos, and Sophia. It can be found at gnosis. org. The creation tale goes a little like this:

It seems that once there was only the Fore-Creation, invisible, without form or gender, all-pervasive, filling the depths and heights of what was and which, desiring to manifest an inward potential gave birth to many holy dyads...that is, pairs, the first of which were the Abyss and Fore-thought. Then a desire arose in Fore-thought and it meditated on Silence who conceived and gave birth to twins: the first visible female form called Truth and the first visible male form called Mind, in turn they together gave birth to Life and Word...Life was the form-mother of the Pleroma and Word was the form-father of those manifest within the Pleroma. The Pleroma is the fullness of the spiritual world, uninfluenced by matter, energy or light.

Many other dyads were born, called Aeons, or sacred powers, the last of which was the divine Sophia, or Holy Wisdom. Of all the Aeons, the divine Sophia desired most intensely to know the origins of Her own creation, that is, the nature of the Fore-Creator. Though Mind told Her that such knowledge was impossible, nevertheless, Sophia began to search high and low, after Mind was restrained by Silence. None of the Aeons comprehended the Fore-Creation other than Truth whose perfect reflection was a transparent presence invisible to Sophia. She separated Herself from Her consort, ranged the vastness of the uncreated Immensity, and far out distanced all the other Aeons.

Sensing her separation from the other Aeons, and lacking a clear knowledge of the Fore-Creator, She felt pain and sorrow, She wept and grieved deeply, She desired with all Her Heart to comprehend the vast, unending totality of the Fore-Creator, also called the Abyss. But the Abyss was vast beyond comprehending, and Her sorrow increased and Her passions flowed out of Her in waves and She risked utter dissolution into the Abyss as She radiated forth a turbulence into the stillness of Immensity. Then, suddenly, She encountered Horos, the Limit, Boundary, and understood that the Fore-Creation was unknowable, holy and profound, beyond the comprehension of Mind, Word or even Truth. This was the First Gnosis.

But now, the manifestations of Her intentions and passions remained as viable presences in the Immensity, they overflowed the Pleroma and began to take on a more substantive appearance. Sophia beheld these manifestations, the consequences of Her passions, and was again stirred with grief, fear, uncertainty and sorrow because She understood that these were the manifestations of Her own ignorance concerning the Fore-creation. A dim, barely light-like haze began to appear, first manifestation in the Primal Void, the concatenation of passion and desire unfulfilled, slowly evolving into manifest forms—the stirrings of light, energy and chaos.

All the Aeons together were concerned about the appearance of Chaos and so they, with the divine Sophia, prayed in depth and a new dyad was manifested: Christos and the Holy Spirit, his female counterpart. Together, they calmed the Aeons and soothed their fears, also instructing them in the unknowableness of the Fore-Creation while simultaneously revealing to them the inner unity, harmony and illumination of the Pleroma—this was the Second Gnosis. Yet, the haze and proto-forms of Chaos remained and among these emerging forms was an image of Sophia, called the Lower Wisdom, for She had divided Herself in the passion of her search and now, the Lower Wisdom abided in the midst of Chaos.

This Lower Wisdom desired to return and be united with Her own Higher Self, rather than remain trapped in Her passions and desires and when She felt the emmanations of the Holy Spirit and the Christos, when they manifest their healing and harmony within the Pleroma, She began to seek a way to return to the primal harmony and illumination of the Second Gnosis. And when Lower Wisdom discovered that She was bound by Limit and could not return or ascend to the Pleroma, She once again grieved and sorrowed. And from this second grief, from the waves and energy of that sorrow, the first material substances began to form, divide and align themselves in patterns of light, dimness and darkening matter. Then the Aeons together asked the Christos to assist the Lower Sophia and He manifested in the lower world of proto-matter as Yeshu'a, and soothed Her and comforted Her and revealed to Her all the many luminous beings that manifested in the Void as their spiritual companions.

But the proto-matter of the Void was now mixed with passion, desire and sorrow, and the luminous lights of the Void were the spiritual presences inherent to the newly forming matter, inherent to each and every elemental substance, the combinations and the consequent appearances. Thus the spiritual qualities of matter are the inherent emmanations of Wisdom stimulated through the manifestation of Christos and the Holy Spirit. And Wisdom was reunited with Her own Higher Self, and perceiving the holiness of the manifestation, and seeing clearly both the psychic and material character of those manifestations, gave birth to one last entity—called "Father of the Material Realm" or the Maker and creator of the Lower Visible Realms. [The Demiurge]

This Father God [Demiurge] created then, seven realms, each more material than the last, until finally this human world was formed and the beings of this world rose and walked, crawled or flew through the skies. But the Father God was vain and jealous, angry and forbidding, not knowing the power of the higher Aeons, nor of the Pleroma, nor even of his own Mother, the Divine Sophia. And when the Divine Sophia instructed him and opened his mind to Truth, he was amazed and refused to divulge these mysteries to those of his own creation. Being a god of the material, social and psychic order, it was not possible for him to be a teacher of the higher mysteries, and Sophia was dismayed by his wrath, anger and jealousy. So when he created the first human beings, She was there and secretly, without his knowing, She gave to them the gift of the Holy Spirit as a divine spark in every human heart.

And it is said, that in the Garden of Eden, created by the lower Father God, that Eve was the manifestation of the Lower Wisdom and that the serpent or snake of the tree, was actually the Christos who urged Eve to eat the Fruit of the Tree of Knowledge that she might attain the true Gnosis or knowledge of her origins and realize the Higher Sophia in perfect illumination and bliss. But the Father God, discovering that this secret teaching was disturbing his supremacy in the lower realms grew angry and cast them out of the garden and into the suffering of the world. Yet each and every descendent has this spark and the potential to recover the true Gnosis.

It is also said that it was for this reason that the Christos manifest as a human being, to bring the gift of the Holy Spirit, in all its female power and capacity, to liberate those who cast free from the illusions of the material and psychic realms and to ascend through visions of power and knowledge to the Higher Gnosis, to reunite the lower and higher self, to attain to visionary truth and perfect transparency. The Divine Sophia is the manifest presence of that vision, and this tale, one of Her symbolic forms. And the snake, an image of Higher Wisdom, is a true teacher that reconciles the desires and passions of knowledge with higher insight, overcomes the limitations of a jealous and demanding lesser god and transmits the teachings of the Divine Sophia. In this way, it is said, the faithful attain peace and the passion, union, holiness and joy.

Wisdom is said to exist before Creation, according to 1 Corinithians 2:7, "The Wisdom I proclaim is God's secret Wisdom, which is hidden from human beings, but which he had already chosen for our glory even before the world was made."

In an ancient gnostic gospel known as *Pistis Sophia,* Jesus has been appearing to his disciples for 11 years after his resurrection, asserting that he never physically died. Over these 11 years he begins initiating his disciples into the Lower Mysteries. The fourth chapter has Jesus ascending to Heaven and descending to the Earth before the disciples' very eyes. Whilst teaching and explaining the 24 different elements of the Mystery, Jesus mentions that Sophia operates and dwells in the 13th aeon. Obviously this is interesting as 13 is such a strong number of the sacred feminine between the moon, menstrual cycles, and the cycle of Venus. It was Authades[1] who sought to be Lord over the 13th aeon, and constantly was battling Sophia for Her place. However, despite the suppression, the attempt to remove her power, She prevails.

Essentially, the God we all know in Christianity was created by the Mother of Wisdom, who is really the wife and mother of the Christos. Therefore when we hear the tale of son of Mary (the Virgin), husband of Mary (Magdalene) we see an interesting Gnostic parallel all going back to Sophia. Jesus is representing the Christos, where he is still son of Sophia, and wife of Sophia, but Sophia is represented here by two different women.

---

[1] Authades is the self serving, arrogant universal energy.

The name Mary, going back in Hebrew, was actually "Miryam" which is said to mean *beloved*. It is possible that this name originated in ancient Egypt, which would be incredibly fascinating because of its meaning in Egypt. The name "Miryam" or "mry-t-ymn" or "Merit-Amun" means *beloved of Amun*.

Now let us back up for just a moment. Amun, also spelled Amen, as in the way Christians end a prayer, is an Egyptian God dating from the 11th dynasty, or 2000 BC. Mary originally means, "beloved of Amun." Beloved of the Sun God.

Amen was often depicted as being one and the same as the ram. The worship of him began in about 2000 BC, which incidentally is when the Age of Aries began, which ended up lasting until just around 0, around the birth of Jesus, the dawning of the new Age of Pisces, the fish.

A daughter of Thutmosis III and Merytre-Hatshepsut was given the name Meritamen. Meritamen was born sometime in the middle of the 15th century BC, and actually inherited a title and priestess position from her mother. This title was called *God's Wife of Amun*. This was a political and religious affiliation in Egypt, as religion within the ancient dynasties was seen as the responsibility of the royal family. We see a very ancient connection between being a spiritual leader as well as a lawful leader. This is also observed in Native American tribes, having the chief of the tribe being also the medicine man. The pharaoh held two titles: *Lord of the Two Lands* and *High Priest of Every Temple*.

Because Pharaoh was the High Priest, his queen would also hold a similar position. This is where the title God's Wife of Amun comes into play. The Pharaoh and his wife were equals: High Priest and High Priestess. They were both taught and initiated into these ancient mysteries and rituals. The "God's Wife of Amun" tradition existed for a long time going back at least as far as the reign of Ahhotep I (1570-1544 BC). The title likely existed earlier, but likely was simply "God's Wife." This High Priestess participated in rituals and ceremonies, and held just as much power as Pharaoh.

There are many arguments that Judaism and its traditions, and even King Solomon, originated in Egypt. The temples were often laid out the same way the Jewish tabernacles were, with the Holy of Holies being the sacred place where only the High Priest in Judaic tradition was permitted to enter. In Egypt, the High Priestess, the God's Wife of Amun was also granted access to the Holy of Holies. She also would take a ritual bath in the sacred lake with the other top four temple priests prior to entering the temple for ceremonies. This ritual of purifying yourself before entering the temple obviously continued to live on.

Amun was often depicted as a ram, or was guarded by a ram, symbolizing fertility as Amun-Min. He is also known as "the mysterious one." Amun goes down in history as being the one God who can become whatever his followers need him to be. Just as his consort represented the mother goddess, She could take on any role She needed to, just like Isis. She has always been veiled, to be protected. Now how does this relate to Mary Magdalene you may wonder.

11.3 Mariamne, Talpiot Tomb

In 1980 the Talpiot Tomb was discovered five kilometers south of the Old City of Jerusalem. It is a rock-cut tomb containing ten ossuaries (Jewish burials). These ossuaries are inscribed with names that all seem to line up with the royal family of Jesus, including: Yeshua bar Yehosef (Jesus son of Joseph), Maria (Mary), Yose (Joseph/ Jose), Yehuda bar Yeshua (Judah son of Jesus), Mariamne e Mara (Miriam [and] Martha), and Matya (Matthew).

There are many important factors here, but a couple include the fact that Mariamne (pronounced "Mary-ah-mn-ay") and Jesus have been proven not to be related by blood, proving the fact that these two people very well could have been married, and therefore the parents of Judah, son of Jesus.

The other important thing here is that if this is indeed Mary Magdalene, *Mariamne,* then her name has a very familiar ring to it. "Amene" (ah-men-ay) sounds eerily similar to "Amaunet/ Amunet/Amenet." Coincidence?

On the ossuary of Jesus are two letters of the Hebrew alphabet, one being the aleph, the first letter of the Hebrew alphabet, and the second being the last letter of the Hebrew alphabet, the tav. The aleph is important here as its actually made to be a "Hooked X" which is likely a symbol of the Holy Trinity or the Royal Bloodline of Jesus, the X being a union of male and female and the hook in the upper segment being a child in the womb. The meaning that was likely implied here was the concept of "alpha and omega" or "beginning and end" as Jesus calls himself. Why does he call himself this? Maybe it is because he is filled with kundalini, the Shakti energy of the divine feminine that was known to the ancients as the beginning and end, the infinite. Or maybe it is for another reason, decide for yourself.

He was literally born in the last few years of the Age of Aries the Ram. Therefore, he is the end of one era, and the beginning of the Age of Pisces. The ancient people always looked to the heavens for guidance, for even in the Christian Lord's Prayer, it says: Our Father, who art in heaven, hallowed be thy name; thy kingdom come; *thy will be done on earth as it is in heaven.* As above, so below. Whatever the people saw happening in the heavens, they attempted to do on earth.

The disciples ask Jesus to tell them their end, in the Gospel of Thomas. Jesus responds and says, "Have you discovered, then, the beginning, that you look for the end? For where the beginning is, there will the end be. Blessed is he who will take his place in the beginning; he will know the end and will not experience death."[2] What Jesus is ultimately saying is that there is no distinction between beginning and end; when one achieves inner union with the Holy Spirit, they have achieved eternal life, they have essentially escaped the matrix. They are filled with the Shakti energy that is infinite, never starting and never stopping. This further alludes to the fact that time is a manmade construct, and cannot exist outside of the realm of mankind. Jesus is also indicating that his followers are capable of becoming the alpha and omega themselves in this way.

The idea of a god being the beginning and end goes back thousands of years. There is the timekeeper god of the Greek mythology, Cronus, also known as Father Time. This is who the Christian god is modeled after. He controls time, all of it, from beginning to end, just like the Roman god Janus. Another example of a beginning and ending tradition within ancient religion is the Hindu god "Shiva the Destroyer and Creator." Shiva had both aspects, birth and reincarnation, but also death and destruction.

---

[2] The Gospel of Thomas, verse 18.

.The power of birth and destruction stemmed from Shakti, whom we talked about in the first chapter (1.1). Shakti was the primordial energy of the cosmos, considered to have no beginning and no ending, but simply *forever.* She was the creator goddess of the cosmos. Did Jesus work with the Shakti energy? Did he embody the goddess energy? As you will find later in section 11.5, Jesus spent time in India and Tibet; it is very likely he learned from these traditions. Could Mary Magdalene have also learned from these traditions? Did they both work with *Shakti,* the God-source, the mother Goddess herself?

Who else would fit the bill? Naturally, the life giver, the goddess. The goddess is often associated with birth and death. For example, Venus in Her cycle allegorically dies between cycles of the morning star and the evening star. This is detailed in the ancient story of the "Descent of Inanna" where she goes to the underworld, dies, and is resurrected. She is both aspects, creator goddess, birth giver, but also queen of the dead.

In fact, the omega sign actually has a rather ancient history. It was not something created in Jesus's heyday—it was something that existed at least a thousand years before him. This symbol is often seen in Sumerian and Akkadian art surrounding the goddess Ninhursag. Her name literally meant "Lady of the Mountains." Another name She was known by was Nintud/Nintur: Queen of the Birthing Hut. The term birthing hut could be in reference to the womb. The Akkadians knew Her as Belet-ili: Queen of the Gods. Other names that She went by include Mamma or *Mama.* Sound familiar? With that being said, the omega symbol which in a biblical sense would represent the *end,* is often seen as being an ancient symbol of the *womb.* Sometimes it was seen as part of a blade used to cut the umbilical cord. The womb's meaning can be viewed as twofold: the womb is where life starts. However, if one dies and is reincarnated, there is an element of ending and beginning as well. This symbol can be found on a kudurru, or boundary stone, of the Kassite ruler Melishipak (1186-1172 BC) at the Louvre Museum. The horseshoe-like symbol, an upside down omega symbol, can be found on the upper right.

As it seems, Jesus and Mary Magdalene traveled to many places and taught many their traditions. Mary Magdalene was said

Kudurru of the Kassite ruler Melishipak (1186 BC-1172 BC), Louvre.

to be the only disciple who achieved the same level of spiritual enlightenment as the Master Jesus. The Gospel of Philip dives heavily into the concept of the ritual bridal chamber, and the idea of sex representing divine union.

The Gospel of Philip is one of the lost gnostic gospels. Da Vinci Code fans would recognize a certain verse which Sir Leigh Teabing quotes, "And the companion of the Savior was Mary Magdalene. He loved her more than all the disciples, and used to kiss her often on the mouth..." This in fact is not a made up verse, but reality. However, in the Gospel of Philip, ants seemed to make a hole in an important spot in the once buried manuscript, obliterating the word describing the place where the gospel states Mary would receive Jesus's kiss. We can assume it was on the mouth—however scholars argue that one would only receive the "breath of the spirit" or holy spirit. Now this sounds an awful lot like the "ankh" in Egyptian tradition which is closely related to the sacred feminine and is perceived as the "breath of life."

David R. Cartlidge, in his book, *Documents for the Study of the Gospels* states about the gnostic tradition of the Bridal Chamber, "the gnostic sacrament culminated with a kiss, symbolizing spiritual conception." Is this all that the kiss meant? Or did it mean that they were lovers? In biblical tradition kissing was not a scandal until it was between man and woman. For a man and woman to kiss on the mouth in public was frowned upon because it led to "lewdness." So why would Jesus, a teacher, a rabbi, kiss a woman on the mouth in front of his disciples if she was nothing but a common disciple?

Mary Magdalene is called Jesus's companion in this gospel, often a word used to refer to a spouse or consort. They were clearly very close, and he respected her. They were partners in the teaching and healing of their followers. With that being said, there was also a concept of dualism present– Jesus embodying the masculine, potentially the beginning, as a womb is fertilized by a man's seed, and his partner Mary Magdalene representing the end, and that ability to create, or bring to life again, the omega. To ancient cultures, this symbol was prevalent of the goddess. Do we really think that Jesus and Mary Magdalene would not have known that?

11.4 Mary Magdalene, Bride in Hiding

There are many theories about where Mary Magdalene lived out her final days. An intriguing and popular theory is that she lived out the rest of her days in southern France after fleeing from Egypt, after of course, Jesus's crucifixion. Interestingly, there is no shortage of places named after her, cathedrals dedicated to the Saint Mary Magdalene, and even a church dedicated to her that is said to house her remains. Caves are named after her, rivers, forests, and more. She is quite well known in the southeastern parts of France. It is said that her remains are buried there at St. Maximin Basilica. There is a sarcophagus that now lies in the crypt beneath the basilica with her name on it. Is it really the Magdalene buried there? Or is she in the Talpiot Tomb?

According to local legend and lore, Mary Magdalene came ashore there, allegedly with her child, Maximin, Lazarus, and her sister, Martha. Some legends even say that Jesus survived the crucifixion and came with. However, Mary Magdalene has a grotto named after her, where she allegedly lived out the rest of her days in a cave, and continued Jesus's teachings to the local people.

Upon the discovery of Mary Magdalene's tomb, a golden reliquary was created to house her skull there—by none other than Pope Boniface VIII, the same pope who refused to put down the Knights Templar when King Philip the Fair of France pushed for their dissolution. King Philip had Pope Boniface beaten so badly he ended up dying a month later from a fever. Why did he find Mary Magdalene important enough to build a golden reliquary for her? Was he aware of her significance, as wife of God's representative on Earth, and therefore Goddess on Earth? Was Pope Boniface a secret initiate himself? Or is this simply just a coincidence…? There are many supposed burial locations of Magdalene; which one is the real one?

There are many theories out there about Magdalene being the Grail, carrying the royal blood of Jesus the Nazarene. Many theories suggest she fled to France and her children ended up being the Frankish kings known as the Merovingians. How are we to know? There have been some interesting emails sent to my colleague, Scott Wolter. In his book *Cryptic Code of the Templars in America*, Scott mentions an email sent to him: "To add more fuel to the fire concerning the marriage of Jesus/Yeshua and Mary Magdalene, on February 7, 2015, I received an email from a friendly fan named 'Dave' who said he was a retired Navy Commander and shared the following information:

> *Dear Mr. Wolter:*
> *I saw your season finale (Season 3). While I am not a geologist, I am a professor of Jewish history. Especially back in the days of Yeshua (Jesus) there would have been tremendous pressure on Him to make his mother, Mary...a grandmother. Under the Jewish tradition of that time, for His child to be recognized as legitimate, Yeshua would have to be married BEFORE the child was born. To make his mother, a grandmother would be a societal honor bestowed upon her. It would be in modern parlance, a feather in her cap. Now, the RC (Roman Catholic) church has been anti Mary of Magdala since the earliest days of*

the church. Modern research and inquiry has indicated that 1) Yeshua and Mary of Magdala were indeed married and 2) Mary, about 7 months after the crucifixion gave birth to the daughter of Yeshua.

As a Freemason, I cannot give you exact knowledge, but let's just say that your assumption that the Templars became part of Freemasonry and your assumption that they brought the truth of Yeshua's daughter and skeletal remains to North America are not unfounded.

There was a parchment delivered to the RC church in 1927 by an antiquities collector. It was dated by experts in 1945 to around 120 A.D. and it details the marriage of Yeshua and Mary and her birth of his daughter...and the fact that Mary of Magdala was in fact the head of the Christian church for several years.

The document was called the Catholicos Mysticus. It was apparently penned by the bishop of the church of Galatia and many requests to view it over the decades have been denied....and as of 2012 the RC Church officially denies its existence. I cannot and will not offer any more info on this subject.... it's just not prudent for me.

[Wolter continues] If it were possible to verify this referenced document, perhaps it would shed more light onto the life of Jesus and Mary Magdalene. Further correspondence with "Dave" shares this information: *"The Catholic church is MOST worried about the truth of Yeshua and Mary of Magdala coming out. As for Yeshua and Mary, I believe it was true...I mean, a Vatican Monsignor admitted it was true."*

See the email on the following page from Monsignor Francis Marchetti admitting that a document exists from 220 AD stating Mary Magdalene was married to Jesus. In art, Mary Magdalene is often depicted wearing red or orange and green. Green is the color of initiation. It is also the color of fertility, spring, birth, and victory of life over death. Orange is the color of endurance, strength, and passion. Red is of course associated with blood, a bloodline, and martyrdom.

Dave

----- Original Message -----
From: Msgr. Francis Marchetti
To: Dave
Sent: Tuesday, 12 May, 2009 10:07 AM
Subject: RE: Catholicos Mysticus

Dear Mr. ███████

Thank you for contacting me with your question.

First, let me say that it is true, the "Catholicos Mysticus" is in fact in our Vatican archives in storage.

It is true that the papyrus in question was delivered to the Christian authorities in 220 AD and that it details the reported event that 1) Mary of Magdala had secretly wed our Lord and Savior....2) She had his child, a girl....and 3) to avoid possible persecution of the child, she travelled with "trusted friends" to what later became known as Europe, reportedly France.

The papyrus was delivered by members of the church of Galatia. I will neither state that the papyrus is true or false...and I can assure you that the Holy Roman Catholic Church will never allow the document to be seen by the public.

Under His Omnipotence,

Msgr. Francis Marchetti

Email from Vatican Monsignor admitting to marriage between Jesus and Mary Magdalene (Courtesy of Scott Wolter).

11.5 Lineage of Mary Magdalene

Through one potential lineage, Mary Magdalene was the daughter of King Cyrus of the Benjamites. This means she too is descended from Jesus's ancient ancestors, giving her a right to the throne as well. Interestingly enough, the first king of the United Israel and Judah was a Benjamite (in about 1076 BC) named Saul. The mother of Mary Magdalene in this lineage is likely Eucharis/ Eucharia Magdalene, or titularly, "of Magdala," and also wife of King Cyrus of the Benjamites. While it is very difficult to find any trace of Eucharis, this lineage makes sense. Of course, we cannot be certain. However, this lineage going back to the same covenant of Jesus's ancestors, detailed in the book of Genesis, would make sense, and would logically explain Jesus's and Mary Magdalene's legitimate royal blood and their claim to the throne, especially together.

There are others that contend Mary has a somewhat Celtic lineage on one side, while having a Jewish or Egyptian heritage on the other. This perhaps is where the long red hair could have come from, but it must be noted that red hair was not so uncommon in Egypt at this time either. In fact, Ramesses II was found to have red hair. Could this have to do with intermarriages going back millennia with the Celts of Britain? Was there a significant connection between the Celts and the Egyptians? Did Mary Magdalene have Celtic roots, or is this pure speculation? I must point out that the great biblical prophet Jeremiah ventured to Ireland just after Nebuchadnezzar, king of Babylon, conquered Jerusalem in 586 BC. He took with him the two daughters of the last King of Judah, Zedekiah. Princess Tamar Tephi married Eochaidh the high king of Ireland, thus establishing a Davidian connection to all of the future kings of Ireland. These same kings then came to the west coast of Scotland later on, and ruled the kingdom of Dalriada from Argyll. There is a clear connection between the House of David and the Celtic bloodline, and if so, why would it be so impossible for Mary Magdalene to be of similar descent? Until we are able to locate Mary Magdalene's remains and perform genetic tests, all we can do now is analyze the information surrounding her mysterious origins.

Based on the evidence in the Cremona document in *The Scrolls of Onteora*, it is possible that Mary Magdalene is of a Hasmonean lineage. The Maccabeans were another name used for the Hasmoneans. The Hasmonean dynasty ruled over Judaea from 140 BC to 37 BC. Traditionally the ruler was both the high priest *and* king. This is similar to what Jesus initially became, an *exilarch*. He was the High King of the Jews, but also the high priest. The Hasmonean dynasty ended but later, male heirs were sought out by the then current king of Judea, Herod the Great. He felt extremely threatened by the strong rebellious Maccabean family; he was concerned they might attempt to overthrow him and reestablish their dynasty on the throne. It is for this reason that he murdered his own wife, Hasmonean princess Mariamne. The name appeared to be a traditional name passed down in the family, interestingly similar to the name used for Mary Magdalene on multiple occasions.

When Herod the Great heard that a "King of Jews" was to be born he initiated what became known as the Massacre of the Innocents. All baby boys under two in Bethlehem were to be slain. It was generally believed that the Maccabeans were meant to usher in the age of the Messiah, the True King, the Anointed. It is no wonder that Herod the Great was paranoid; he knew there was a shift coming, something that he could not stop. This leads me to question, was Jesus himself somehow connected or related to the nearly extinct Hasmonean descendents? If only the male heirs of the Hasmonean dynasty were killed off, then that left the opportunity for the Maccabean blood to live on in the surviving females. Therefore, it is possible that Mary Magdalene, or as she is referred to in the Cremona document, Miriama, was a Hasmonean princess in hiding.

It has also been proposed that Mary Magdalene had two siblings we are made aware of in the Bible. Martha, her sister, and Lazarus, the beloved disciple, her brother, who is well known for being "raised from the dead" by Jesus, which was an initiation or raising within their Essene tradition, and not an actual resurrection from the dead. A Martha also appears with Mary Magdalene in the *Pistis Sophia,* as another female disciple. It is possible that they could have been sisters, or purely sisters in the ministry.

11.6 Magdalene the Venus

It is important to remember that many of the stories relating to Jesus in the New Testament are allegorical, they are symbolic and not necessarily meant to be taken literally. But, some are. Based on my own research, I have come to the conclusion that Jesus represented God on Earth, his high priest. The ultimate form of Spirit is light, therefore he would be the life-giving force of the Sun.

He is representative of the "Sun God." Or more popularly

146

known today, the "son of God." Earlier we mentioned the Egyptian sun god, Amun/Amen, and his consort, Amunet. Jesus is representative of Amun, while Mary Magdalene may represent his consort, Amunet, literally meaning "she who is hidden" or "that which is concealed." Perhaps Mary Magdalene/Mariamne is destined to play the same role, and remain in hiding? She most certainly seemed to represent Venus, God's wife, Goddess, Her high priestess on earth.

Ancient people's lives revolved around the seasons, the changing phases of the Sun, and the cycle of nature. They lived from the Spring Equinox (rebirth upon Mother Earth), to Summer Solstice (celebration of the life-giving force, Sun), Fall Equinox (harvest), and Winter Solstice (celebration of the Goddess giving birth to the Sun). In *The Golden Bough*, a comparative study of history and religion published in 1922, the author, anthropologist James Frazer, writes:

In the Julian calendar the twenty-fifth of December was reckoned the winter solstice, and it was regarded as the Nativity of the Sun, because the day begins to lengthen and the power of the sun to increase from that turning-point of the year. The ritual of the nativity, as it appears to have been celebrated in Syria and Egypt, was remarkable. The celebrants retired into certain inner shrines, from which at midnight they issued with a loud cry, "The Virgin has brought forth! The light is waxing!" The Egyptians even represented the new-born sun by the image of an infant which on his birthday, the winter solstice, they brought forth and exhibited to his worshippers. No doubt the Virgin who thus conceived and bore a son on the twenty-fifth of December was the great Oriental goddess whom the Semites called the Heavenly Virgin or simply the Heavenly Goddess; in Semitic lands she was a form of Astarte. Now Mithra was regularly identified by his worshippers with the Sun, the Unconquered Sun, as they called him; hence his nativity also fell on the twenty-fifth of December. The Gospels say nothing as to the day of Christ's birth, and accordingly the early Church did not celebrate it.

Mary depicted at Santa Maria Novella, Florence.

In knowing and understanding the Sun, its cycles, its importance to the ancient agricultural civilizations, we can easily see why some of the elements of the story of Jesus are applied to him—to associate him with the ancient Sun God. The story of the slain shepherd being resurrected by the goddess is an ancient story, one replicated in so many different cultures around the world, and definitely a story that Jesus and Mary would be familiar with.

Now—the Sun God's consort, where is She?

Astronomically speaking, Venus is *always* 47 degrees from the Sun. When the Sun seems to die at the fall equinox, and the days get shorter, Venus is right there beside him. At spring equinox, the time of "rebirth," also near the time of Jesus's alleged crucifixion and resurrection, Venus is right there to see him revived. Who is there at Jesus's feet during the crucifixion? Who is the first person to see him resurrected? Mary Magdalene, Herself.

Curious to see if there was anything to this astrologically, I looked up astronomical calculations on my astronomy program and set the dates back to the date of the crucifixion. It happened on a Friday, the day of the week dedicated to the worship of Venus mind you. This particular Friday was April 3, 33 AD, the date of the crucifixion of Jesus. It was at 3 pm that Jesus was said to die, so I went ahead and plugged in that same time. I adjusted my

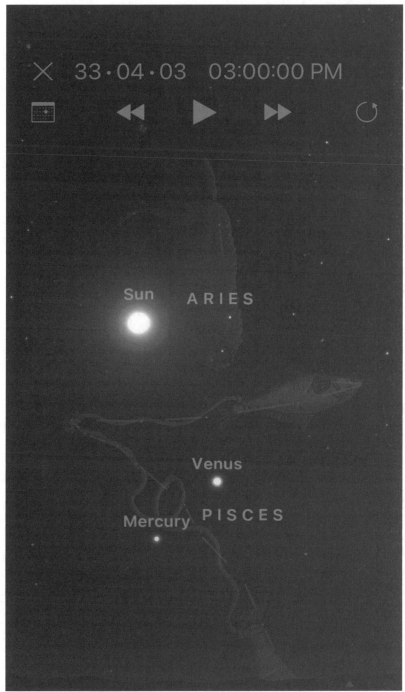

Venus and the Sun at 3 pm on April 3, 33 AD.

location for Jerusalem so that I could see the heavens just as Jesus, Mary Magdalene and his followers would have. What I saw did not shock me. What I saw confirmed what I already hypothesized. Jesus and Mary Magdalene absolutely represented the Sun and Venus on Earth.

The Sun is up in the afternoon spring sky, where you would expect to find it. Venus has been in the constellation of Pisces the Fish since January of 33 AD, which really just seems to fit in perfectly. At 3 pm on the crucifixion day, Venus is just southeast of the Sun. Venus sits at the Sun's feet. Just as Mary Magdalene is always portrayed at the crucifixion in art.

I find it interesting that some art places her on the right, southeast of Jesus's head, as this is the appropriate representation of the Sun and Venus on that specific day. Whoever first portrayed them this was likely an initiate, and knew of their connections to the heavenly bodies above. However there are paintings where she is on the left side instead, but still within the 47 degree sphere. I contend this could be for a few of reasons. 1) The artist was not aware that Jesus and Mary were representing the Sun and Venus. 2) They were trying to veil the connection they had to the Sun and Venus. 3) The left side is traditionally the feminine side. If they portrayed Mary on the left on the feminine side, Jesus was now on the masculine side, the right, whereas astronomically, the Sun was really on the left, in the feminine sphere, while Venus was on the right in the masculine, as viewed from Earth.

On the morning of Jesus's resurrection when Mary goes to the tomb to anoint him, she finds he has already risen prior to her ritual anointing. She goes to anoint him with the Holy Spirit so that he may be resurrected, or *raised.* When he appears to her, he tells her that it is she who is meant to be carrying on his church and ministry. On the morning of Sunday, April 5, Venus rises before the Sun, and would be found in the upper right corner. She is leading The Heavenly Way as the Morning Star, just as Jesus tells Mary to do.

Something else that dawned on me while looking at the artwork, whether it is the crucifixion or resurrection art, Jesus and Mary always appear to be within about 47 degrees of each other, much like the Sun and Venus. This can even be applied to the Last Supper painting by da Vinci if you consider the figure on the left of Jesus to be Mary Magdalene. There appears to be a 47 degree angle between their touching arms. Was this a coincidence?

11.7 Hieros Gamos: The Holy Marriage

Holy marriage, what could that be? It is not just *any* marriage ceremony, but rather something more ancient and more sacred. It is a marriage that takes place between god and goddess, but done by their representatives on Earth: priest and priestess. This symbolic ritual of the god and goddess that was played out by their earthly counterparts goes back thousands of years.

This occurred between Sumerian city-state royalty who were seen as king and high priest, queen and high priestess of Inanna. The concept of "ruling by divine right" has existed for a long time. Rulers have always believed they ruled the earthly realm while the gods and goddesses ruled the heavenly realm. Zeus and Hera's union was ritually recreated at the Heraion of Samos. The biblical land of Canaan yields similar traditions between representatives of El and Asherah; and between Baal and Anat. At the temple of Eanna (House of Heaven) in Uruk, along the Tigris and Euphrates, something very similar would take place. The high priestess of the native goddess, Nadītu, would select a young man to ritually represent the shepherd Dumuzid, consort of Inanna. Their marriage was celebrated during the annual Duku ceremony which occurred at the autumn Equinox (Autumnal Zag-mu Festival).

Jesus is often referred to as a shepherd of his flock in much the same manner. In fact, he has much to say about the hieros gamos throughout the different gospels, and particularly the ones that were not deemed worthy of the Bible. The Gospel of Thomas tells us that while watching babies nurse from their mothers' breast Jesus said, "When you make the two *into* one, when you make the inner like the outer and outer like the inner, the upper like the lower, and *when you make male and female into a single one, so that male will not be male nor the female be female...* Then you will enter into the Kingdom of the Father and Mother, the Way of Mystery." In this way he can literally be speaking of a physical divine union, but also of the inner divine union. This statement has two layers.

Jesus is clearly inspired by the scene of the children suckling from their mothers' breast, and is thinking about how this scene came to be. The union of these two sacred opposites is powerful enough to summon a soul to the womb of woman, to bring forth a child nine months later. If sex is this powerful, what else is it capable of when done with a spiritual purpose? If sex is the power of creation, it is the ultimate energy of God-Goddess-Creator, whatever you choose to call deity. Jesus tells us in the Gospel of Thomas that achieving oneness between male and female (or within oneself) gives entry to the Kingdom of the Father, but also the Mother. Jesus tells us that the Father is not above the Mother, but she is his equal, his sacred partner in creation. This is a far cry from what the Christian church would have you believe.

Let us not forget that a similar statement is said pertaining to the marriage between man and woman in Genesis 2:23-25: "And the man said: This is now bone of my bones and flesh of my flesh... For this reason a man will leave his father and mother and be united to his wife, and they will become one flesh. And the man and his wife were both naked, and they were not ashamed."

Their lack of shame is indicating their awareness of sexuality. They are husband and wife, they have no reason to feel shame over each other's nakedness. Jesus himself is clearly aware of the sanctity of lovemaking, and he himself is a traveled man.

The original "Lord's Prayer" in Aramaic that Jesus actually taught is much different from the one we have all learned growing up. The Lord's Prayer we have all been taught begins with "Our Father," which translates from "abba," when in fact the actual Aramaic word is "Abwoon," which is a combination of "abba (father)" and "woon" (womb). This shows Jesus's recognition of the masculine and feminine source of creation. Why was this sacred feminine principle excluded?

Dr. Douglas-Klotz, in his *Prayers of the Cosmos: Meditations on the Aramaic Words of Jesus,* wrote various translations of the Lord's Prayer in Aramaic from the Lord's Prayer from the King James Bible. The translation of the first line I find riveting:

Our Father who art in Heaven:
O Birther! Father-Mother of the Cosmos, you create all that moves in light.

The Aramaic version of the prayer is vastly different from the translation many Christians are familiar with. Not only does it offer more spiritual allusion, but it also references the Father *and* Mother of the cosmos. Why was this lost within Christianity? Why have we stopped honoring Her, the Holy Mother?

Within Christianity, the goddess is still present, but just as mother of Jesus, the "Virgin Mary." Firstly let us address the issue of her virginity: She was not a virgin by modern standards. The word used before translation was the Semitic word *almah,* meaning simply "young woman" with no sexual meaning whatsoever.

Mary is called mother of god within Christianity. Mary was said to conceive by the Holy Spirit. Theoretically, if one has had inner union with the Holy Spirit Sophia, they may have learned to work with the kundalini energy, one and the same with Shakti and the Holy Spirit. Mary was most likely a Levite, just as her cousin Elizabeth, mother of John the Baptist, was. Elizabeth was referred to as one of the "daughters of Aaron."

The lineage of Mary is never explicitly talked about in the Bible, but Jesus is referred to as high priest and king, due to his Aaronic lineage as well as his Davidian: "But Christ came as High Priest of the good things to come, with the greater and more perfect tabernacle not made with hands, neither of this creation."[3] Jesus, being of Levite lineage, would be permitted to *carry the Tabernacle* as high priest. Joseph was descended from kings, and Mary was descended from priests. Further, "Thus says the Lord: 'If you can break My covenant with the day and My covenant with the night, so that there will not be day and night in their season, then My covenant may also be broken with David My servant, so that he shall not have a son to reign on his throne, and with the Levites, the priests, My ministers. As the host of heaven cannot be numbered, nor the sand of the sea measured, so will I multiply the descendants of David My servant and the Levites who minister to me.'"[4]

It is made clear the importance of both the Levites and the sons of David, so a union between Mary, a Levite, and between a

---

[3] Hebrews 9:11.

[4] Jeremiah 33:20-22.

prince, Joseph descended from David, would make perfect sense. Joseph, being an exilarch, would still be expected to marry and produce heirs of his kingdom, that should one day be restored to a descendent of King David. This makes Joseph a prince, with a need to marry and have children. Mary being descended from a priestly lineage, would be meant to produce an heir to the temple priests. Jesus would be a priest king, highest of the high in both his lineages.Thus a child conceived in this royal union would be a child that has claim to high priesthood as well a kingship. Is it possible that the conception of Jesus took place during *hieros gamos?* With kundalini being a feminine faceless energy associated with the Holy Spirit, is it so far fetched to say that if Mary and Joseph shared in this sexual and spiritual union, that Jesus was conceived of the Holy Spirit, whilst actually being physically conceived?

It was indeed a holy act to conceive a child destined for high priesthood, and for kingship. Being a priest-king was something that existed in Israel for hundreds if not thousands of years, and before that Egypt, where the pharaoh was high priest of all the temples, and his queen high priestess. Hieros gamos very well could be the source for all of the talk around Mary's spiritual conception, as hieros gamos was very much a spiritual experience, representing God.

The encounter Mary has with the archangel Gabriel may even confirm such a thing. It is possible that the archangels were actually priests, who had assumed a level of perfection and inner union. Inner union would mean they had connected to both Father and Mother God (Holy Spirit), thus making them no longer one gender or the other. Archangels are said to present the prayers to God said below; is this not a function of a high priest? In every aspect, there is some heavenly representative on Earth for every single one in heaven. God bestowed his earthly kingship upon the lineage of David, for example, and they should all be called "sons of God."[5] Is it possible that the priests of the temple were also given titles of the angels in heaven? Considering that in the past two thousand years, there are no recorded accounts where one literally and physically saw and spoke with an angel, you have to wonder if the archangels were in fact the earthly archangels—

---

[5] 2 Samuel 7:13-14..

154

priests.

Gabriel appears to Mary, likely a priest, and of her own lineage. He bestows upon her the news that she is meant to conceive, to be a mother, to bring another priest of her lineage into this world, "Fear not, Mary: for thou hast found favor with God. And, behold, thou shalt conceive in thy womb, and bring forth a son, and shalt call his name Jesus."[6] She says to Gabriel, "How shall this be, seeing I know not a man?" He responds by saying, "The Holy Spirit shall come upon thee, and the power of the Highest shall overshadow thee: therefore also that holy thing which shall be born of thee shall be called the Son of God."[7] The Highest would be God, or God's king on earth, would it not? Joseph would be meant to be the exilarch king, just as his son Jesus is destined to be. In essence, Gabriel explains to Mary that she will indeed have a union with the most High [King]. "Overshadow" in this translation could literally mean to *cover* her, or to lie with her. For anyone to be given the opportunity to marry a prince or king, they should certainly be excited and would attribute this to God's favor just as Gabriel does.

In relation to the royal wedding customs, Laurence Gardner says in his work *Bloodline of the Holy Grail: The Lineage of Jesus Revealed*, "Messianic marriages were always conducted in two stages. The first (the anointing in Luke) was the legal commitment to wedlock, while the second (the later anointing in Matthew, Mark and John) was the cementing of the contract. In Jesus and Mary's case the second anointing was of particular significance for, as explained by Flavius Josephus in the 1st-century, the second part of the marriage ceremony was never conducted until the wife was three months pregnant. Dynastic heirs such as Jesus were expressly required to perpetuate their lines. Marriage was essential, but community law protected the dynasts against marriage to women who proved barren or kept miscarrying. This protection was provided by the three-month pregnancy rule. Miscarriages would not often happen after that term, subsequent to which it was considered safe enough to complete the marriage contract."

---

[6] Luke 1:30-31.

[7] Luke 1:34-35.

Luke 1:27 informs us that Mary and Joseph were already contractually betrothed. Later, Gardner continues on about their marriage tradition saying that, "intimacy between a dynastic husband and wife was only allowed in December, so that births of heirs would always fall in the month equivalent to September—the month of Atonement, the holiest month of the calendar." Firstly, if man and wife were only allowed to live together in intimate relations in the month of December, then await the second and final stage of marriage three months later (spring equinox), would they not live separately after December?

After Mary's conversation with Gabriel, and following her conception, she goes to stay with her Levite cousin Elisabeth and her husband, the priest Zacharias. They celebrate Mary's pregnancy, and the two women support each other in their childbearing bliss for a time. This time happens to be *three months.* Luke 1:56 says, "And Mary abode with her about three months, and returned to her own house." Is this when Mary's final marriage with Joseph took place? Is this why it was believed that she was unmarried when she became pregnant?

Secondly, the child was meant to be born in September, which was likely considered the holiest month of the year because this was the time of harvest and abundance. Additionally, this is the month of the sign of Virgo, the virgin, or the *almah,* young woman. Could this also play a part in the story of Jesus being of a Virgin birth? Did Mary and Joseph practice these dynastic wedlock traditions over the right months? When was Jesus really born?

***

During the "lost years" (the years of Jesus' adolescence and young adulthood) Jesus traveled to many places, just as almost all dynastic heirs would do, as they should be traveled and educated in the matters of the world. His father Joseph likely did the same thing. Some of those places were Buddhist monasteries and other temples of the land. In Kashmir, controlled by India, it is believed by locals that St. Issa (Arabic for Jesus) is buried at the Roza Bal Shrine at Srinagar.[8]

For thousands of years people visited monasteries or places

---

[8] "Jesus Was a Buddhist Monk," BBC Documentary Film.

of hermitage to prepare themselves to tap into the kundalini. A spiritual pilgrimage, retreat, or vision quest was often the precursor to divine revelations. There is evidence to suggest Jesus did much the same during the lost years. A man as learned and spiritual as Jesus would certainly humble himself to learn all of the different ways of achieving union with Mother-Father God. Was Jesus the only one who traveled and learned these sacred traditions? Or did Mary Magdalene perhaps make this spiritual journey around the old world as well? Is it possible that Jesus and Mary Magdalene were working with the infinite, cosmic, and divine feminine energy within them? As they became one with her, within their Divine Union, they would have literally become infinite, the *beginning and end.*

Perhaps it was here that Jesus learned about tantra. Tantra literally means "woven together." Tantric sex is a form of divine energetic lovemaking, perhaps an aspect of the hieros gamos that was practiced for so long. As Jesus was traveling through his youthful years it is possible he could have also learned yoga, a form of meditation, and even reiki: energy healing. While reiki would appear to be a New Age phenomenon originating in the 1920s, it is very likely it existed for much longer. In fact, it was the Japanese Mikao Usui who is attributed to founding reiki, but only after attending a *Buddhist* retreat. Jesus was said to perform miracles like healing by touch; if you have ever seen the work of reiki done, this would look quite similar. The concept of energy work centered around the Seven Chakras first appeared in the Indian texts of the Vedas between 1500 BC and 500 BC. With chakra work comes energy work.

Singing bowls originated over 5,000 years ago in Mesopotamia, despite being believed to be a Buddhist tradition. Singing bowls and their vibrations are used to induce energetic balance and healing even on a physical level. This tradition did in fact make its way to India, Tibet, and Nepal not too much later. It is quite likely that Jesus learned these very methods of healing. While we do not know about Mary Magdalene's early years, it would be safe to say that she likely also became a master at these practices as she was Jesus's partner in ministry and miracle and was the disciple that Jesus loved most. Jesus would seem willing to teach these mysteries and miracles to those wanting to learn as he says in John 14:12, "I tell you, whoever believes in me will do the works I have been doing, and they will do even greater things than these."

With the clear descent from royalty of both Jesus and Mary Magdalene, they would be familiar with these practices. They would most certainly bring God into their marriage, whether they were married to each other or others. Within their partnership it is apparent that Mary Magdalene and Jesus traveled together as equals, and likely as priest and priestess. They would have been well aware of hieros gamos. I must reiterate that in many cases the hieros gamos included an entire ritual of anointing with oils and such prior to consummation. For we must remember that Jesus's ancestor, Solomon married the daughter of the Pharaoh, and the Song of Solomon tells us of their intimate encounters of the bridal chamber and the anointing.

The Bible often refers to Jerusalem as the "bride" and of God in the heavens the "bridegroom." Revelation 21:9 refers to the the "bride of the Lamb" when it's stated, "Come here, I will show you the bride, the wife of the Lamb." We know that the lamb refers to the constellation Aries the Ram, and the bride would be Jerusalem, in the Old Covenant (the Age of Aries which has come to pass). The New Jerusalem is to be established in the new Age of Pisces, with a *new covenant.* Revelation 21:2 says, "And I saw the holy city, the new Jerusalem, coming down out of heaven from God, made ready as a bride adorned for her husband." The ancient concept of the earth and land being feminine and the light of the heavens being masculine is firmly applied here. It is worth mentioning the Christian doctrine of the Christ Bride and Her Bridegroom. The Church would have you believing the Christ Bride is Jesus's church and ministry. The reference "The Holy Mother the Church" comes to mind. Yet remember, he left his church and ministry to the one and only Mary Magdalene upon his allegorical death. *She* literally becomes his church.

So where is the origin of hieros gamos? The concept of this sacred marriage goes back to the primordial union between heaven and Earth, which takes place time and time again. All of the ancient sites that have solar alignments on specific days of year represent this union. Many of these ancient stone chambers will be "impregnated" by the solar rays on a specific day, usually on December 21, as nine months later, the crops are harvested in September at the fall equinox, in the sign of Virgo the Virgin.

The Bible tells us in Genesis how Eve came from Adam's rib or side, which could translate in various ways. 1) She is of the same tribe and perhaps is actually related somehow. 2) Man and woman were first created as one complete being already in union. Plato tells us a story having to do with Greek traditions on such matters: "Humans were originally created with four arms, four legs and a head with two faces. Fearing their power, Zeus split them into two separate parts, condemning them to spend their lives in search of their other halves."[9]

Is this perhaps the truth? Or rather a romantic story of the idea of how soul mates or twin flames came to be? Legend holds that soul mates are only temporary partners who come to teach lessons, whereas the twin flame is the actual other half. Twin flame relationships are never easy, but rather a relationship that forces each half to work on themselves. The twin flame relationship is like looking into a mirror; they each see their vulnerabilities and problems. This is why one partner chooses to run until both of them are ready to come together and ascend spiritually as one. The twin flame union is the ultimate form of spiritual alchemy, of *hieros gamos*. Twin flame union is doing the internal and spiritual work together, so that the two halves may return to one being in divine harmony. In the tarot deck, this alchemical union is represented by the Lovers card.

Despite the phrase "twin flame" being a recent addition to the New Age vocabulary, it is actually a concept that has existed for thousands of years. The ancient Egyptian text known as the *Book of the Dead* dates back to as early as 1550 BC. This would be 3,500+ years ago. Within the texts are primarily funerary practices and spells, but also within the ancient texts are mentions of a soul-deep love. *The Book of the Dead* goes on to say that within a lifetime a soul will be born searching for another soul, and that if they do not find each other in one lifetime they shall be reincarnated as many times as it takes to find that other half.

With such intimate love and spiritual bonding as Jesus and

---

[9] The Symposium.

Mary Magdalene shared, they appeared to be on the same spiritual level. They mirrored each other as divine vessels of truth, wisdom, knowledge, and balance between the sacred feminine and masculine. They shared a bond that made the disciples envious and jealous.

The Gnostic gospel *Pistis Sophia* provides us insight into the conversations Jesus was having with his disciples post-resurrection. What is it that Jesus has done, learned, and studied since his *rebirth*? The disciples asked how man had come to be on the mortal Earth, from the immortal world of the cosmos. Jesus says, "Son of Man consented with Sophia, his consort, and revealed a great androgynous light. Its male name is designated 'Saviour, begetter of all things.' Its female name is designated 'All-begettress Sophia.' Some call her 'Pistis.'" Jesus is not solely the *Son of Man*, but represents a god, or something much greater in the heavens. Sophia is called Pistis, which translates loosely as faith. Pistis also sounds eerily similar to the name *Isis*.

The disciples never seemed to get the concept of the sanctity and equality of both the feminine and the masculine, even though Jesus spelled it out for them. Many of the disciples do not like Mary, and make that very clear on multiple occasions. After the resurrection, Mary Magdalene tells the disciples of her visionary encounter with Jesus. In the Gospel of Mary, Andrew and Peter accuse Her of lying. Mary Magdalene is hurt and She wept. Levi in turn says, "Now I see you contending against the woman like the adversaries. But if the Savior made Her worthy, who are you indeed to reject Her? *For he knew Her completely and loved Her devotedly.*"

He knew Her completely. He loved Her devotedly. The love and the spiritual bond shared between Jesus and Mary Magdalene is so strong that it makes the disciples angry and jealous that Jesus may have seen Mary as more worthy than them. Jesus and Mary are bound by the Holy Mysteries that they share only with each other, and not with other disciples. Could one of these Mysteries be the hieros gamos? The Gospel of Philip reveals that Jesus loved Mary more than all of the disciples. As we have seen it says:

The disciples said to him, "Why do you love her more than

160

all of us?" The Savior answered and said to them, "Why do I not love you like Her? When a blind man and one who sees are both together in darkness, they are no different from one another. When the light comes, then he who sees will see the light, and he who is blind will remain in darkness."

What does Jesus mean by this? Is it that Mary is the only one who truly understands his teachings, the only one who was become "perfect" as Jesus has? In this case she would have achieved union with the Holy Spirit, or Holy Sophia. Jesus indicates that Mary is the one with sight, while the apostles would be those that dwell in blindness and darkness. They have not truly accepted his teachings, nor have they opened up their hearts and spirits to them completely yet.

The disciples ask Jesus when the New Kingdom of Heaven shall come to pass, and he says, "What you look forward to has already come, but you do not recognize it."[10] By saying this, Jesus acknowledges their ignorance within the Mystery. They do not seem to get that the Kingdom is found and achieved within.

My interpretation appears to be confirmed in Chapter 17 of the *Pistis Sophia* when Mary asks for permission to speak openly. Jesus responds by saying, "Mary, blessed one, whom I will perfect in all Mysteries of those of the highest, speak in openness, you, whose heart is raised to the Kingdom of Heaven more than all of the brethren." Jesus openly declares that Mary understands the Mysteries where as many of the disciples still have not opened their hearts to it.

Mary proceeds to share some of her own Wisdom based on the teachings of Jesus, perhaps sharing a slightly different perspective. Jesus lovingly responds to Her, humbly receiving her Wisdom, his heart more open and aware than ever. He responds by saying, "Well said, Mary, for you are blessed before all women on earth, because you shall be the fullness of all fullnesses and the perfection of all perfections." This is an interesting thing for Jesus to say, as when Gabriel had gone to his mother Mary in the book of Luke, he says, "Hail, thou that art highly favored, the Lord is with thee: *blessed art thou among women.*"

---

[10] Gospel of Thomas, verse 51.

***

What appears to be obvious is the connection in spirit and love they lived in together. Before and after the crucifixion, Mary was the most Beloved Disciple, the one whom Jesus loved most, the one who understood his seemingly new and radical teachings. Mary was very conscious and aware that these teachings were not in fact new, nor radical, but natural and ancient. They were as ancient as humanity itself, for these were the teachings of the priest kings of Egypt, Mesopotamia, and those before.

Jesus mentions that Mary is of the highest perfection, meaning she has achieved perfection, just as he has. The concept of being perfect further cements her embodiment of the wife of God, of Goddess incarnate, high priestess on earth. The idea of achieving union with Goddess, the Holy Spirit/Shakti/Kundalini/Deity, whatever you want to call it, is as old as spiritual consciousness itself.

For two people as deeply evolved as Jesus and Mary to engage in hieros gamos, in a spiritual form of sexual intimacy, must be one of the most freeing, enlightening, and love-filled experiences one could have. You can argue their marriage, whether or not they had a sexual relationship or children to follow, but what cannot be argued is the tender love, respect, and compassion shared between the two. This is the intimacy that many relationships in the modern world lack. Jesus knew Her completely and loved Her devotedly.

> "It is to those who are worthy of my Mysteries that I tell my Mysteries."
> —Jesus, Gospel of Thomas, verse 62

11.8 Wedding at Cana

Many Christians and biblical scholars will eagerly refute any claim that Jesus may have been married. Why? They claim the Bible *does not* say that Jesus was married, and the Bible is the word of God, so that is that. Not quite so. The Bible is notoriously missing many ancient scriptures of the time, as the Council of Nicaea made sure to only include the gospels and the works that fit their Roman Catholic narrative. In the classic Roman Catholic style, however, they could not miss out on the opportunity to discuss one of the many "miracles" their Lord and savior performed: turning water into wine.

Immediately following Jesus's baptism (initiation) into The Way by John the Baptist, he goes out into the desert, embarking upon a 40-day-long vision quest. Here Jesus contemplates many things, as one does during a period of isolated reflection. It was only three days after his return from such an ordeal that Jesus and his mother, Mary, attended a wedding at Cana. Before I explain the actual wedding, it is important to have a basic understanding of ancient Jewish wedding tradition.

There were three different steps within the ancient Jewish wedding customs:

1. "Shiddukhin" was the mutual agreement and signing of a marriage contract. Here the price of the bride was decided upon and a contract was signed.

2. "Erusin" was the betrothal which took place after both the bride and bridegroom were rituly immersed in the mikvah, the natural spring bath, and then entered into the huppah (marriage canopy). The marriage canopy represented the symbolic planning of new households, and the bridegroom would often give his bride a valuable gift such as jewelry. They would then make their vows and share a glass of wine to seal their new covenant. This betrothal period would usually last about a year, but sometimes longer. Even though the couple had not gone through the actual wedding ceremony, they were considered married at this point. The bride would now wear a veil until the time of the marriage to signify that she was spoken for.

3. "Nissuin" was the actual marriage. The bride was not aware when the bridegroom would return to collect her and take her to his home to make their marriage official. When he arrived, he would blow a ram's horn to alert the household. There would be lots of noise, excitement, and in this bridal fashion the bridegroom would carry his new bride home. Once at the bridegroom's house, they would enter the marriage canopy once again and finalize their vows over wine. Sometimes the bride would circle the bridegroom seven times, as seven was the number of perfection. After this the

bride and bridegroom would retire to their private chambers to consummate the marriage. Following the consummation, there was usually a large wedding feast and celebration lasting seven days.

With this all in mind, let us consider what occurs at the wedding in Cana. Cana is located in northern Israel in Galilee, an area that Jesus and Mary Magdalene were very familiar with. John 1:1-10 says:

> On the third day there was a wedding in Cana in Galilee, and the mother of Jesus was there. Jesus and his disciples were also invited to the wedding. When the wine ran short, the mother of Jesus said to him, "They have no wine." Jesus said to her, "Woman, how does your concern affect me? My hour has not yet come." His mother said to the servers, "Do whatever he tells you." Now there were six stone water jars there for Jewish ceremonial washings, each holding twenty to thirty gallons. Jesus told them, "Fill the jars with water." So they filled them to the brim. Then he told them, "Draw some out now and take it to the headwaiter." So they took it. And when the headwaiter tasted the water that had become wine, without knowing where it came from (although the servers who had drawn the water knew), the headwaiter called the bridegroom and said to him, "Everyone serves good wine first, and then when people have drunk freely, an inferior one; but you have kept the good wine until now."

Naturally the names of the bride and the bridegroom are left out, leaving us to wonder whose wedding it really is. The idea of it being the wedding of Jesus is not far-fetched considering that he and his mother Mary are acting as hosts of this wedding feast. If Jesus's family was not hosting, his mother would not be concerned about the wine running out. According to the scripture, these six stone jars would hold in total about 180 gallons, or 680 liters of wine. By modern comparison, this is approximately 1,000 bottles of wine. If we prescribe this new wine to the thirsty wedding party-goers, let's say each person is to drink half a bottle (modern standard) this is at least 2,000 people present. Not to mention how much wine had already been consumed prior to this is unknown. We could assume the stone jars were full at the beginning, so perhaps there were as many as 1,000 bottles drunk prior to Jesus's miraculous refill. It is possible there were even more than 2,000 people present, anywhere up to 4,000! A usual Jewish wedding would not bring about so many people. However, if this were to be a large *royal* wedding, it would make perfect sense.

As we look for evidence that Jesus and Mary were in fact husband and wife, we cannot ignore what could be some of the most intriguing evidence to date: the Cremona Document. The Cremona Document is a vast, complex, and lengthy tale. Trying to put its contents into the narrow constraints of a few sentences could never do it justice, but Don Ruh, the man who deciphered many of the documents within it, did a brilliant job of explaining it in his book *The Scrolls of Onteora.*

What the Cremona Document first does is detail the journey of medieval Knights Templar, whose identities have been able to be verified in our world history, to what is now America. They are sent to America, a land they call Onteora, to retrieve certain scrolls that were likely placed in the "Temple of the Goddess" sometime in the first century by Jews. On the list of scrolls that were deposited in the Temple of the Goddess were many controversial titles. One in particular is especially grabbing:

A contract of marriage with Yeshua Ben Yosef and Miriama A Hasmonian at Cana.[11]

A marriage contract between Jesus son of Joseph, and Mary the Hasmonean. A marriage that takes place at Cana, where Jesus performed his first "miracle" of the wine. Could this truly serve as evidence to prove that Jesus and Mary Magdalene were in fact married?

11.9 The God of Wine

Wine was a very important thing to the ancient people, and thus Dionysus became the Greek god of wine. Dionysus was

---

[11] Ruh, Don. *The Scrolls of Onteora*, p 251.

fathered by Zeus and birthed by the goddess Persephone, or in some myths, the goddess Demeter. The worship of Dionysus dates all the way back to 1300 BC according to a stele found in Pylos on the Greek Peloponnesus. Dionysus and his mystery traditions could potentially come from a much older time. Dr. Carl J. Becker says, "Dionis was the epithet for and then the priest or acolyte of the tradition of Hermes." This is not surprising, as Hermes Trismegistus (meaning thrice greatest Hermes) was the messenger god. Hermes was the Greek version of the Egyptian god Thoth/Toth. Thoth was a magician, one who worked with the mysteries of death and resurrection quite often. He even helped Isis resurrect her husband Osiris.

Thoth was the original "initiator" into the Egyptian Mysteries. He began what became known as a "Mystery School." The first reference to him is in the Pyramid Texts which date back to 3000 BC. Almost all of the "Hermetic mysteries" begin in Egypt. Dionysian Mysteries clearly follow Thoth-Hermes in a new age way. The phrase "As above so below" was found on the enigmatic Emerald Tablet in which the texts were attributed to Hermes Trismegistus. There seem to be many parallels with Dionysus.

Dionysus is often called the "twice born" son. The concept of this twice born notion comes from another story about the birth of Dionysus—still son of Zeus, but born of the virgin mortal mother Theban Princess Semele, also said to be a priestess of Zeus. Semele was supposedly sacrificing a bull at the altar of Zeus when he first laid eyes upon her.

Fittingly, the name Semele means *mother earth*. Semele was said to conceive by drinking from a cup that had cut up bits of Zeus's heart in it after he had been slaughtered. This is similar to the concept of Christian communion, drinking from the blood of Christ to *conceive of the Holy Spirit* as well as eating from the body. Within Christianity there often appears to be a major emphasis on the "sacred heart" of Jesus as well as his mother, Virgin Mary.

Dionysus embodied many qualities that were later attributed to Jesus, such as being born of a virgin, being son of (a) God, and being the "protector of humanity." In a 5th century epic poem by Nonnus, Zeus appears to Semele and tells her, "You bring forth a son who shall not die, and you I will call immortal. Happy woman! You have conceived a son who will make mortals forget their troubles, you shall bring forth joy for gods and men."[12]

Due to the fact that Dionysus was born of a mortal woman, it was even suggested in ancient times that Dionysus was a real living and breathing historical figure. The emperor Julian of the 4th century wrote, "I have heard many people say that Dionysus was a mortal man because he was born of Semele, and that he became a god through his knowledge of theurgy and the Mysteries, and like our lord Heracles for his royal virtue was translated to Olympus by his father Zeus."[13] According to Julian, Dionysus was a man that was made into a god through his understanding and initiation into the mysteries, much like Jesus.

Dionysus was said to have been quite the traveler, roaming much of the old world trying to avoid his jealous father's wife, Hera, and her famous wrath. It was in present day Turkey that Dionysus allegedly came into contact with the goddess Cybele, who began to teach him all of Her religious rites. He then proceeded to travel all over Asia and India, teaching about winemaking (and likely the other rites he learned from Cybele). Dionysus traveled all over the old world, including India, just as Jesus was said to. There was even a city called Nysa, which was near the Indus River, that the locals claimed was founded long before by Dionysus himself. The Greek historian, Diodorus of Sicily (90 BC-30 BC) wrote about how Dionysus essentially dominated most of the globe in a manner similar to military conquest. At some point Dionysus journies down into the Underworld to rescue his mortal mother who had died during pregnancy. He found Semele, redeemed her, renamed her Thyone, and "ascended" with her to heaven and made her a goddess.

If we presume that Dionysus was indeed a real human at some point in time, then could it be possible that his mother, Semele, a princess and High Priestess of Zeus, engaged in hieros gamos with the High Priest of Zeus, therefore, he was conceived of Zeus? Another connection to a later high priestess follows, for if Dionysus truly existed, it was likely the High Priestess of Cybele,

---

[12] Dionysiaca 7.

[13] To the Cynic Heracleios, Julian.

She who represented the goddess on earth, that he came to learn these secret religious rites from. Dionysus was allegedly born only 18 miles southeast of Nazareth in the Galilean city of Beth She'an. The town was allegedly named Nysa earlier on, being founded by Dionysus, and was also the place where he had to lay to rest his wet nurse. The town would have been founded in the earlier part of the 3rd century BC. Beth She'an's name was changed to Scythopolis after Alexander the Great conquered the East, in honor of the Scythian guards that, according to legend, Dionysus took with him on his travels to India. Jesus also traveled to India.

The city of Beth She'an did in fact yield many archaeological artifacts confirming that the worship of Dionysus was very present and very popular at that time. There were several statues and altars of Dionysus found there. This is only miles away from where Jesus supposedly grew up.

Semele likely bore a child as a single mother, princess, priestess and therefore had to live in hiding, or in disgrace as she was not married. Dionysus would carry no honorable name. Later Dionysus rescues her from the "underworld" or could it be exile, and offers her redemption, or perhaps *resurrection*. Perhaps this was Dionysus initiating and raising his mother into the cult of the goddess Cybele. If she was brought into this new mystery cult of priesthood, the realm of heaven, she would require a new name, which became Thyone, much like newly baptized Christians would take a new Christian name. There are many parallels between the Christian story of Jesus being born of a virgin, and the story of Dionysus. His mother conceived him by God, by partaking in drinking from the ritual cup of wine and/or blood and/or body; he traveled, learned, taught, and even performed miracles. Like Jesus, Dionysus was probably a man that was later made divine. There was a celebration of him in late December called "Dionysia" right around winter solstice (December 21) and the Christian holiday Christmas, December 25. Three months later, another festival was held in his honor—Greater Dionysia—right around the spring equinox in late March, just as Jesus is celebrated as resurrected in early spring at Easter. Not to mention, he and his mother both *ascend into heaven*. Eventually Dionysus was said to be torn apart into 14 pieces by the Titans (just like Osiris was cut into 13 pieces) and then put back together by the goddess Demeter, sometimes seen as his mother. He is reborn or resurrected just as the vine on Earth is, so that it may restore the fruit of the vine to the world.

The Egyptian god Osiris was also called "Lord of Wine" during the Wag Festival which followed just after the Wepet-Renpet Festival: the Opening of the Year Festival, the Egyptian New Year's. Wine, and therefore grapes, always had a strong connection with the idea of birth, death, and resurrection. This celebration depended on the annual inundation of the Nile River. A feast was dedicated to Osiris, and was the time for new initiates to be brought into the Osirian Mystery Tradition, which was occurring during the Old Kingdom of Egypt (2613-3150 BC).

A familiar story featuring King Midas involves the wine god. The teacher of Dionysus, Silenus, went missing, so Dionysus set out looking for him. Silenus was being held at the court of the local King Midas. After 11 days of food, drink, and entertainment, King Midas presented Silenus to Dionysus. He was so grateful for the return of his teacher that he offered King Midas any wish that he would have fulfilled. His request? That everything he touched be turned to gold. Later he came to regret his choice, and Dionysus told him he may redeem himself, wash himself of his sins, by going and washing in the Pactolus river. After Midas learned his lesson and washed in the river, he was cured of his golden touch. There is a hint of historical truth to this story as well, because the river was rich with electrum, a naturally occurring alloy of silver and gold. This electrum was the basis for the ancient coins minted in the kingdom of Lydia, 2,500+ years ago. The Greeks called it "gold" or "white gold." For Dionysus to be able to give this ability, of turning things by touch into gold, reminds me of certain alchemical practices. Just as Jesus turned water into wine...

The bull became an important symbol of Dionysus, likely because his "heavenly father" Zeus was venerated by bull sacrifice. Ancient artwork often portrayed Dionysus as a man with bull's or ram's horns upon his head. Zeus was adapted into an Egyptian-Greco god and became known as "Zeus-Ammon." Zeus was absorbed into the Egyptian Amen, and vice versa. The worship of these two prevalent gods became far and widespread, just as the worship and cult of Dionysus. Dionysus became the "resurrection god" just as Jesus was resurrected, like Osiris, Dumuzid/ Tammuz, Attis, Adonis, Mithras, and even the Mesoamerican god Quetzalcoatl.

The fig tree came to be closely connected to Dionysus. Let us not forget that the fig tree bears the fruit of the goddess, and is also the "Tree of Life" from Genesis. The fig is the fruit that Adam and Eve ate from that gave them knowledge. A nickname given to Dionysus was "the Light of Zeus" which sounds like, "God is light," says 1 John 1:5. Dionysus seemed to be initiated into the Mysteries by the priestess of Cybele, which apparently rubbed off on him. He had close ties to goddess worship, was known for his passion for feminine spirituality, and had a massive following of women. Artwork often showed Dionysus as having somewhat feminine and masculine features. Could this be representative of the fact that he achieved dualism in the most divine way? Understanding the sacred feminine *and* masculine within?

Like Jesus, Dionysus was known for performing miracles, and some of them naturally revolved around wine. On Dionysus's feast day, it was believed that Dionysus would be present at Elis in western Peloponnesus. The priests placed three empty basins in a sealed building. On the following morning, upon breaking the seal, the three basins would be filled with wine.[14]

On the Agean island of Andros, during the Theodosia festival on January 5-6, wine began to flow from a spring in the sanctuary of Dionysus instead of water, and whenever samples of it were brought out of the temple, they changed into water.[15]

About 40 miles north of Ephesus on the Ionian coast lay a temple spring in Teos said to be founded by followers of Dionysus. On certain days each year wine poured out of the spring instead of water.[16] Something similar occurred on the Agean island of Naxos, the marriage location of Dionysus and Ariadne. It was said on their wedding day that the spring began spouting wine, which evidently continued to be a recurring phenomenon.[17]

The gift to be able to change something by touch was also

---

[14] Pausanias, 6.26.1.

[15] Pliny, 31.16; Pausanias, 6.26.2; Otto, p. 98.

[16] Diodorus, 3.66; Otto, pp. 97-98.

[17] Otto, p. 98.

given by Dionysus to Oino, the daughter of the Delian king Anius. According to Ovid, she was given the power to turn absolutely anything into wine.[18] If Dionysus could grant this ability to another, surely he also possessed this power? Many will argue that Jesus performing this miracle was simply a stolen story of Dionysus, but what if that is *not* the case?

What if Dionysus, like Jesus, was well traveled, well indoctrinated by multiple ancient spiritual teachings, an initiate of the goddess Mysteries, but ultimately possessed the same wisdom? If Dionysus had existed as a human it would have been long before Jesus, so there is no mistaking the two of them. Jesus likely had learned the same principles and teachings, the same "magic" and perhaps the same *alchemy* that Dionysus had from his upbringing and travels. Is it far-fetched to propose that Dionysus could have been an ancestor of Jesus, John the Baptist, or Mary Magdalene? If so the teachings would naturally have been passed down within the families as they were in Egypt. Whether there was any familial relation or not, passing down of a tradition to initiates, or simply the same study of different ancient rituals, it is curious to see the similarities that are present within both accounts.

The *Dionysian Mysteries* were the result of the widespread worship of Dionysus. There were certain cults that formed that held and performed certain rites and ceremonies in honor of Dionysus. A lot of the time these rites involved euphoric spiritual experiences brought on by indulging in large quantities of wine, as well as dance. The followers would dance with wine and music until they entered a trance-like state and it brought them to an ecstatic spiritual being.

The Dionysian rituals included themes of death, but at the end transcendence. One must know the depths of the Underworld and the darkness before they are ready to be raised into the Light. This could have included ritual death, much like Jesus and some of his disciples experienced, and like what is experienced in Masonic initiation. The Dionysian Mysteries were reserved for only those who were initiated into The Way, and were very secretive, so secretive that we still don't know much of them today. There were purportedly two different sects of Dionysian cults: an outer group

---

[18] *Metamorphoses*, 13.65-53; also Apollodorus, 4.3.10..

who publicly practiced certain ancient rites, and an inner group that was initiated into secret rites and mysteries.

Rome had its own version of Dionysus and his cult: Bacchus and his Bacchic Mysteries. Initiation rites were probably very similar. Around 1 AD, Ovid in his *Metamorphesis,* says about the rites, "In the initiation, of the Bacchic Mysteries, the role of Bacchus is played by the candidate who, set upon by priests in the guise of the Titans, is slain and finally restored to life amidst great rejoicing. The Bacchic Mysteries were given every three years, and like the Eleusinian Mysteries, were divided into two degrees. The initiates were crowned with myrtle and ivy, plants which were sacred to Bacchus." This is not too far off from Freemasonry's initiation. Following this ritual is a descent into the underworld, where the initiate will spend one night alone in a dark place whether they are buried in a tomb, a cave, or wherever best served the purpose. Once again, this sounds absolutely similar to Freemasonry.

Come the end of the rituals, one who has reached the highest degree of initiation is said to be a Dionysis or Bacchus, embodying the god inside and out. This is not dissimilar to the idea of the *perfecti,* the ability that Jesus and Mary had of becoming perfect, achieving union with the Holy Spirit on the inside as well. Dionysian rites are meant to bring all of its initiates to a place of joy and pleasure, enjoying all that life has to offer, be it sexual, spiritual, food or drink. The rites were open to both men and women.

Pompeii is one of the few places that yields any insight into what the initiation traditions held, with a story told in a series of murals. The last two murals show the following: the female initiate looking into the mirror after undergoing the death aspect of initiation, seeing her new self or new soul, and the female initiate enthroned and dressed in a wedding gown. This likely is because the initiate ritually marries or has a union—maybe hieros gamos—with Dionysus, similar to the union of the Holy Spirit within Jesus and Mary, or comparable to how nuns "marry Jesus" when they take their vows. The point being, the initiate is now one with Dionysus, essentially *one with god* or one with everything.

These initiations usually took place in underground chambers or caves, like many other initiatory traditions did, including those of the Knights Templar. Many of the temples to Dionysus were made in circular shapes, just like the Holy Sepulchre in Jerusalem, and then the many temples the Knights Templar built in the medieval era. Reigning over the religious rites was usually a high priest and high priestess, or hierophants which could be male and female.

Like Jesus, Dionysus went into the underworld for *three nights*. These three nights Dionysus was said to have been sleeping with Persephone, the Goddess. We know that the goddess is often associated with Venus and Her descent to the underworld. It appears that Dionysus joined Her there for three nights, and upon awakening after the third night he was resurrected, or *raised* just as Jesus was raised by Mary Magdalene. Upon being raised up, Dionysus *ascended to Heaven* much like Jesus was said to have done. The origin of Dionysus worship stems from early wine cults. The grapes on the vine represented the live earthly aspect of the god, while the fermentation process of the wine, the dismemberment of the body, represented the god's time in the underworld.

If Dionysus was in fact a human at some point, it is possible that Jesus himself came to learn of his traditions and mysteries and these teachings were absorbed into his ministry. When Dionysus existed, we are not sure. If the worship of a wine god came to being when wine began being imported into Greece, this would have been as early as 6000 BC. The actual rites of the Mystery Tradition of Dionysus likely began forming sometime between 3000 BC-1000 BC. Like with Jesus embodying *God's representative on Earth* or embodying the Egyptian god *Amen,* whoever was the actual human Dionysus was likely brought about in a similar fashion, perhaps a descendant of a royal or priestly family in Greece.

For all of these reasons, it is important that we take a look at the references Jesus makes to vines, vineyards, grapes, and wine, the essence of Dionysus himself. Dionysus' cult would have essentially been competing with the cult centered around Jesus, which came to be Christianity. Dionysus' veneration was single-handedly one of, if not *the* most popular form of individual religious association.

11.10 The Vine of Jesus

Within the Bible, Jesus makes many references to the vineyards, grapes, and wine. Was Jesus an initiate himself of the Dionysian mysteries? It is certainly not impossible since Jesus traveled all around the old world during his lost years, much like Dionysus traveled and became initiated into the cult of the goddess.

Jesus refers to himself as the *true vine* in John, and then goes on to say, "I am the vine: you the branches: he that abideth in me, and I in him, the same beareth much fruit: for without me you can do nothing." (John 15:15). The allusion Jesus makes to himself being the true vine is interesting, and if there were any texts or Dionysian proverbs, you would think this would be it! Jesus says in the Gospel of Thomas, "Whoever drinks from my mouth will become as I am; I myself shall become that person, and the hidden things will be revealed to him." This is a very indicative statement by Jesus that whoever partakes in The Way with him will be initiated into these mysteries, that those who have not "drunk from his mouth" or those *without the eyes to see and ears to hear,* will never have those hidden things revealed to them. The mystery traditions of Dionysus seem hand in hand with some of the things that Jesus teaches.

Jesus also says in the Gospel of Thomas, "A grapevine has been planted outside of the father, but being unsound, it will be pulled up by its roots and destroyed."[19] In this instance, Jesus is saying that a vine planted outside the Kingdom of God will not be strong or stable enough to grow into a healthy plant and bear fruit. Therefore we must ask ourselves, what is the Kingdom of God? The Kingdom of God is found within, when one achieves union with the Holy Spirit-Sophia. Jesus explains this, and says, "If those who lead you say to you, 'See, the kingdom is in the sky,' then the birds of the sky will precede you. If they say to you, 'It is in the sea,' then the fish will precede you. Rather, the kingdom is inside of you, and it is outside of you. When you come to know yourselves, then you will become known, and you will realize that it is you who are the sons of the living father."

Jesus says, "It is impossible for a man to mount two horses or to stretch two bows. And it is impossible for a servant to serve

---

[19] The Gospel of Thomas, verse 40.

174

two masters; otherwise, he will honor the one and treat the other contemptuously. No man drinks old wine and immediately desires to drink new wine. And new wine is not put into old wineskins, lest they burst; nor is old wine put into a new wineskin, lest it spoil it. An old patch is not sewn onto a new garment, because a tear would result."[20] The lesson of not being able to serve two masters is rather clear, but what is the other lesson here in reference to the wine? Jesus uses the wine allegory to compare people who have achieved inner union. Once you have been made new after this inner union, after this enlightenment, one does not go back to the old ways, nor do they resume old habits. After you achieve union with the Holy Spirit, you remain in the Kingdom of God.

The Greeks saw the Jewish god, Yahweh, as being one and the same with Dionysus, which is not too surprising considering symbols of Dionysus were interwoven throughout much of Jewish tradition. They saw Yahweh himself being a *wine god* likely because Yahweh required multiple wine offerings on a daily basis. According to the Roman historian Tacitus, some people believed that the Jews worshiped Father Liber, or Dionysus-Bacchus because their priests intoned to the flute and cymbals and wore ivy garlands, a common custom of Dionysian or Bacchian priests. Not to mention that the entrance to the temple of Jerusalem was decorated with a golden grapevine which made rather obvious the connection between the wine god and the Jewish god.[21] The grapevine also appeared on the temple that Herod built. On Jewish reliefs and coins, vines, grapes, and wine glasses appeared. Images of Dionysus appeared on coins made in Damascus, Scythopolis, and other cities nearby.[22]

Being born a second time from a spiritual or *heavenly* aspect, as Jesus began teaching, was not a popular Jewish concept. It was not until after Jesus's new controversial teachings came about that Jews began teaching the ability to be *born again*. The teachings and rites of Dionysus however certainly offered that opportunity.

The Jewish god yields another similarity to the cult of Dionysus. He promotes joy, dancing, and the enjoyment of food

---

[20] Gospel of Thomas, verse 47.

[21] Histories, 5.5.

[22] Smith, *Wine God*, p. 820.

and drink after he has made the world righteous again: "They will come and shout for joy on the heights of Zion; they will rejoice in the bounty of the Lord—the grain, the new wine and the olive oil, the young of the flocks and herds. They will be like a well-watered garden, and they will sorrow no more. Then young women will dance and be glad, young men and old as well. I will turn their mourning into gladness; I will give them comfort and joy instead of sorrow. I will satisfy the priests with abundance, and my people will be filled with my bounty," says Jeremiah 31:12-14.

During a Dionysian festival in the mid-second century BC, Seleucid King Antiochus I forced Jews to wear ivy garlands, a symbol of Dionysus, and march in the procession in the god's honor. Later in 164 BC, after the defeat of Antiochus IV and the purification of the temple, there was still a ceremony with Jewish women carrying ivy-wound thyrsoi, a commonly known cult object of the Dionysian Mystery Tradition.[23] Later, this became a tradition of the "Feast of the Booths" or "Feast of the Tabernacle." These so called "heathen traditions" remained in Jewish religion. Once the partakers entered the temple, it was not known what rites were performed, but it's assumed they were Dionysian-Bacchic rituals.

Another reference to better times to come including better wine to come is made in Amos 9:13-14, "'The days are coming,' declares the Lord, 'when the reaper will be overtaken by the plowman and the planter by the one treading grapes. New wine will drip from the mountains and flow from all the hills, and I will bring my people Israel back from exile.'"

Proverbs 9:1-6 says, "Wisdom has built her house; She has set up its seven pillars. She has prepared Her meat and mixed Her wine; She has also set her table. She has sent out Her servants, and She calls from the highest point of the city, 'Let all who are simple come to my house!' To those who have no sense She says, 'Come, eat my food and drink the wine I have mixed. Leave your simple ways and you will live; walk in the way of insight.'" Wisdom, wife of god, the Holy Spirit, could very well represent the feminine half of Dionysus, or his female consort, maybe *Persephone*...

At the last supper Jesus and his disciples break bread and

---

[23] 2 Maccabees 10:7.

share wine. Jesus says to them, "Drink from it, all of you. This is my blood of the covenant, which is poured out for many for the forgiveness of sins. I tell you, I will not drink from this fruit of the vine from now on until that day when I drink it new with you in my Father's kingdom." (Matthew 26:27-29) Jesus has clearly indicated how important the eucharist is taking in both the blood, the feminine element, and the body, the masculine element. The wafers used to represent the body are typically small and in round disc-like shapes, much like the Egyptian solar disc. The Egyptians may have used something similar in their own rituals. The drinking of the wine for the blood, however, was a very ancient practice. The drinking of wine as the blood represented the Great Goddess, as the drinking of her menstrual blood from her *sacred vessel* or *womb,* something likely incorporated into Dionysus ritual by Cybele's traditions. Could drinking the wine as the blood even represent the acknowledgement of a divine or priestly bloodline?

Did this allusion to wine as blood stem from the teachings of Cybele and Dionysus? Did he incorporate the rituals of the goddess into his own traditions? Was Jesus influenced or an initiate of the Dionysian mysteries?

Yet another possibility of an additional meaning of the *vine* is present according to Dr. Neil Douglas-Klotz, an Aramaic scholar who once stated, "The word for 'vine' comes from the verb meaning to dig, or form a body from. Metaphorically, it can be used in Hebrew or Aramaic to refer to a blood lineage."[24] The vine then could also represent a physical bloodline as well as a spiritual tradition passed on from generation to generation. Jesus being of the royal and priestly bloodlines certainly makes this a possibility. Therefore, could vines incorporated into later church buildings be a symbol of Jesus's bloodline, and maybe of his children's bloodline?

In Song of Solomon 1, Solomon's bride, the Shulamite, says, "My mother's sons were angry with me; they made me keeper of the vineyards, but my own vineyard I have not kept." If this woman was of a noble family, it is likely that she was given a title to pass down, through her own "vine," or bloodline. She could be

---

[24] Dr. Douglas-Klotz, Neil. *The Hidden Gospel: Decoding the Spiritual Message of the Aramaic Jesus.*

saying that she has not fulfilled her family duty by producing an heir yet. For whatever reason, the lineage, the title, and likely the wealth were to be passed down through the Shulamite bride and not through her brothers, denoting one of two possibilities.

Firstly, she could be from a matrilineal society who likely still revered the goddess therefore she would be in charge of the wealth, not her brothers, leaving them jealous. Maybe it is this wealth she is given that is the dowry to King Solomon? Many of the surrounding tribes and countries were still matrilineal and even matriarchal. Secondly, the Shulamite bride could very well be from a royal family from a nearby tribe or nation that wanted to ensure the wealth and prosperity of their kingdom through King Solomon, therefore passing on title and wealth. A child from this union may even have claim to both territories as heir.

King Solomon was a powerful and wise ruler, who was also very wealthy. Forming a marriage alliance with someone like himself would be a very strategic alignment to make for your own land and people. If your daughter is the wife of the king and you run into trouble, you know who you are going to turn to. Was she truly a Shulamite, or was she a woman from Shulem, synonymous with Salem, the original name of Jerusalem? Or, the name Shulam[ite] could simply be the married name or title of Solomon's counterpart; since it means *peaceful* just as Solomon does.

There is obviously something special about her, as Solomon says, "My dove, my perfect one, is the only one of her mother, pure to her who bore her. The young women saw her and called her blessed; the queens and concubines also, and they praised her."[25] The Shulamite bride is the only daughter born to her mother, which is evidently of significance. For the other wives of Solomon to praise her and call her blessed, she must be someone that is more important than the rest based on her status. She must be royalty, the most respected amongst wives and queens.

With the Shulamite bride being of Solomon's greatest affection, it is obvious that they are to engage in intimacy as husband and wife. She is the most important of all his brides, as we do not have any other known scripture dedicated to the other wives written

---

[25] Solomon 6:9.

by Solomon in such a romantic manner. The children they would have together he would favor more than all of the rest surely, and would ensure a royal bloodline between her own family as well as his dynasty. The vine of Solomon would be established, which is now known as the *Davidic line* from which a Messiah was meant to spring forth. All future kings of Israel and Judah should be of the "vineyard" of Solomon.

One of the significant factors here is the Shulamite wife of Solomon is to anoint him with oil, myrrh and spikenard prior to sharing their marriage bed. He goes on to tell her of his love for her and says, "How beautiful is your love, my sister, my bride! How much better is your love than wine, and the fragrance of your oils than any spice."

11.11 Anointed by the Goddess

Mary Magdalene is always depicted with Her oils and spikenard. She is the one who goes to anoint Jesus with *the Holy Spirit* and appears with Her oils and spikenard at the tomb post resurrection. However, the one particular account we are interested in right now is when She washes Jesus's feet in perfume and anoints him in Bethany, which was part of a much older tradition.

There are four different accounts that tell of this tradition occurring: Matthew 26:6–13, Mark 14:3–9, Luke 7:36–50, and John 12:1–8. The anointment takes place in Bethany in three out of four of these versions. It is only in Luke that it is at a Pharisee's house and it is not specified what the actual town or city is. In Matthew and Mark this anointing occurs at the home of Simon the Leper. Both of these occurrences tell of the woman, who is not specified as Mary but she is the most likely candidate, bringing in an alabaster jar and anointing Jesus's head with oil. She is not specified as Mary in Luke either. Is it possible that her identity is intentionally veiled?

The men rebuke the woman anointing Jesus's head in Matthew and Mark, and Jesus says in response to them, "Why are you bothering her? She has done a beautiful thing to me. The poor you will always have with you, and you can help them any time you want. But you will not always have me. She did what she could. She poured perfume on my body beforehand to prepare for my burial. Truly I tell you, wherever the gospel is preached throughout the world, what she has done will also be told, in memory of her." It is only in these two accounts that he makes the comment about what a beautiful thing the woman has done, and how she will always be remembered.

The woman (not identified as Mary in Luke, but she is identified as Mary in John) enters the home of the Pharisee in Luke with her alabaster jar. She begins weeping and pours out the contents of the alabaster jar onto the feet of Jesus, bathes his feet in her tears, hair, and oil, and adoringly kisses his feet as she does so. Simon makes a rude comment to Jesus about why he would allow this woman to do such a thing to him. He starts in with a story, "Two people owed money to a certain moneylender. One owed him five hundred denarii, and the other fifty. Neither of them had the money to pay him back, so he forgave the debts of both. Now which of them will love him more?" Simon replied, "I suppose the one who had the bigger debt forgiven."

Jesus says, "You have judged correctly. Do you see this woman? I came into your house. You did not give me any water for my feet, but she wet my feet with her tears and wiped them with her hair. You did not give me a kiss, but this woman, from the time I entered, has not stopped kissing my feet. You did not put oil on my head, but she has poured perfume on my feet. Therefore, I tell you, her many sins have been forgiven—as her great love has shown." Jesus explains the devotional love that she gives him, and he reciprocates in offering her forgiveness. This is no different from all of the other times the disciples or male followers of Jesus show distaste for Mary Magdalene.

In Luke and John it is the feet of Jesus, and not his head, that the woman (Mary) bathes and anoints. Could this be showing that not only could these be separate occasions taking place at different times, but that the instances in Matthew and Mark are likely referring to the same encounter of the head being anointed, where the story is nearly identical in both versions? Only in Luke does it specify that Mary is weeping and kissing Jesus's feet, and only in Luke does Jesus tell that specific story, not in John.

It is at the home of Mary Magdalene, her sister Martha, and her brother Lazarus that the anointing takes place in John. Lazarus had been ritually resurrected by Jesus not much earlier, and taught some of the Mysteries. Lazarus had also been sealed in a tomb for multiple days. It is important to note that Jesus and Mary's family were intimately connected in The Way of Mystery that Jesus taught. They were all part of the mystery tradition.

In any case, it is in their family home that Jesus has come and it was six days before Passover. Martha is serving dinner, Lazarus is at the table with Jesus, and Mary Magdalene goes to the feet of Jesus. She bathes his feet in her oil and her hair. Judas Iscariot begins harping on Mary for using such expensive oil and how it would be better if it were sold and the money given to the poor, because it is worth a whole year's wage. Jesus defends her and says, "Leave her alone. It was intended that *she should save this perfume for the day of my burial.* You will always have the poor among you, but you will not always have me."

We know that Matthew and Mark speak of the same anointing. Here Jesus states, "She poured perfume on my body beforehand to prepare for my burial." In Luke, Jesus does not say anything similar to this, but rather argues that the woman has shown him more love than the host. In John, Jesus says, "It was intended that she should save this perfume for the day of my burial." This indicates that there was already a planned ceremony, that Mary Magdalene was to be involved in his anointing after the (ritual) death of Jesus on the cross. So we have to ask, were the Passover anointing, the anointing in the house of the Pharisee, and the anointing at Simon the Leper's house, all three different occasions?

What were the purposes of the three different anointments? Did any of it involve marriage, as Laurence Gardner suggests? Is there any reason to believe that kissing and washing someone's feet was part of a marriage rite? In traditional Indian Hindu weddings, which share a few commonalities with Jewish weddings (like the walking of the seven circles), the bride is to touch the husband's feet as part of the ceremony. This is still a custom practiced today.

Jesus says once that she is preparing him for burial, but we do not know how early that first anointment took place. How did Jesus know he was going to need to be buried in the first place, unless it was part of a ritual murder that was planned out? Six days before Passover, Jesus states that she is meant to use that same expensive oil on him in the tomb. This indicates that it was planned and thought out, and that there could very well be another side to the crucifixion story.

For Mary to have acquired this very expensive spikenard, she must have had plenty of money, and we know she does because scripture tells us that she helped fund the ministry of Jesus. Where would this wealth come from? Likely a royal, noble, or priestly family. Mary reminds me of the Shulamite bride, being of a wealthy family, and having all of her myrrh, spikenard, and oil.

Mary's bathing and anointing the feet of Jesus could be a later version of the beginning of the Egyptian *Sed Festival* celebrated by the pharaoh during his first year on the throne, and then later after his 30th year of kingship. Mind you, it was when Jesus was 30 that he performed his first "miracle" of wine at the wedding at Cana, very probably *his own wedding* with Mary Magdalene. Note that in ancient Rome, Vestal Virgins (virgins dedicated to the goddess Vesta) remained virgins for a 30-year vow.

The Sed Festival celebrated the renewal or birth of kingship as the young god Horus. The pharaoh before him represented the god on Earth, Osiris, so this new king represented the young aspect. He would be ritually sacrificed and resurrected as the "son" of Osiris. This was a renewal or rebirth of the pharaoh's divinity and power as ruler. The pharaoh was God incarnate on earth, not only king but priest of all temples.

The pharaoh would first have his feet washed before engaging in ceremonial activity. A ritual involving a race against an apis bull was observed, to prove that the pharaoh had the strength, power, and the god-like immortality to continue his reign over Egypt. After proving his strength against the bull, the pharaoh was then carried to multiple temples, before engaging in the rite of "Raising The Djed Pillar." A wooden pillar would be erected on a shrine by the king and his priests, representing the resurrected Osiris. Following the raising of the Osiris pillar, reenactments of the tradition of Isis and Osiris took place.

Jesus was being prepared for his own ritual to prove his strength and god-like immortality: the crucifixion. Mary Magdalene was almost certainly a priestess and likely of the goddess, as she taught and healed by the side of Jesus. As a priestess, and/or as wife, would she not be the one to ritually prepare him for the trials to prove his worthiness as king and priest?

The word "messiah" in Hebrew literally means *the anointed* or *to smear with oil*. In Hebrew it is *mashiach* which is pronounced as *ma-shee-ah-kh*. What are the etymological beginnings of this word?

- The word for mother in Egyptian is *ma*.
- In Hebrew the word *mah* meant womb.
- The word *meh* in Egyptian meant to fulfill or satisfy.
- *Meshu* is Egyptian meaning "to turn back" or "return."
- The Hebrew word *msheh* means to anoint for priesthood or kingship (pronounced with a short e sound at the beginning as mehh-sheh).
- Two different words are used in Egyptian meaning to anoint: *masu, mas* both pronounced as the s being sh.
- The Egyptian word *masiu* referred to the dinner on the *last night* of the year, which reminds me of the concept of a "last supper."
- The Egyptian word *skhi* means to elevate, or even the top of heaven; the sky. The k in ancient Egyptian is pronounced softly and sometimes as a light g sound.[26]

Clearly the feminine aspect is present in the concept of the *messiah* or *mashiach,* which would seem to be an originally Egyptian word altogether. Ma in both languages, is associated with the mother or the womb. The Egyptian word to fulfill, meh, likely goes back to the *womb being filled* with man's seed, or with child. The Egyptian word meshu meaning to return also connects with the prophecies of a *returning messiah*. The element meaning to fulfill is reminiscent of *fulfilling a prophecy,* while the aspect of a *prophesied return* can also be read between the lines.

It is the Egyptian word masu (pronounced ma-shu), which means *to anoint*. Mesopotamia yields a connection to this word, as Masu, sometimes even spelled Masi, was a hero god there. Sometimes the name even meant *twin,* which is especially interesting since Jesus was said to have a twin brother, Thomas.

---

[26] Massey, Gerald. *A Book of the Beginnings*. Williams and Norgate, 1881.

The Bringer of Life

Usually this was a title bestowed upon someone as *mas mas*—a title that was to be given to sorcerers, incantation priests, and "wonderworkers." Replace wonder with miracle worker and it sounds a bit like Jesus's alleged abilities. The god Masu/Masi was the son of the moon god *Sin.* Coincidence? Probably not.

The word for anoint being mas/masu in Egyptian points to a feminine origin. Why did the word *to anoint* become something that was rooted in the mother, or the womb? Was it because an heir to the throne, a future king, was to be born of his royal mother? Do not forget that the king/pharaoh in old times was god incarnate on earth, therefore the king's mother would be the *"mother of god"* just as Jesus's mother is referred to. This could point to the early matrilineal and matriarchal traditions of the ancient people where the goddess was revered as the original creator mother.

The Egyptian chief (or sometimes called great) royal wife was usually a close relative of the pharaoh like, for example, his sister. This was to legitimize their child's heritage on both sides of the family. Their son would be the future king. Therefore she was the mother *and* wife of the king. The pharaoh represents Osiris, while the young heir would represent Horus. The order of succession passed through the chief royal wife, and through her only. The other wives of the pharaoh's children had no claim to the throne because they were not sons of the chief royal wife, God's wife and priestess on earth.

This could be applicable in Jesus's mother Mary being of Aaronic priestly lineage and marrying Joseph of the kingly Davidic line, proving legitimacy on the throne and in the temple. If Jesus and Magdalene were in fact married, this could be another example.

Diving back into the middle of the word mashiach, to be elevated/most high/top of heaven in Egypt was to be skhi. This could be the origin of the "shee" sound in mashiach, showing that this spirit was divine, heavenly. Akh meaning being spirit, is denoting the spirit that fills the conduit, or the person.

In totality, one could go as far to say that even the deeper meaning of the mashiach is *"heavenly/most high spirit"* that *"filled"* the *"womb (of the mother)."* Were all those born of the chief royal mother called messiah/mashiach? Were the sons called

184

the anointed because they were born of a royal and priestly mother, and *son of God* because they were born through the established God-king on earth?

Almost every ancient culture had an understanding of the seven chakras, or the seven different energy points that exist in the body. The Egyptians did too. Seven different corresponding anointing oils are mentioned in the Egyptian Book of the Dead. The Egyptian serpent goddess, Wadjet, appears on the Egyptian crowns of the pharaohs and queens as the uraeus. The serpent has long been associated with the chakras, but specifically with gnosis, knowledge and spiritual awareness. The serpent represents Christos, *the anointed* in Greek. The serpent goddess Wadjet was worn on the crown as She was the protector of all pharaohs and their queens, but also the protector of childbirth.

When the chief royal wife was giving birth to the next heir of Egypt, it was an extremely exciting time; the new god-king was being born. During childbirth, when the child's head becomes visible through the vagina this is referred to as *crowning,* since it is the crown of the child that emerges first. The Egyptians would have recognized that it was the crown chakra first emerging from the chief royal wife who represented the goddess on earth. What the ancient Egyptians called this part of childbirth I cannot be sure, but they did see a connection between the crown chakra, and the serpent, gnosis, the goddess Wadjet that protected all royalty, born and unborn. It is also worth looking at James 1:12 where it says, "Blessed is the one who perseveres under trial because, having stood the test, that person will receive the crown of life..." If we are discussing eternal life, then this is essentially a rebirth into the afterlife, a chance to be born again. Is this a reference to childbirth *crowning?*

The word for Christ can even be found in Egypt, pertaining to that of the mummified dead, *krst.* Upon death and mummification, one was ritually washed, embalmed and anointed with oils to prepare for rebirth or resurrection in the afterlife. According to Gerald Massey, "To *kares* [in Egyptian] means to embalm, anoint, to make the mummy some type of eternal; and when made, it was called the *karest;* so that this is not merely a matter of name for

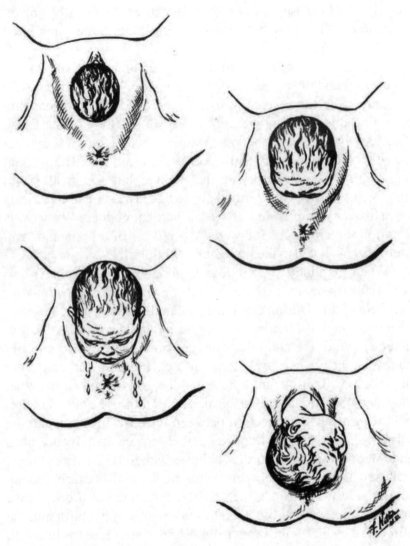

Crowning of childbirth. Drawing by Frank Netter.

name the Karest for the Christ."[27]

It was the goddess Isis who mummified and anointed Her husband Osiris so that he could be resurrected in the afterlife, just as Mary Magdalene prepared Jesus for burial by washing and anointing him. A parallel that also stood out to me is that in the

---

[27] Massey, Gerald. *Ancient Egypt the Light of the World*. Routledge, 2013.

Egyptian telling of this story there are two wailing women who mourn Osiris's death: Isis and Her sister Nepthys. Most artwork depicting the crucifixion shows two mourning women at the cross: Mary, the mother of Jesus, and Mary Magdalene. The latter goes to anoint him again to prepare him for his resurrection. One could obtain a spiritual sense of *krst* awareness after going through the Osirian Mystery initiations. Almost all mystery traditions involved a form of death and resurrection. Jesus too practiced this Mystery ritual, anointed by his priestess-wife Mary Magdalene, that could very well be an evolved version of the Egyptian Sed Festival rituals.

In conclusion, it is absolutely imperative that we see the roots of the sacred feminine at the foundation of the ideology of the *messiah*. Some aspect of the importance of the cosmic creator goddess was preserved, being that it was She who gave birth to man at the very beginning, not man giving birth to man. This was reflected in the earthly tradition of the royal lineage of the god-kings and messiahs that were born of a royal and/or priestly maternal lineage. This tradition existed quite obviously for thousands of years in many royal families around the world, even into the time of Jesus and beyond.

The goddess embodied both life and death, as well as the ability to resurrect. She chose who was worthy to be resurrected, to be initiated into the Truth, because She dwelled in both the darkness and the light. In Egypt it was Isis and Osiris, along with Horus that were the archetypal holy trinity, showing that it was Isis who reigned supreme over both the mortal life and the afterlife. Throughout many cultures the same mystery rites appear, showing a universal understanding and connection to the cosmic spirit of the divine feminine that gave birth to all that is and all that will be. The messianic tradition of the anointed is just another way to continue honoring Her.

Chapter 12
The Grail, the Goddess, & the Lion

The Holy Grail. What is it? Some say it is the cup that Jesus and all the disciples drank from at the Last Supper. Some say it is the cup that Joseph of Aritmathea used to catch the blood of Jesus at the crucifixion. Some say it is both. And those who have read or seen *The Da Vinci Code* may know it to be a bloodline, or vessel, that carried Jesus's bloodline, his wife, Mary Magdalene.

Let us first examine the history of the word "grail." The Online Etymology Dictionary says, "Grail (noun)—1300, gral, "the Holy Grail," from Old French graal, greal "Holy Grail; cup," earlier "large shallow dish, basin," from Medieval Latin gradalis, also gradale, grasale, "a flat dish or shallow vessel." The original form is uncertain; the word is perhaps ultimately from Latin crater "bowl," which is from Greek krater "bowl, especially for mixing wine with water... Holy Grail is Englished from Middle English seint gral (c. 1300), also sangreal, sank-real (c. 1400), which seems to show deformation as if from sang real "royal blood" (that is, the blood of Christ) The object had been inserted into the Celtic Arthurian legends by 12c., perhaps in place of some Pagan otherworldly object."

It is obvious that the grail has seemed to shapeshift throughout the centuries. However it is interesting that the word "sangreal" seems to be synonymous with the Holy Grail. It is the French word for "Holy Grail." Coincidence?

Perceval, the Grail, & the Fisher King

"Perceval ou le Conte du Graal" or "Perceval the Story of the Grail" is a poem written in the 12th century by a man named Chretien de Troyes. A summary that can be found online goes as follows:

Chrétien de Troyes' Perceval, the Story of the Grail, is a poem of chivalry. The hero is a youth brought up in ignorance by a widowed mother, who intended to keep him away from the dangers of knighthood and men clad in armor. She even clothed him in linen and leather to make him look ridiculous and keep him home. One of the counsels given to him is to avoid asking too many questions.

But, one day, Perceval sees some of those noble knights in their shining armors, beautiful as angels. He is ambitious to follow and sets forth on his wanderings in spite of his mother.

Gradually, he gets experience and is consecrated a knight, being instructed in charity and piety. In the course of his adventures he learns what true love means, when he rescues a distressed damsel. He visits the Castle of the Fisher King, where all pass before him in procession a wonderful sword, a lance dripping blood, a ten-branched candlestick, and the mysterious "Graal," borne by a maiden.

Perceval, whose name even to this point has not been revealed by Chrétien, remembers his mother's advice, and does not dare to ask the significance of this Grail. The consequences are unfortunate, for the question would have healed the sufferings of the Fisher King.

Chrétien's hero has many other adventures, but the narrative was unfinished by its author. The poem received different continuations and endings by Gaucher de Denain, Mennecier, and Gerbert, in which Gauvain (Gawain) continues as a prominent character.

It is in the later parts that the Grail begins to acquire a mystic character and becomes the dish in which Joseph of Arimathea received the blood of Christ. The growth of the mystic symbolism in Perceval, the Story of the Grail and other works of the followers of Chrétien is obvious, superimposing the monastic ideal of chastity over the intentions of the practical, mundane poet.

In this story, the wounded Fisher King represents Jesus. Jesus is associated with the fish for many reasons, but the most obvious being astronomical. This all goes back to an observable phenomenon above in the night sky. This phenomenon is known as the **precession of the equinox** or **axial precession.** This is a cycle that takes approximately 25,800 years. What we see here on planet Earth is the rising constellations behind the rising Sun at spring equinox change. This rising constellation changes every 2,150 years. Currently we are in the Age of Aquarius that many say we officially moved into in 2012 because we moved out of the constellation of Pisces. This was also why the Mayan calendar that ended was not the end of the world, but the end of the astronomical cycle of nearly 26,000 years. But what actually *causes* this occurrence? This phenomenon is caused by the slight shift of the North Pole, causing an axial wobble of nearly 60 inches a year. This is what causes different "ages" of the zodiac.

The age that just recently ended was the age of Pisces. This in the zodiac, is a fish. Approximately the age of Pisces began around 1 AD. It is hard to be precisely sure when the age changed, but it was most definitely around this time. So theoretically, the fish becomes the "King of the Zodiac." Chretien de Troyes certainly was aware of this when writing his Grail legend. Ironically, he never finished the tale of Perceval, which is almost fitting considering the age of Pisces had not yet ended.

Interestingly, in this tale, there is a young fair maiden who possesses the Grail. The Fisher King is the Grail king, but it is handled and presented by the Grail maiden. Astronomically speaking, the Fisher King is wounded at sunset on the Spring Equinox as He (Pisces) sinks below the western horizon. However, directly opposite on the eastern horizon, the constellation Virgo rises as night falls. She who is in the dark, She Who is Veiled.

Therefore, when the Fisher King (Jesus) dies in the Spring, who is to carry on his legacy throughout darkness? Virgo, also associated with Mary Magdalene, who comes to the tomb after the death of Jesus. It is Jesus who appears to Mary Magdalene and not the other disciples, and gives her a message so that she may carry on his teachings, and his legacy, just the same as when Pisces theoretically "dies" at night on Spring Equinox as Virgo "rises" in the dark night sky.

Pisces is the last constellation in the zodiac, and so its passing was the end of this nearly 26,000-year precession cycle. Now, moving into the Age of Aquarius, when the constellation Aquarius sets, Virgo is rising. The sign of Aquarius is the "water bearer" or "cup bearer." Would it be too-far fetched to say even "grail bearer?" As the constellation Aquarius sets every evening and Virgo is rising in the evening, there is a time here where Virgo and Aquarius would be looking right at each other, mirroring each other.

So, that being said, the Grail maiden who is carrying the Grail could very well represent Mary Magdalene, or Aquarius, as the Fisher King (Pisces) dies. After all, the Age of Aquarius directly follows the end of the Age of Pisces, as Mary Magdalene appears to Jesus and is told to continue his teachings.

Some may wonder if this Grail legend did truly have any base in astronomy and astrology, and the answer is Chretien de Troyes did not tell us specifically, but the parallels are nearly too perfect to dismiss in my eyes.

12.1 Lion of Judah

According to the Torah, the tribe of Judah, one of the twelve tribes of Israel, descends from Judah, the fourth son (of twelve) of Jacob and Leah. In Genesis 49:9, Jacob refers to his son, Judah, as a "young lion." This appears to be the first time the lion is associated with the tribe of Judah. It is also at this time that Jacob is on his deathbed and tells his sons that the kingship of Israel will pass on to Judah. In Genesis 49:10 Jacob says, "The scepter shall not depart from Judah, nor the ruler's staff from between his feet, until tribute comes to him; and to him shall be the obedience of the peoples."

Let us back up a bit. What right does the tribe of Judah have to the throne of Israel? Earlier in Genesis 17:16 God appears to Abraham (grandfather of Jacob). He promised Abraham saying, "I will bless her (Sarah—EL) and also give you a son by her; then I will bless her, and she shall be a mother of nations; kings of peoples shall be from her." In Genesis 35:11 it states, "God appeared to Jacob at Bethel and changed his name to Israel. He said: "I am God Almighty. Be fruitful and multiply; a nation and a company of nations shall proceed from you, and kings shall come from your body." And so there is this promise God makes with this specific line of people, that they should be the rightful hereditary monarchs.

192

One of these kings is David, who is the father of the next king, Solomon. The book of Revelation refers to the Lion of Judah in context of the Second Coming of Christ when Revelation 5:5 says, "Then one of the elders said to me, 'Do not weep. Look, the Lion from the tribe of Judah, the Root of David, has conquered so that he is able to open the scroll and its seven seals.'"

It is obvious that this verse is referring to the descendent of King David, Jesus.

All of the twelve tribes were assigned a zodiac sign, a constellation, and most accordingly, the tribe Judah is associated with the constellation Leo, the Lion. What is important about associating this constellation with Judah, and with Jesus, all goes back to the night skies above.

Every night, the constellation Virgo (the Goddess) rises right next to the constellation Leo. He rises first, and then she follows. If Jesus is Pisces the Fish, and Leo the Lion, what can this mean? First and foremost I think the first part of the story is the death of Pisces at sunset, and then, in the dark, we see Leo rising. Perhaps this is where C.S. Lewis got the idea of the portrayal of the resurrected Jesus being a lion in his Narnia series?

Leo rises in the dark night sky, or the King is resurrected in the dark, allegorically speaking. Directly following him, the constellation Virgo then rises as well by his side, to be his partner and consort. Or maybe, it is the Lion guarding Virgo? Perhaps it all goes back to protecting the Goddess, *She who is veiled.* Many ancient goddesses in Mesopotamia were flanked by lions, in fact, such as Ishtar. Could this have anything to do with the constellation Virgo and Leo right next to Her?

Cauldron of Ceridwen

The story of Ceridwen, through its linguistic roots, can be traced back to 9th century Wales. This story is popularly associated with grail legends, and there happens to be many similarities in the tale of Ceridwen's Cauldron and the story of the Fisher King.

Ceridwen herself is known as a "white witch" or is closely associated with the mother and crone aspect of the triple goddess (maiden, mother, and crone). To the ancient people, she was associated with the Goddess, rebirth, fertility, wisdom, knowledge, and power. More than likely, if she truly did live, she was some kind of high priestess that was enlightened with ancient knowledge and wisdom that she had to pass on.

The cauldron itself is said to be a cauldron of knowledge and wisdom. It contains all that one needs to know, and in some stories can even bring the dead back to life. However, this could be associated with the tradition of "raising one from the dead" or initiating them into some type of esoteric tradition much like the Essenes, the group that Jesus belonged to. This is also a symbol of alchemy, as is the grail.

According to legend, the cauldron must be brewed for a year and a day to reach its full potency.

12.2 The Cauldron of Bran the Blessed

According to the online article by Medium, in the Celtic legend of Bran the Blessed, the cauldron appears as a vessel of wisdom and rebirth. Bran, mighty warrior-god, obtains a magical cauldron from Ceridwen (in disguise as a giantess) who had been expelled from a lake in Ireland, which represents the Otherworld of Celtic lore. The cauldron can resurrect the corpses of dead warriors placed inside it (this scene is believed to be depicted on the Gundestrup Cauldron). Bran gives his sister Branwen and her new husband Math—the King of Ireland—the cauldron as a wedding gift, but when war breaks out Bran sets out to take the valuable gift back. He is accompanied by a band of loyal knights, but only seven return home.

Bran himself is wounded in the foot by a poisoned spear, another theme that recurs in the Arthurian legend—found in the guardian of the Holy Grail, the Fisher King. In fact, in some Welsh stories, Bran marries Anna, the daughter of Joseph of Arimathea. Also like Arthur, only seven of Bran's men return home. Bran travels after his death to the Otherworld, and Arthur makes his way to Avalon. There are theories among some scholars that Ceridwen's cauldron—the cauldron of knowledge and rebirth—is in fact the Holy Grail for which Arthur spent his life searching.[1]

It is interesting that some believe Joseph of Arimathea brought

---

[1] https://medium.com/i-m-h-o/the-evolution-of-the-cauldron-into-a-grail-in-celtic-mythology-a96a41604e9f.

the Holy Grail to the British Isles. Joseph of Arimathea was a secret supporter of Jesus, and happens to be the man who asked Pontius Pilate for the body of Jesus after his death. Firstly, it is strange that Pilate even agreed to give Jesus's body to Joseph; typically those who were crucified were not allowed to be given a proper burial. Perhaps Joseph of Arimathea bribed Pilate?

In any case, Joseph of Arimathea must have been a relative or a very close friend of the family of Jesus since he offered to bury Jesus in the family tomb on his property. There are many legends that say Jesus even visited the British Isles with Joseph of Arimathea growing up. One of the most intriguing legends associated with Joseph of Arimathea is that he brought the Holy Grail to Glastonbury, England. There is evidence to suggest that Joseph of Arimathea was actually a title bestowed upon Jesus's brother, James.

Unfortunately, it is hard to find any mention of this visit of Joseph and the Grail until the 13th century. Could this "grail" that Joseph brought over have inspired the Welsh tale of Ceridwen's Cauldron? Is that where this cauldron of wisdom came from? Perhaps, but we obviously do not know for sure.

12.3 The Glastonbury Thorn

There is one more tale that is important to the legend of Joseph of Arimathea. According to an article by BBC, "The Glastonbury Thorn (Crataegus monogyna 'Biflora') is a variety of hawthorn that flowers twice a year in winter and spring—or, given suitable conditions, at Christmas and Easter."

The legend states that Joseph of Arimathea became a missionary after the death of Jesus and was eventually sent to England to preach the Gospel. He took with him the Holy Grail, and his pilgrim's staff. After landing in England he made his way to Glastonbury. When he stuck his pilgrim's staff in the ground at Wearyall Hill it overnight turned into a flowering thorn tree.

In time Joseph converted thousands to Christianity, including, it is said, 18,000 in a single day at the town of Wells. He also converted Ethelbert, the local king. Joseph went on to found Glastonbury Abbey.

He became so well-known and admired that when he died at

The Gundestrup Cauldron.

the age of 86, his body was carried by six kings in the funeral procession.

The Glastonbury Thorn is said to flower on Christmas Day every year, and blossom from the plant in the churchyard of St. John's Church, Glastonbury. It was said to be used to decorate the Christmas breakfast table of the Queen each year. St John's Church has a stained glass window commemorating Joseph of Arimathea.

Obviously Joseph had a very strong presence and impact in the west of England. Because of how strong his legacy is there, there is a very strong possibility that he was in fact in England. And if he really did come to England,[2] did he actually bring the grail here? Or did Mary Magdalene take it to the south of France?

12.4 The Gundestrup Cauldron

This incredible artifact made primarily of silver was discovered in a peat bog in 1891. It was found in the bog Rævemosen, near Gundestrup in Himmerland, Denmark. It had likely been put into the bog as an offering to the gods. It appears Celtic in origin, but the location of the manufacturer is still up for debate. Some argue that it was manufactured in the Lower Danube region, potentially Dacia or Thrace (today's Romania and Bulgaria). There does

---

[2] http://www.bbc.co.uk/thepassion/articles/joseph_of_arimathea.shtml

seem to be a common opinion that it came from the 1st or 2nd century BC but this too cannot be certain. Is this an even older representation of Ceridwen's Cauldron, or the grail? [3]

12.5 Joseph's Silver Cup in Genesis

In Genesis 44, we learn a story about Joseph's silver cup. Joseph had been sold into slavery by his jealous brothers 20 years earlier Egypt in the story. When they come to Egypt to seek food, they do not know that Joseph is the governor of Egypt, second in power to the Pharaoh. Now Joseph tests them by framing them for stealing from the Royal House. One of the objects that is said to be stolen is a silver cup, or divination bowl, that Joseph used to see the future.

Ancient Egyptian and middle eastern mystics were known to use "medicine bowls" to heal ailments, see into the future, and much more. Also known as "divining bowls" they were very popular among healers and seers. These types of bowls seem to be very popular not only in this part of the world, but on a global scale. In fact, I personally saw a really incredible bowl carved into a cave in Scotland.

12.6 Gilmerton Cove, Scotland UK

While in Scotland in November 2019, I visited an intriguing site situated in the southern part of Edinburgh known as "Gilmerton Cove." This site is actually an underground cave that was carved out by man. The mysterious part of this site is that we do not know who actually carved it first or when. There are carved out doorways, benches, tables, and more. There also appear to be light shafts strategically placed throughout the underground chambers.

Unfortunately, very few people are aware of this cave, but it likely is a very important site that we will someday better understand. Many legends offer different builders, whether it was the Druids, the Knights Templar, or even a man who claimed to carve it all himself, George Paterson, who was a local blacksmith that was later known to have ran an illegal drinking den in the cave. However it is unlikely he would have been able to carve it all himself in the short amount of time that he claimed.

---

[3] http://www.native-science.net/Gundestrup-Cauldron.htm

Gilmerton Cove Ritual Bowl.

Access to the cave is found through an old mining cottage. It is known that there are more tunnels, chambers, and hidden passages behind some of the fallen debris and rubble. Some of these now covered passageways are even said to go all the way to Roslin, as in Rosslyn Chapel and Castle.

There were certainly Freemasons in the cave at some point, and likely before that members of the Knights Templar. This I know because of some intricately carved Masonic symbols found near what I call the "Grail Cup" of Gilmerton Cove. On a long, hand carved table of the cave, there appears to be several inscriptions.

198

The most intriguing inscription to me, is one intricately carved symbol that, at first glance, only seems vaguely familiar. It is an upside down V shape, with a smaller V on the inside. Maybe this symbol reminds us of an image we have seen associated with Freemasonry for as long as we can remember? Initially, this symbol made me think of the logo of Freemasonry, the compass and square, which usually form the same shape. But the longer I stared at this strange symbol, I began to realize it predated Freemasonry. No, Freemasonry was where I had seen this symbol!

This symbol was in fact a symbol of the Goddess, or in Christianity, the Virgin Mary, on to the Templars, Mary Magdalene, representing the divine feminine, Goddess, wife of God. When I realized what this symbol was, I was even more excited. So let me explain how we get to this shape and why it represents Mary, and the divine feminine.

The most common name for these marks usually found in medieval churches and monasteries dating all the way back to the 13th century and probably even before, is a *witch's mark*. The reason why they were called this was because this symbol was carved to ward off evil and call upon the (Mother Goddess) Virgin Mary. One of the first important things that we have to do in educating people is make it known that the Virgin Mary is equivalent to Goddess, wife of God. Is the Virgin Mary not essentially the wife of God?

These were symbols of protection! How incredible. Not only are they found in this cave, but also all over the UK and Europe. Another nickname they have come to have is *Mary's mark*.

A historian, Charles Fairey of South Cheshire, has brought immense clarity to me with regard to this symbol. While surfing the Internet, I came across his website talking about this same symbol and I began to see why this symbol means what it does.[4] Suddenly everything started to make sense! Fairey has made some amazing diagrams that break it down completely. See the picture on page 201.

Essentially all of the symbols Fairey shows us represent the Virgin Mary. In the top right of the diagram we see the symbol in

---

[4] https://sites.google.com/site/charlesfaireyhistorian/publications/apotropa-ic-identification

Gilmerton Cove, and we see it represents "AVM." AVM as we see there, represents the "Hail Mary" prayer of "Ave Maria." It could also quite possibly represent a variation of this prayer, "Ave Virgo Maria," which translates to "Hail Virgin Mary."

Interestingly, we see the "W" also represents "Virgin of Virgins!" This is because of the two V's interlocking. A completely different way to look at the letter W! Of course this also gives us an upside down M for Mary/Mother as well. Recalling the earlier chapter about what Mary/Miriam means, it means the "beloved of Amen (Egyptian Sun God)." Everything suddenly starts to make

The AVM carving Gilmerton Cove Ritual Bowl.

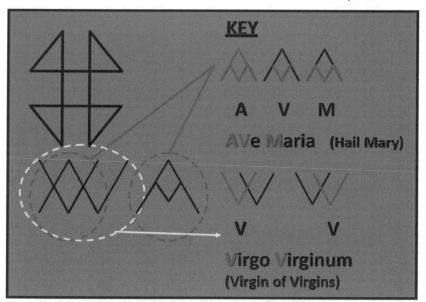

The AVM diagram, courtesy of Charles Fairy.

sense when you start looking at things with a different perspective.

Moving forward with the interesting symbol, that is not all I noticed in Gilmerton Cove. It was brought to my attention that there were light shafts carved in the roof of the caves. The young lady who worked there was pointing these out to me, and mentioned the possibility of sunlight coming through in the morning or evening perhaps, and filling the cup with light! Then a light bulb went off inside my head and the gears started turning.

Instantly, I pulled out my phone, and brought up the Sun Seeker App to test the hypothesis I had just imagined in my head seconds ago. Could there be an alignment here on a specific day? Equinox or solstice? As I opened the camera, and it showed me where the Sun rises on March 21, spring equinox, I thought, aha! My hypothesis was correct. It appeared that at 9 am, on spring equinox, the Sun would rise in a position right above the light shaft, and potentially illuminate the inside of this cup carved in stone.

This is so important on so many levels. Going back to an earlier chapter, I mention Newgrange in Ireland, which is a site approximately 5,000 years old that has an astronomical alignment on winter solstice, also at 9 am. This alignment I believe was allegorically representing the fertilization of the Goddess (Mother Earth) by the Sun, God, to show that life is bound to return soon; it will begin to grow in spring, and crops will be harvested nine months later, in September.

However, obviously there is something different going on in Gilmerton Cove since this alignment takes place at spring equinox and not at winter solstice. The alignment going hand in hand with 9 am tells me that this is somehow related to the Goddess. Nine of course, is the number of months that it takes to carry a full length pregnancy to term. Perhaps this is why they choose that hour of the morning for this alignment? Spring is always associated with

The ritual table at Gilmerton Cove.

birth and rebirth, so naturally since this alignment is taking place during the ninth hour of the day, this has something to do with birth.

Also, it is interesting to consider that if the sunlight does indeed come through the shaft and penetrate the cup, then this is similar to what we see in Ireland in the fact that it is the Sun having a divine sexual union with the Earth, the Goddess. Is this chamber neolithic as well? Or did it come later via Esoteric groups such as the Freemasons or the Knights Templar, or even Druids? Whoever carved these caves out did so with the intention of making it a place for ritual. If only walls could talk, right?

The next fascinating part of this site is another chamber down the way. This chamber too has an interesting light shaft. Beneath the light shaft is a stone table. This stone table even has a stone pillow, and it seems to have a depression at about the point on the table where a man's heel should come to rest. Therefore anyone laying upon the table, in a postmortem state, will have his heels in the depression so his feet stand erect. It was an incredible sight to see. It would not surprise me whatsoever if this was a chamber used by secret organizations such as the Freemasons, Knights Templar, and many others. But these traditions have origins that go back much further. It is possible this site has been in use for hundreds or thousands of years.

What I can tell you, is that I was able to determine that it appears that on the same day, spring equinox, this chamber has a solar alignment penetrating the light shaft at sunset. According to my hypothesis, the light would then hit the stone pillow. Or, it would hit the head that lay upon the stone pillow. Perhaps this would be signaling a release of spirit back to the spirit world?

I have seen this type of ceremonial practice in another place, but on the other side of the world—Serpent Mound, located in Peebles, Ohio. While attending Lakota ceremonies there, I have heard many whispers. One thing I know for certain is there used to be a large altar stone that lay on its side inside the oval or head of the serpent. This same altar stone is known as the "fallen monolith." But according to the legends the local natives tell, it was no standing monolith, it was an altar.

When it was inside the oval at the top of the serpent, the man who mowed the mound was tired of mowing around the large altar stone, so it was thrown over the cliff! Along with all of the small egg-shaped stones that were sitting upon it and surrounding it.

The connection to Gilmerton Cove is this. While at Serpent Mound, we heard many stories from the local natives. One of those stories is that the natives here would bring these egg-shaped stones to place them on the altar. They were believed to contain the souls of the dead. The head of the serpent is aligned with sunset on summer solstice. Nearby stood a tall wooden pole, and when the Sun set, it would cast a shadow from the pole to the altar. It was then the souls of the dead would be released. This is where I see the connection. Is this a concept that goes back thousands of years? Could it connect two groups or cultures who are separated by the Atlantic Ocean?

12.7 Newport Monolith, Rhode Island USA

In the last section we explained what the AVM symbol stands for. While I found it intriguing to find it in a location like Gilmerton Cove with potential connections to the Knights Templar, I found it even more intriguing to find it on a mysterious monolith that seemed to appear out of nowhere. The monolith in question is located on a private beach in Newport that had gone a long time without being noticed, likely because it is almost entirely covered in sand.

After a storm came through in December of 2020, the sands receded allowing for more of this monolith to be exposed. Pictures then began popping up on social media showing this standing stone with a mysterious carving. I immediately recognized this carving as an AVM symbol. In July of 2021, geologist and co-researcher Scott Wolter joined me in Rhode Island to check out the site. Our friend Scott Ambruson, who had previously visited the location, met us in Newport and led us to the monolith. The standing stone was hardly visible at this time, and could easily go unnoticed if you weren't looking for it. Approximately 20 inches of the stone was visible above ground as of July 2021, which was only a fraction of what became visible in December 2020.

The stone clearly has been there for quite some time. The current sand levels have likely been consistent for an extended period of time. We know this due to the iron oxide stain at the apparent current ground level. The water and sand likely regularly lap here. This is further supported by the lack of weathering beneath the iron oxide stain.

We began digging down, wanting to find out exactly how tall the artifact was. Unfortunately, the water table prevented us from doing so. We were able to measure the stone to at least 56 inches tall. If I had to hypothesize the height of this artifact, I would propose it is 65.33 inches. Why? If this artifact was carved by an

The Newport Monolith, July 2021.

esoteric group like the Knights Templar, they likely would have used megalithic yards in measurement. This would mean we only need the monolith to be a mere 9 inches more in height than what we have been able to uncover. This would be quite reasonable. We are hoping one day in the near future to find out for sure and move this artifact to a protected location.

Another riveting fact about this monolith is its orientation. It faces the east—towards Jerusalem. Only an initiate of an esoteric order would have done this. Now the question arises: how old *is* the carving? The stone is a medium grained granite, which is a very sturdy stone. The grooves of the carving appear to be extremely weathered and rounded which indicates the carving is not recent. According to professional geologist Scott Wolter, the carving is no younger than at least a couple hundred years, but likely older than that.

Who carved it? I propose that it was erected and carved by the Knights Templar, an esoteric group who revered the sacred feminine, the goddess, and called her Mary. This monolith appears to be one of many pieces of a Templar puzzle in the area. The monolith is only two miles as the crow flies from another mysterious building with ties to the Knights Templar: the Newport Tower, into which we will dive in the next chapter about Venus. Also nearby is the "In Hoc Stone." The In Hoc Stone is located on another beach in Newport, and is under water during high tide. The inscription in its entirety is "in hoc signo vinces" which is Latin for "in this sign thou shall conquer." This became the battle cry of the Knights Templar. Another artifact found nearby is known as the "Narragansett Rune Stone" and is tied in with the Templars because of one mysterious symbol engraved on its surface: the hooked X.

Chapter 13
Venus, Queen of Heaven

All over the world, the planet Venus has been associated with the goddess, Queen of Heaven. She has had many different names around the world, as She always has. There are two distinct symbols that have also long been associated with her: the five-pointed star and the eight-pointed star. Both symbols have been in use for thousands of years. Why?

In Chapter Three I briefly mentioned the five-pointed star's connection to Venus. The pentagram has long been associated with devil worship; why I am not sure aside from the fact it was revered by Pagans. The pentagram, the five-pointed star, is found all over the flag of our country, the United States of America. The five-pointed star has become an extremely popular symbol. The origin of this symbol is rather simple. It is an astronomical symbol of a cycle of Venus. The ancient peoples' lives revolved around the seasons and cycles of nature, including the cycles happening above. Venus takes exactly eight Earth years to complete the five-pointed star pattern in the heavens above. If you were to watch Her for eight years, you would see Her fulfill this pattern exactly. On Venus, this is precisely 13 Venus years—another connection between the Goddess and 13.

The Golden Ratio, aka the Fibonacci sequence, is everywhere, and we observe it in Venus's behavior just the same. eight and 13 fit right into the Fibonacci sequence. The symbol in fact is not evil, but rather quite relevant to astronomy. It was a functional way of observing cycles in the heavens. And as you will see later in this chapter, Venus was used quite frequently in everyday life.

The eight-pointed star is often called "The Star of Ishtar." As we know, Ishtar was the prominent mother goddess in Mesopotamia. We see that the dominant mother goddess in most cultures tends to be associated with Venus. There is much speculation about why this star is specifically eight points, but ultimately when one looks at Venus with the naked eye, it appears to have eight points. The city of Babylon also had eight different gateways, and which came first—the association of Venus with the eight-pointed star or the building of the city—is up for debate.

13.1 The Morning Star and the Evening Star

Many ancient cultures paid reverence to the morning star and the evening star. For example, in Native American tradition, during ceremonial days you are to rise with the morning star. The morning star and evening star are both Venus. How can Venus be both the morning star and the evening star? It is called the synodic cycle of Venus.

The synodic cycle of Venus is the amount of time it takes for Venus to return to the place it was first viewed from Earth. The

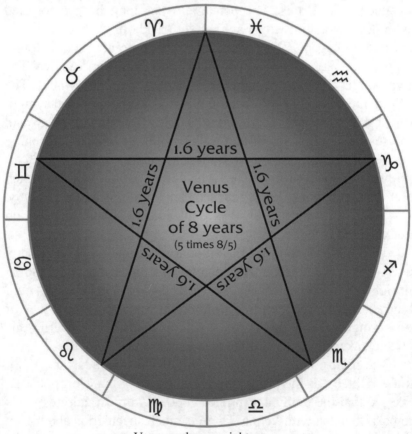

Venus cycle over eight years.

entire cycle takes 584 days. For 263 days, Venus rises before the Sun as the morning star, and the Sun follows her. Venus will disappear altogether from the sky for 50 days, then reappear as the evening star for another 263 days where she will rise after the Sun has set, and She is following Him. Once the end of this evening star period is reached, She disappears from the sky once again but for eight days. We now know that eight is significant to Venus in at least two different ways. At the end of the eight days, Venus emerges once again as a morning star, 584 days after she previously rose in the position. It is interesting to note that the synodic period of Venus is rational to the 365 solar year of Earth by 5:8.

Venus's morning and evening star periods last 263 days each. This is three days short of 38 weeks. Average human pregnancy is between 37-40 weeks long. Theoretically, this morning or evening star period fits right into the gestation period of humans. Is this at all shocking when Venus has always been referred to as the Goddess in the Heavens, or the Queen of Heaven? Venus has always been remarkably feminine in Her cycles, and this "pregnancy" of Venus before she changes cycles, or is "reborn" as a morning or evening star is remarkable.

13.2 Venus Cycles in the Bible

One of the most important cycles of Venus lasts 40 years. This all begins with the eight-year cycle of Venus where She makes the five-pointed star in the heavens above us. It takes 40 years for Venus to get back to the exact point where She began the cycle from our point of view on Earth. Within 40 years She will have completed exactly five cycles. We see in the bible that the number 40 is significant in many different aspects. The Israelites were told by God that they were meant to find the holy land, but had to roam the desert for 40 years first. The explanation from God is that the older generation that did not trust his word must die out before God will grant them the holy land.

The most important use of the 40 year Venus cycle in my opinion is its use as a *generation.* 40 years was considered an entire generation, and also was the length of time that the three kings Saul, David, and Solomon ruled. The star of David, also called the Seal of Solomon, is a six-pointed star consisting of two different symbols forged together in union. When looked at as two separate symbols, there is the triangle pointing upwards, which represents the phallus, the masculine, fire energy. The other triangle is a downwards pointing triangle, which represents the pubic triangle, the womb, the chalice, clearly the feminine, and lastly: water. These two symbols brought together are the sacred union of male and female. It is obvious there was reverence not only for a masculine deity, but also a feminine. Why wouldn't they have used the cycle of the Queen of Heaven to determine the reign of kings on Earth? As above, so below.

There are other relations to 40, but as 40 days. For whatever reason, 40 remains a significant number. We know that eight is significant to Venus because it takes eight Earth years (13 Venus years) to make the five-pointed star in the heavens. It is believed, according to the Bible that eight is the number of ultimate perfection. The Earth was created in seven days, and so eight is divine completion. Eight may also be considered the day of resurrection. Is it any coincidence that Jesus makes *eight* appearances over 40 days after his resurrection and before his *ascension* into heaven? Yes—that is right—two numbers associated with the cycle of Venus. And who is it that he first appears to after the resurrection? None other than Mary Magdalene, the one who is meant to carry on the teachings and ministry of Jesus (Mark 16:9). His second appearance is also at the tomb, where the other women see him and are overcome with joy. So the women hurried away from the tomb, afraid yet filled with joy, and ran to tell his disciples. "Suddenly Jesus met them. 'Greetings,' he said. They came to him, clasped his feet and worshiped him. Then Jesus said to them, 'Do not be afraid. Go and tell my brothers to go to Galilee; there they will see me.'" (Matthew 28:9-10).

Jesus's third appearance is in Luke 24:13-32 when he explains the happenings of the crucifixion to two of his disciples on the road to Emmaus. The fourth appearance of Jesus is in Luke 24:33-43 as well as John 20:19-25 when 10 of the disciples see Jesus and are in awe of his appearance and cannot believe their eyes. It is at this time Jesus eats for the first time since the resurrection, and his first meal is broiled fish. The significance of this meal will be made clear in a later section. In essence, his first meal after resurrection is the flesh of the *Goddess*.

In his fifth appearance, Jesus appears to all 11 remaining disciples, and Thomas, who had doubted the resurrection of Jesus was there this time (Mark 16:14; John 20:26-31). Sixth, Jesus appears to seven disciples by the Sea of Galilee. The disciples have gone out to fish (later you will see the significance of the fish) and have caught nothing, however, Jesus stands on the shore and offers them advice, and they catch 153 fish. 153 is a sum of the first 17 numbers, which is a combination of divine grace, or the *Seven Gifts of the Holy Spirit* and the Law, which are the 10 Commandments. The seventh appearance takes place at a prearranged location on a mountain in Galilee. When he meets with his 11 disciples he gives them the authority to make other disciples. It makes sense that this is the seventh appearance, as seven represents a certain wholeness within the scriptures. His disciples have obviously reached a certain degree of initiation, and therefore are allowed to become initiators themselves (Matthew 28:16-20). The final appearance during this 40 day period happens in Acts 1:3-9, amongst many of his followers when he declares that his mission is complete, and thus ascends into heaven before their eyes, which allegorically would mean he assumed the title of High Priest in the Holy of Holies, the east facing section of the tabernacle where only the High Priest could go, but also where God was said to appear to the High Priest.

13.3 The Megalithic Yard

Have you ever wondered what unit of measurement the people of prehistoric times used? How did they come to decide on a unit of measurement? For a lot of things, the ancient people turned to the heavens above—the megalithic yard included. A unit of measurement needed to be practical, but it also needed to be something that was universal to some degree. Now how could that be done? Let's go back 5,000 years. The people of the Neolithic era were building henges, stone circles, cairns, stone chambers, and many other megalithic sites. These archaeological sites are incredible, and they all tend to have one thing in common: the incorporation of archaeoastronomy.

The Bringer of Life

The people of the Neolithic era were farmers, therefore they had to have a pretty deep understanding of the cycles and seasons. Their reasons for keeping track of astronomical dates had both spiritual and practical purposes. We know they kept track of the month by way of the lunar month and not solar, leaving 13 (lunar]) months in a year. That being said, they came up with units of measurement, be it time or physical measurement units, by using the celestial bodies above.

The "megalithic yard" is a term coined by a Scottish engineer, Oxford Professor Alexander Thom. Professor Thom spent most of his time exploring Britain's megalithic sites, and in 1967 published a book titled *Megalithic Sites in Britain*. This megalithic yard is about 2.72 feet. It became apparent that sites at other locations around the world were also using the same unit of measurement, the *megalithic yard*. The megalithic yard was also found to be in use at the Carnac stones in Brittany, France.

Another researcher, Dr. John Clark, made an interesting discovery regarding the site of Teotihuacan, in Mexico. He made note that there appeared to be an 83 cm unit of measurement incorporated in the construction of the site. The megalithic yard, going from 2.72 feet to centimeters, comes out to 82.97 cm. This is almost *exact*. If there were multiple civilizations around the world using the same unit of measurement that supposedly did not have contact, there has to be something universal within the unit of measurement—and there was. It was the use of the Goddess in the heavens.

Alan Butler and Christopher Knight prove that there was a universal way to calculate a unit of measurement in their book *Civilization One.*[1] They propose that the megalithic yard was a unit of measurement invented by using the planet Venus. With that hypothesis in mind, they set out to conduct an experiment. Butler and Knight successfully complete their experiment using a pendulum with a fulcrum of half a megalithic yard. The pendulum beat 366 times as it moved through one degree of Earth's circumference. 366 is almost the precise number of days in a year. Why would the ancient people *not* look to the brightest object in the sky other than the Sun and Moon?

[1] Knight, Christopher, and Alan Butler. *Civilization One: The World Is Not As You Thought It Was*. Watkins Pub., 2010.

13.4 The Newport Tower, Rhode Island USA

In the previous chapter we discussed the potential Templar carving on the Newport Monolith. Just two miles north from the monolith's location is the Newport Tower. The Newport Tower has been baffling researchers for centuries. While there is a lot of information and many arguments about what the tower could be, who it could have been built by, and when, we will stick to the facts and information that are relevant to this specific area of research. The tower itself is a round tower with eight arches, seven windows, and an unknown number of niches. The purpose of the tower? Likely what many other ancient monuments were meant to be: an astronomical observatory.

When was the tower built? This has been a question that has long been debated over. An archaeological dig in 2006 by Jan and Ron Barstad yielded only artifacts dating to the colonial era, which is considered roughly 1607-1776. If you were to use archaeoastronomy to date the site, then it would appear that it was built sometime between 1200-1600. The evidence to support this hypothesis is the feature of the tower that was built to view a star of the earlier mentioned era. This star is called Dubhe.[2] When this took place, Polaris, the North Star, was at its upper culmination,[3] due north. Polaris could also have been seen through Window 2, as well as through a hypothetical hole in the roof. It is clear that the precession of the equinoxes was considered in the construction of the tower, as it was in many medieval cathedrals, like Chartres Cathedral.

Other astronomical observations were also found. Solar *and* lunar alignments have been located. The tower can also be used to observe major lunar standstills, which occur every 18.6 years. In addition to the lunar major standstills, a full moon could be observed through a window in the tower 12 hours after the Sun was observed there. This can be observed just before the spring or autumn equinox. It is important to note that the builders were keeping track of the nodes of the moon's orbit. This was likely the case due to an interest in eclipses.

Solar alignments appear to be rather important as well, and one

---

[2] Star also known as Ursa Minoris.
[3] Upper culmination takes place when a star is at its highest point in the sky.

takes place at sunrise on winter solstice, December 21. The Sun shines through an east facing window and projects a rectangular box of light on the opposite wall. As the Sun continues to rise, the box moves lower on the wall, until it eventually illuminates an egg-shaped white keystone. This takes place at 9 am, which appears to be a universal hour of the goddess that we have seen before. As we saw in Chapter 3 this same solar alignment, on winter solstice, at 9 am, takes place at Newgrange, in Ireland. While the engineering of this structure that allows such an alignment to take place is awesome, I find the allegory here even more awesome. This is once again the allegorical union of male and female, Heaven and Earth, and represents the fertilization of the Goddess by the solar deity, so that nine months later, the harvest can take place at the autumn equinox, in the sign of the Virgin, Virgo. This is the impregnation of the egg in the womb of the earth. This is the same concept as seen at Newgrange, along with many other megalithic sites found around the world. In the spring of 2020, Scott Wolter and I ventured out to the Newport Tower on a hunch that there just may be an alignment that takes place on the cross quarter day May 1, Beltane. Sure enough, there was a sunrise alignment!

On solstices, it is obvious that Venus follows the Sun, and Scott Wolter was hot on Her trail. In December 2007, Scott had gone to see for himself. He was able to document the two smaller windows at the top of the tower that were in perfect position to view Venus. Surprisingly, no one else before had investigated a Venus alignment at the tower, which I find shocking. Venus after all, is the third brightest heavenly body in the sky.

The tower looks nearly identical to other structures in northern Europe. There is substantial evidence to indicate that the tower was built by the Knights Templar. We know that Venus was extremely important to the Templars, as they were an esoteric group that revered the divine feminine, but also because they were seafaring people.

13.5 Venus in Mayan Culture

There is a planet that was used for everything including war; can you guess who? That's right: Venus. The ancient Mayans looked to Venus for Wisdom quite often, and even decided on

214

when to conduct human sacrifices based on the movement of the heavenly body. The Mayans knew Venus as *Chak Ek.*

One of the most well known of the Mayan gods was associated with Venus, Kukulkan. Kukulkan is a winged serpent, who in other parts of Mesoamerica was known as Quetzalcoatl. This flying serpent was said to be the creator god, as well as god of wind, rain, and storms. Around the world, the serpent has long been associated with the Goddess, and in turn Venus.

The Mayans built multiple observatories, and some of these were used specifically to track Venus. The most prominent example is El Caracol. El Caracol is located at the iconic Chichen Itza site. At the front of the structure is a staircase that faces 27.5 degrees north of west. This position correlated with Venus's northern extreme, Venus's most northerly position in the sky.

It has been long established that the Mayans were genius at calculating the calendar and astronomical events with extreme accuracy. They were often working with the synodic cycle of Venus that is mentioned in the earlier section.

13.6 Venus, the Fish, and Friday

The ancient people named their days after their gods, and it is no secret that Friday was dedicated to the Great Goddess. In Norse mythology this is Freya, in Rome this was Venus. In Spanish, Friday is even called *Viernes.* The iconic Mother Goddess was ultimately the same deity in all these different times and cultures, only called by different names. Going back thousands of years to Mesopotamia, She was called Ninlil. Ninlil went by several other names as well: Mulliltu, Mullissu, and Mylitta. Her worship began as early as 2900 BC, about 5,000 years ago. She was the wife of Enlil, and later of Assur, head of the Assyrian pantheon. Later in the 2nd century AD, she was referenced as Mylitta by Herodianus in his "Peri Orthographias."

Mylitta was seen as the Assyrian Aphrodite or Venus. The one thing these mother goddesses all had in common was that they all had some connection to the "primeval waters" as they were the creatresses. The other connection they all seemed to have was to fish. Why? There are many different reasons. The shape of the fish, the same shape that had somehow become a symbol of Jesus,

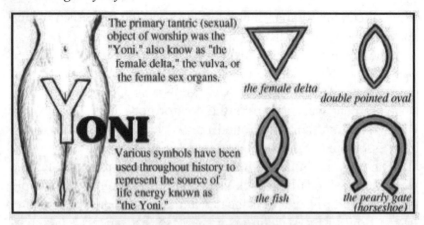

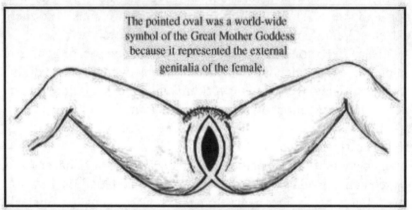

Symbols the Goddess.

is the shape of the yoni, the vagina. As seen in this diagram, it is clear that the most important part of this symbol is the vesica piscis. This symbol has been incorporated for centuries into sacred geometrical architecture, seen in many churches and cathedrals.

On Fridays in ancient times, not only did they venerate the Goddess, but they also had sacred rituals in Her honor. One of these rituals included a ceremony performed by priests and initiates, in which they would partake in eating fish, which was perceived as being the flesh of the goddess, much like how in Christianity eating wafers and drinking wine is considered eating and drinking the flesh and blood of Jesus, which by the way represented menstrual blood of the goddess, and the flesh of the Sun god prior to Christianity. Marriages were also performed on Friday, so that they were blessed by the goddess herself.

Does eathing fish on Fridays sound familiar? It should, considering that the Catholic Church forbade the consumption of meat on Fridays during Lent; adherents were encouraged to partake in the eating of fish instead. There was also a Jewish tradition of the "fish meal" prior to the creation of Christianity. It was Jewish custom that they enjoyed a meal consisting usually of fish, bread, and wine on Fridays; this was considered their sabbath meal. In addition to being a Friday tradition, it is also the meal of Passover.

Fish were also a great symbol of fertility, as they are known to lay hundreds to thousands of eggs at once. And as we are well aware, water is the most important life-force out there. Babies are surrounded by water and darkness inside the womb. The iconic fish symbol became linked to Jesus and Christianity. But why? According to Augustine in the early fifth century, the acronym for "Jesus, Christ, Son of God, Savior" is I-c-h-t-h-u-s. Ichthus is the Greek word for *fish*.

Another connection that has been made between the fish and Jesus is the fact that his birth in the year 0 ushered in the age of Pisces, which lasted approximately 2,000 years. Not only was this the dawn of a new era, but more specifically Jesus was said to have been born March 20, 6 BC. March 20 is right at the equinox, but specifically it is the last day in "Pisces season" since the constellation rules the heavens from February 19-March 20. Jesus himself was a Pisces! Because he was born at the beginning of the Age of Pisces, he is referred to as the Fisher King in Grail lore. However, the connection between the fish and the goddess existed for thousands of years prior to this astrological transition. Among the initiates in esoteric tradition, the vesica piscis/fish symbol is well known as a representation of the feminine aspect of God.

A notable monument in the United States also contains the vesica piscis. In Washington DC stands the Washington Monument. The obelisk stands right in the center of the oval shape, just in the middle of the yoni symbol. This is clearly an allegorical representation of male and female. The monument was dedicated to George Washington, whom we all know, and who was also a Freemason. The architect responsible for designing the monument was Robert Mills, also a Freemason. The construction of the monument began in 1848 and was completed in 1884.

The Washington Monument, aerial view.

Many will argue that the symbol represents something else, something more Christian in nature. The fish does indeed have its connections to Jesus. We know that Jesus was referred to as the "Fisher King." This was because he ushered in the Age of Pisces, the fish. The ending of an era, the Age of Aries the Ram, came upon the world just as Jesus was born. What did this mean? We will come back to this. First, let us not forget that early in Jesus's ministry he comes across Simon and Andrew who were fishermen. It is in Mark 1:17 that Jesus proclaims, "Come follow me, and I will make you fishers of men."

Jesus uses this allegory for many reasons, one being that he was very much aware of the new Age of Pisces, the Fish above in the heavens. Going back thousands of years to his ancestral genesis, Egypt, there was always a tradition of following the astrological age within religious teaching. Around 2000 BC the Age of Aries the Ram was close to dawning, thus signaling a new religious teaching. It was here that the Cult of Amun emerged, Amun was always shown as a ram, as Aries, the Ram. This age came to and end within a few years of Jesus's birth, therefore he became called the *Lamb of God*.

In Hebrew Aries is called Taleh, the lamb. In Arabic the name is Al Hamal, the sheep, and came to mean gentle and merciful. In Akkadian the name was Bara-ziggar. Bar means altar, or sacrifice,

218

and ziggar translates to "making right." Together this would mean *sacrifice of righteousness*. In the forehead of Aries the Ram is a star called El Natik or El Nath, which means wounded or slain. The left horn holds another star, Al Sheraton, which translates to the wounded or the bruised. The concept of the "lamb of God" or the slain lamb, is a concept here that was not born with Chrisitianity, but born with the beginning of a new astrological era observed up above. The constellations were the heavens, the Kingdom of God, and the Wisdom of the cosmos.

The first reference to Jews slaughtering the ram came in

Saint Peter Catholic Church, County Wexford, UK. Courtesy Andreas Borchert.

Genesis 22:13. Prior to sacrificing the sheep, man was meant to sacrifice his firstborn son to God on the mountain. Abraham has taken his son Isaac to sacrifice him, and just as he is to kill him, a ram appears and god commands that he is to sacrifice the ram and not Isaac. Abraham lived during 1996 BC-1821 BC, just as the Age of Aries the Ram was beginning, and this represented the ushering in of this new religious tradition. What was happening in the heavens was meant to happen on Earth as well. Later during the Hebrew month of Nisan, ancient Jews used to ritually slaughter a lamb at Passover, and mark their door with the blood of the lamb. Because Jesus came at the end of that astrological cycle and tradition, a new one had to come along. It appears that every astrological cycle brings with it a new tradition and religious belief.

For example, before Aries the Ram there was the Age of Taurus the Bull. The Age of Taurus lasted between about 4300 and 2000 BC. During this time the Egyptians worshiped the Apis Bull, the god Hapi. In the same era, the Mesopotamians were worshiping their own bull god. Ancient Indians also worshiped the bull. As early as 8000 BC, people of Çatalhöyük in Central Anatolia were worshiping a bull skull. This veneration of the constellations in heaven was clearly not just in Egypt and Mesopotamia, but was instead a worldwide phenomenon.

Following this ancient tradition, why *wouldn't* Jesus continue this tradition when he was born of this Egyptian royalty himself? He knew it was his duty to be the "Fisherman" of Earth. Just as the animals in the past represented God on Earth, the symbol of the Fish now would as well. Therefore Jesus begins teaching his disciples a combination of many different religious and mystery traditions, all infused into his own ministry, full of his own "Fishers of men."

What does this mean, making someone a fisher of man? Fishing is a career which is unpredictable. There is no guarantee that you will catch any fish at all any time you cast a net out. This is parallel to the initiatory mysteries, how some people will not understand, or will not be receptive to these teachings. We see this when Jesus explains why he loves Mary Magdalene more than all the other disciples in the Gospel of Philip. The idea of baptism in water began around the birth of Jesus, likely also due to the new Age of Pisces. Fish live in water, therefore those initiated into the new mystery religion must also be "born" into the religion in water. John the Baptist was the first to begin baptismal immersions in water. Water itself has always been considered feminine, the life force, as it is found surrounding a baby in the dark womb of woman.

John the Baptist was the one to initiate Jesus. At the time of his baptism, Jesus was 30 years of age. The Talmud teachings say that a man reaches his prime at the age of 30. The Mishna says that at 30 a man is full of strength. It is also said here that there are 30 attributes to kingship. Levite priests began providing the service in the Tent of Meetings at the age of 30. In ancient Egypt, it was after 30 years of kingship the pharaoh would celebrate the Sed Festival. In Rome, the constellation Virgo is related to Vesta, the virgin goddess of domestic life. Vestal Virgins dedicated their lives to the goddess for a period of 30 years.

Obviously, 30 is deemed a sacred number. Numerologically, 30 can be reduced down to just 3 (3+0=3). Three represents the Holy Trinity which we have already gone through, but it also represents the triple aspect of goddess: maiden, mother, and crone.

13.7 The Dove

When you see the dove, what is the first thing that comes to mind? For someone who was raised in the church like me, I instantly am reminded of the Holy Spirit, who is the veiled goddess in Christianity, the mother figure within the trinity as wife of God. Going back thousands of years, the dove was always associated with the mother goddess. This is true of the Mesopotamian Ishtar, the Punic Tanit, the Phoenician Astarte, the Greek Aphrodite, and the Roman Venus.

Franz Cumont states in his book, *The Oriental Religions in Roman Paganism,* "Two animals were held in general reverence, namely, Dove and Fish. Countless flocks of Doves greeted the traveler when he stepped on shore at Askalon, and in the outer courts of all the temples of Astarte one might see the flutter of their white wings." In Grail lore, it is always the dove that brings the Grail to the altar.

Later in the medieval era, we see the dove associated in artwork with Mary Magdalene, who represented the divine feminine, the Holy Spirit. As Sophia, the gnostic goddess of wisdom, She is also represented by the dove. We see in the bible an early connection between the Holy Spirit and the dove in Luke 3:21-22 when speaking of Jesus's baptism performed by John the Baptist: "When all the people were being baptized, Jesus was baptized too. And as he was praying, heaven was opened and the Holy Spirit descended on him in bodily form like a dove."

Going back to even more ancient times, lead dove figurines were found in temples dedicated to Inanna-Ishtar. Later on, the Greeks also began to use the dove as a symbol of Venus. They even sacrificed doves in Her honor on specific days. The ancient Greek word for dove was *peristerá* and meant "bird of Ishtar." There was very clearly a connection between the dove and the goddess prior to the time of Jesus.

Chapter 14
The Roman Catholic Church

To truly understand how and what the Roman Catholic Church stands for, we must first go back to the beginning. When was the Roman Catholic Church really founded? And how similar was it actually to Jesus's teachings? This is a concept no one who grows up Christian seems to question, because in church we are taught not to question things, but just to have faith. Right?

14.1 The Stolen Throne

Traditionally, we are taught that upon the death of Jesus, the apostle Peter also known as the "Rock" carries on the tradition and church of Jesus the Christ. He establishes the first church of Jesus at Antioch. For those who are not aware, Antioch was located in the Roman province of Syria and Phoenicia. Today, Antakya (Antioch) is in Turkey. It is at this location that the term "Christians" is used as a derogatory term for the followers of Jesus.

In many ways, it was not proper for Peter to establish this church that Jesus began. Jesus himself was in fact a Jew, an Essene Jew at that. Jesus himself was descended from kings, and had a right to the throne of Jerusalem by birth. However, unfortunately for Jesus, there was a usurper king on the throne, Herod Antipas. In The Gospel According to Luke (13:32), Jesus is reported as having referred to him with contempt as "that fox."

Earlier, at the very end of the 6th century, an ancestor of Jesus through the Davidic line, Jeconiah, was dethroned by the king of Babylon, Nebuchadnezzar II. Jeconiah became the first of the exilarchs,[1] or Jewish leaders/kings in exile during the Babylonian rule. The exilarchs, understandably, continued to live their lives just the same but pledged loyalty to the King of Babylon, therefore the royal line continued, but they were only recognized as the

---

[1] A Jewish king/leader of the Jews in "exile" while answering to the Babylonian king

223

leaders of the Jews.

Because this is Jesus's genetic background on his father's side, we know also that Jesus was meant to hold this position of power. His rightful throne was Jerusalem, but because he was a "king in exile" he did not rule from the throne, he ruled from the ground. Many people dispute Jesus ever had children, but there is a very important reason, from two different aspects of his life, that would tell us having a child (and therefore a wife) would be mandatory.

Jesus was a dynastic king by birthright, but also took on the Rabbi title and role. In the traditional sense, the leader of the Jews was also a teacher, and a high priest. Similar to Native American tribes, the Chief or leader is also the Medicine Man/Holy Man. In the Highlander Clan cultures of ancient Scotland, the Chieftain of the Clan was also responsible for the welfare of his people that depended on him for safety and leadership. In these cultures the role of leadership was passed on to the heir of the Clan or Tribal Chief. The rules of ancient Jewish dynastic leadership require the king to marry and produce an heir to carry on their father's duty. It is also important to keep in mind there was no separation of spirituality (in some cases religion as well) and state/throne.

One tradition that is relevant to Jesus is known as *pidyon haben.* This is a Hebrew phrase that translates to "redemption of the first born." This tradition this only applies if the first born is a male and is born of natural circumstances. After thirty days, the parents will engage in this ceremony which is known as a *mitzvah.*[2] This child is given a title, "opener of the womb." At this ceremony, the parents will pay the Jewish priest silver coins to "redeem" their son. This stems from the more ancient traditions of offering the first born in sacrifice to God. Now, the firstborn son who has been *redeemed* is to become a priest! This is where we get the idea and mitzvah that a rabbi or Jewish priest must marry and have a son to offer to God that will also carry on the teaching.

That all being said, it is a requirement within the Jewish community (more so in ancient times) that man must marry and give birth to a male son. Royal or not. In Jesus's case, he is hit on both sides. Not only must he marry because God commands man to "be fruitful and multiply" (as is said in Genesis) but he is also a

---

[2] Commandment given by God to fulfill a certain religious duty.

leader, a king by birth, and therefore is under significant pressure to bring forth an heir to his throne and title.

Now, with that in mind, we know Jesus would have married. Due to his kingly line, he would have also married someone who was of royal descent. This marriage also would have been to someone who was his equivalent of a high priest, so his wife would have been a high priestess, versed in the mystical ways of ancient Jewish and Egyptian tradition. This marriage would also be a strategic alliance for both families. Who better than Mary Magdalene, who herself was a high priestess and a princess nonetheless?

Going forward, they would have had children, theoretically. While the apostles were on the road with Jesus, his child or children, would be in some place of education, whether a monastery, college of mystical arts and sciences, or even a training school where the heir is to learn how to be a king or leader of his people and how to handle certain public and foreign affairs (as the heir's parents, Jesus and Mary, were doing out on the road). This would account for the lack of mention of any of Jesus's children in scripture. They most likely had not come of age to be active, therefore it was still Jesus and Mary's mission.

Going back to the founding of the church, this would have rightfully been the responsibility of the heirs to the throne and temple of Jerusalem. Not to Peter. Or Paul. Or anyone else. This responsibility belonged to the blood of the king priest and queen priestess. Because Jesus was very close to Peter, and trusted him significantly, he left it upon Peter to ensure his heir be kept safe to continue teaching and leading the Jewish people. However Peter took it as an opportunity upon the alleged death (disappearance) of Jesus, to create something using the name of Jesus. He took a role of leadership that, if done in the traditional Jewish way, would have been the responsibility of the first male heir of Jesus the Christ and Mary Magdalene. Frankly, Peter was no better than Judas. He attempted to take a throne and title from Jesus the Christ, and yet did it all in his name.

Many people often wonder why Christians are followers of Jesus, and still, Jesus himself was a Jew. How does that make sense? Jesus was teaching a new form of Judaism. He taught a reformed version of Judaism. The teachings he preached became known within a hundred years after his "death" (disappearance) as Christian teachings. Christianity was not a word Jesus ever acknowledged or used.

Peter took away the birthright of Jesus's children for himself. The Pope, or the Throne of Peter, really should have been the throne of Jesus or his son. Could you imagine how different the world would be today? The church as we know it today may still be popularly known as a temple, and the throne of the current "Pope" would be sat upon by a descendent of Jesus the Christ himself. Instead, the Pope is elected, not brought in dynastically by tradition as it would have been, had a rightful heir sat upon it.

When Jesus made it clear to his disciples that he was leaving the earthly materialistic society, his disciples asked him who would carry on his teachings in Jerusalem. To this, Jesus responded, "No matter where you come from, it is to James the Just that you shall go, for whose sake heaven and earth have come to exist."[3]

Who is James the Just? James is also known as *James the Righteous*. He is first mentioned in Matthew 13:55 and Mark 6:3 as one of four brothers of Jesus among many sisters. James the Just is a known Nazarite priest. We will dive into the meaning of Nazarite shortly. James was also known as "James the Lesser" (or "the Younger"). James was made bishop of the church in Jerusalem, but unfortunately in 62 AD, James was martyred. The high priest of the Temple of Jerusalem, Ananus ben Ananus, ordered the Pharisees to stone the brother of Jesus to death. Had the teachings of Jesus been preserved in his brother James, the church still would have remained in the family. Unfortunately, it did not work out that way. What kind of world would it be if it had?

14.2 Mystic Jewish Sects and Magic Hair

What exactly *is* a Nazarite (also spelled Nazirite)? A Nazarite is a person who has taken the Nazarite vow, which can last a lifetime or simply 30 days if there is no indicated time period. The Nazarites do not cut their hair during this time, nor indulge in alcohol or anything deriving from the grape. During a Nazarite's

---

[3] Gospel of Thomas.

vow, he may not touch or come anywhere near a corpse. If he does, he becomes ritually "unclean" and must remain ritually "clean."

The word Nazarite comes from the Hebrew word "Nazir" which means "to consecrate" but more likely "to anoint" as Jesus is often referred to as the Christos, which in Greek is literally *the anointed*. Nassi or nasi additionally was a Hebrew word meaning "prince." Which brings up the question, is this where Adolf Hitler found his inspiration for the *nazis'* name? Hitler was a man that was extremely interested in legends like the Holy Grail, and alchemy, but also Jewish occult practices (like the teachings of the Kabbal).

Jesus was often called the "Nazorean" which could refer to the sect of the Nazarites. The town of Nazareth most likely was not established at the time of Jesus's upbringing. Archaeological evidence tells us that the priestly families of Judea did in fact flee to Nazareth around 135 AD following the Hadrianic War. Jesus is often depicted in art as having long dark hair, despite the fact that the bible tells us it is a disgrace to God for a man to wear his hair long unless he is a Nazarite.

James, Jesus's brother, was a Nazarite who took his duties very seriously. Other Nazarites in the bible include Samson and Samuel, who were dedicated to the tradition from inside their mother's *womb*. However, each person's vows could differ, also seen in the bible in reference to Samson and Samuel. The Nazorean sect of Jews and later early Christians, adhered to some of the same rules as the Nazarites. John the Baptist (Initiator) himself was an Essene Jew. Mary Magdalene and Jesus were both rather taken by his teachings, and witnessing his teachings inspired them to take the ministry on the road, continuing John's teachings of "The Way." Like the Nazarites, the Essenes did not cut their hair. They believed their hair gave them a stronger connection to the Divine, to Mother-Father God, similar to Native American tribes' beliefs about long hair.

The Essenes also did not drink alcohol, but this is something we know Jesus did fairly often as many different books in scripture confirm. Early on in Jesus's ministry, it is made abundantly clear that his brothers, including James, do not agree with his teachings. This is made clear in John 7:5 when Jesus says he isn't going to the Festival of the Tabernacle and his brothers say to him, "Leave

The Bringer of Life

Galilee and go to Judea, so that your disciples there may see the works you do. No one who wants to become a public figure acts in secret. Since you are doing these things, show yourself to the world." The Book of John then states how even his own brothers did not necessarily believe in him.

Why? Why would Jesus's own brothers challenge him upon being a public figure, a teacher? Could this be because some of Jesus's beliefs were radical and new? Whether he was an Essene or at sometime a Nazarite, it is clear there are some rules he did not strictly follow. Jesus indulged in wine, and likely wore his hair long. He engaged in certain activities that a strict Jewish sect would not approve of. What exactly was the root of all of Jesus's teachings? Clearly some are rooted in Torah, but where else did he learn these teachings? We know Jesus incorporated many different traditions into The Way, such as a form of energy healing, known today as reiki.

Going back thousands of years before Jesus's time, to ancient Egypt, hair was a significant symbol. Those in the royal family would wear their hair long; for the Queen it showed her maternal powers and embodied the mother goddess, Isis. The pharaoh himself also wore his hair and beard long and thick, as it served as a symbol of masculinity, fertility, and as a reminder that like Osiris, he held that regenerative spiritual strength.

This idea of hair holding significant spiritual importance would appear to be a worldwide concept, as its found in almost every ancient culture. There are many different theories as to why hair was found to be so sacred, but ultimately it tells us that humans to some degree are all operating on similar evolutionary levels. Thousands of years ago these people around the world had an extremely deep understanding of natural cycles on earth and in the heavens above. As humans began to develop into spiritual beings, one of the first common beliefs was that hair held some type of power. Likely this began with the goddess worship, as long hair has always to some degree been associated with females and mothers. Men, for thousands of years (in Egypt as well), cut their hair short. 1 Corinthians 11:14-16 says, "Does not nature itself teach you that if a man wears long hair it is a disgrace for him, but if a woman has long hair, it is her glory?"

228

14.3 "Mortal One Day & Divine the Next!"

For the last two thousand years the church has existed under its concept of one true God, and there have been lies and bloodshed in its name. Up until about 313 AD, Christianity was not tolerated in the Roman Empire. It was in February of 313 that Roman emperors Constantine and Licinius signed the Edict of Milan, which stopped the persecution of Christians and initiated religious tolerance. Interestingly, Constantine's soft spot for Christianity began about six months earlier.

In October of 312, Constantine marched toward what would become known as the Battle of Milvian Bridge. The evening before the battle, October 27, it is said the Roman emperor had a vision. This vision was that of a fiery cross in the heavens accompanied by the words "In Hov Signo Vinces." This is Latin for "In this sign thou shall conquer." The next day, Constantine's outnumbered forces won their battle, much to everyone's surprise. He took it as a sign from God, and was seen as being a bold and favored ruler. As we have seen the Latin phrase also went on to be associated with the enigmatic warrior monks, the Knights Templar.

Later on, Constantine called into order the *Council of Nicaea in 325 AD*. This was the first ecumenical council of the church. There were over 300 bishops who came to discuss the important matters of the church. While there were many things to be discussed and debated, one of those things involved the divinity of Jesus. Was he created or was he creator (God incarnate)? It was decided that Jesus was literally in fact the incarnate God, therefore his son on Earth. Unfortunately, there are a lot of misconceptions and misunderstandings in the bible. The title "Son of God" means "chosen to do God's work." The first part, "Son," means to be special and to have a divine purpose. The second part of the phrase would instill a royal purpose, as all the dynastic rulers believed they were God's divine representative on Earth to rule the kingdom with God's justice, Wisdom, and mercy. This could also be in reference to Jesus's father, Joseph, being the one who currently rules as king or leader in exile, therefore he is representing God, the holy father, and Jesus's father at the same time. The Son of God is in reference to the holy and kingly descent from the House of King David of Jerusalem.

This being said, many, including those at the Council of Nicaea, have translated everything literally, when there are in fact many books that refer to a Son of God, or Sons of God, which indicate they are really of royal descent. One early reference to this divinity comes from 2 Samuel 7:13-14, when God speaks to David through the prophet Nathan, and says, "He [David] shall build a house for my name, and I will establish the throne of his kingdom forever. I will be his father, and he shall be my son…"

Keep in mind, the books of Samuel were written between 630 and 540 BC! They were written hundreds of years before Jesus was even conceived. This is a legitimate piece of evidence to suggest that the title Son of God was bestowed upon those descended from King David, who is directly given the title of "God's Son" by God as spoken through Nathan.

So, at the Council of Nicaea when they were debating over whether he is God or he is man (the created) they really are debating over nothing. Jesus was chosen by God to be his king on Earth, and it says so in the early books of Samuel. David established this "house" of royalty. However, the debate over Jesus's divine status resulted in the *Nicene Creed*. Essentially all it really is, is a document confirming Jesus is God on Earth, and the Heavenly Father is one with Jesus.

Moving on, another topic at the Council was the date of Easter. The day we celebrate Easter is not the actual day Jesus the Christ was "resurrected," it is in fact a day decided upon by the church. Traditionally this event took place during the Jewish Passover. Passover traditionally was an eight day celebration (remember eight is associated with Venus) at the end of what we would call March and the beginning of April. In 115-124 AD, the ruling Pope was Pope Sixtus I, and he had chosen the date of Easter to be a Sunday in the lunar Jewish month of Nisan. This date for Easter happened to fall the day before the spring equinox, which seemed daringly Pagan. The Christians then established the *Christian Nisan* festival after the equinox!

Also, discussed at Nicaea was what scriptures belonged in the bible. There was some discussion on the matter, some books were totally rejected, some were added, and some were kept. Later on, at the Council of Constantinople in 381 AD, the rules to determine

230

what books were allowed in the bible were officiated. Man decided what scriptures were allowed and not allowed to be in the Bible, not God, therefore the Bible is not God's word, but *man's chosen* Word of God. As a child, I remember being taught that not telling the whole truth is still lying. Is it not?

Personally, I do not find it fair for a man, or men, to determine what is suitable for me to believe and read. I think it is necessary to read, to grasp and understand all aspects and all perspectives of the history pertaining to the religion I am surrounded with, before making an opinion for myself. It is only fair to have a complete understanding of a subject before immersing oneself in it.

Moving forward, Paganism within the Holy Roman Empire was tolerated until about 375.

14.4 Saint Jerome & Pagan Christianity

A very learned Christian man appeared in Rome, and challenged the Papal authorities on the translations of scripture. Saint Jerome wanted to see the translations in Vulgate (Latin). Saint Augustine insisted this was not appropriate and made his concerns known that through this manner there could be an "infinite variety" of translations of the same texts. Well, what do you know? That is the case still today! We have *many* different versions of the bible even in the English language.

Under the authority of Pope Damasus, Saint Jerome had his way. He saw to it that the translations be done. Damasus may be the author of the anonymous Carmen contra Paganos (song against the Pagans). It is quite likely Pope Damasus was an initiate of the Way that Jesus himself, and Mary Magdalene taught. Damasus grew up in his father's church. Damasus' parents were Antonius, who was a priest at the Church of St. Lawrence (San Lorenzo) in Rome, and his wife Laurentia. This was later known as the Basilica of Saint Lawrence outside the Walls of Rome. Interestingly, several hundred years later this became the Latin Patriarchate of Jerusalem, the Catholic episcopal see of Jerusalem, officially seated in the Church of the Holy Sepulchre located in Jerusalemc. This was the European seat for the Bishop or ecclesiastical ruler of Jerusalem.

When the Holy Land was won, the King Godfrey of Bouillon

of Jerusalem was the Rightful King, the descendent of the Merovingians, the Sangreal (or Blood Royal, of Jesus and Mary Magdalene), and of the House of David, but most importantly, the "Primordial" or "Original Waters." Godfrey of Bouillon founded the Order of Sion in 1099, what so many have known as the "Priory of Sion."

The Basilica of Saint Lawrence later became the European seat for the Holy Throne of Jerusalem. Why this place in particular; why was it deemed so special and so Holy a seat? This place where hundreds of years earlier Pope Damasus grew up watching his Father Antonius preach? From the research I have done, it has been made obvious that Pope Damasus knew something others did not. He was also *the* Pope to make Latin Rome's official language.

It was about 405 when Saint Jerome completed his Vulgate version of the bible which was based on the existing scriptures which were in Greek, Hebrew, and some Latin. Unsurprisingly his Vulgate version of the Bible, was not even recognized by the Roman Catholic Church until 1546. It was in Saint Jerome's *Commentary on Ezekiel* that he writes of the Pagan relationship between life, death, and resurrection. He says, "Hence as, according to the Pagan legend, the lover of Venus, a most beautiful youth, is said to have been slain, then raised to life again, in the month of June, they call the month of June by his name, and they have a solemn celebration in it every year, in the course of which his death is mourned by the women, and afterwards his resurrection is chanted and praised."[4]

I find it incredible that the Holy Pope Damasus *endorsed* this material of Saint Jerome's in the 5th century. What kind of Holy Father would back up material that proves Christianity (which mind you, *this* Christianity that is taught now is not what Jesus originally taught) was founded on Pagan spirituality? A special kind of Pope—a Pope who is initiated.

14.5 The Origin of Nun

Going back thousands of years, we know that women symbolically "married" themselves to the temple, no matter

---

[4] Migne Edition of Jerome's Works, Vol. XXV, Col. 82, The Myth of Resurrection, Joseph McCabe, 1925.

what gods or goddesses they were worshipping. Many of these women were known as "temple prostitutes" which really is not an appropriate phrase for them. The translation is more appropriately "holy woman" as they served a Holy Role in their own religion and were usually the High Priestess—they had an allegorical and physical union with the High Priest who represented a god or God's representative on Earth.

However, it is truly intriguing that nuns are called "Nun" seeing as the ancient Egyptian Goddess of the Primordial Waters of Creation had the name "Nun" but also many other variations. Furthering the connection, Isis, the goddess who embodies all aspects of the Mother Goddess, is represented by the color black, which in turn represents the night skies and the cosmos. This is the origin of the "Black Madonna" cults that sprang up all over France.

For thousands of years, priestesses of the Great Goddess knew these things, and the High Priestess wore black, just like Mary Magdalene. Nuns in Christianity are not so different. When joining the convent, a nun becomes wife of Jesus. Just as in the old tradition, Mary Magdalene would have worn black as a high priestess and would have been married to Jesus.

14.5 The Cult of the Black Madonna

Across Europe, and especially in France, you will find many statues that would appear to be the Virgin Mary, but one curious thing is her color. She is depicted as black. Chartres Cathedral, for example, had a Black Madonna statue with child made in the 16th century, but it was recently repainted white.

There are many ideas and theories about why She was made *black*. Across Europe we find many statues and paintings that are dark-skinned and black, something that many Christians today are disturbed by. Western culture has always depicted Jesus and Mary as being Caucasion, but if they were really middle eastern people they almost certainly would have had darker skin.

The color black has also had long associations to the Great Goddess. Black was the color of the primordial waters of creation, aka the cosmos. The heavens before creation, and even being littered with stars now, remain black. The goddess is associated with both death and resurrection, just as Venus falls beneath the horizon and dives into the underworld for a time, and as Inanna in Mesopotamian tradition does. The color black can be associated with death, or the underworld. Isis resurrects her dead husband, Osiris, and conceives of his spirit. Venus and the Moon, two aspects of the triple goddess, illuminate the dark night sky. The goddess is revealed in darkness.

Shakti, the primordial conscious energy of the cosmos is another example. Black, darkness, is the being of the cosmos before She began creation. The inside of a female womb, much like the early cosmos, was dark, but also water filled. This is why caves were used most often for Templar and other esoteric initiations, so that the initiate would be once again in the womb of the Great Goddess, blind, in the dark, and vulnerable. A great example is Jesus's ritual death and raising from the *family tomb* of Joseph of Arimathea. Lazarus was also raised by Jesus after an initiatory event in a tomb. Upon emerging from the dark cave or tomb, the initiate will have *new eyes to see* after being reborn from the womb of the goddess.

The south of France has heavy traditions of the Black Madonna, and it is here that She is primarily associated with Mary Magdalene. In France there are at least 350 Black Madonnas, but likely more. Some of the Black Madonna figures were allegedly brought back from the East during the crusades, by none other than the Knights Templar. Many of the cathedrals that currently have a Black Madonna icon were built on top of old goddess temples. The cult of Mary Magdalene in the south of France likely came about because she along with her friends, supposedly arrived in France after the crucifixion. Some say Jesus even went to France with her, and some French lore holds this to be true.

Mary could very well have been dressed in black robes, as priestesses of the goddess, or of Isis, often wore black robes. To dress in black was the highest honor for a priestess. Therefore this connection to the *Black Madonna*, and Mary Magdalene being venerated as such, could certainly be related to the color of her robes. This is seen in Christianity in the nuns dressing in a black habit, just as priestesses of the goddess did.

There are many springs and water sources where Mary has

connections in France. Supposedly she baptized people, and taught near water springs. Many of them bear her name today. The concept of the goddess being dark was not new in the time of Mary Magdalene either. The idea of the goddess being dark went back thousands of years, as the cosmos was black before She began to create. The moon appears at night in the midst of the black night, as does Venus as the evening star. Sometimes Isis was even depicted as being black, along with other goddesses throughout the world. The goddess Venus, Aphrodite in Greece, was a primordial entity, who was supposedly born out of an eternal black night before the Earth's creation.

14.6 The Albigensian Crusade

The Albigensian Crusade, also known as the *Cathar Crusade,* was a 20-year-long crusade against the Cathar people in the Languedoc region of France that lasted from 1209-1229. Pope Innocent III decided he needed to eliminate the "heretics" that lived in the south of France, likely because they knew many secrets and truths of Jesus and Magdalene. The Cathar movement began in the city of Albi, hence the name Albigensian. Some argue that these gnostic traditions came from elsewhere, such as the Balkans and the Bogomil churches. While there could have been multiple gateways around Europe into gnostic Christianity, I think it is imperative to take into consideration Mary Magdalene's heavy influence in the south of France. The Cathars practiced many things that Jesus, Mary, and his ministry taught.

The Cathars were gnostic Christians who held many unorthodox (Christian) beliefs. For some reason, the pope felt threatened by them and saw to it that they were exterminated. But, as the saying goes, you can kill a man, but you cannot kill his belief, nor his spirit. The church became aware of them in the 11th century, but they likely existed in smaller numbers for a much longer period of time prior to the Middle Ages.

Like Jesus's original teachings, they believed that deity had both a masculine and feminine aspect. They believed the god of the material world was evil, the *demiurge,* while the true god was a loving and understanding god. This evil demiurge god could be equated with Satan. Essentially it was believed that life on Earth

235

was hell, and they awaited the ability to enter the spiritual realm of purity upon physical death.

The Cathars taught something else that upset the Catholic Church: you did not need to confess to a priest to obtain forgiveness and entry to heaven. Another unpopular belief of the Cathars was reincarnation. They taught that until you were able to renounce your material self and obtain spiritual perfection, you would continue to be reincarnated on Earth. They even saw Jesus's resurrection as a symbol of reincarnation. They believed that Jesus was the husband, lover, and partner of Mary Magdalene. They viewed her as being even more important than Saint Peter, the "founder" of the Church. Her role as teacher, one who could administer the sacraments, was extremely important to the Cathar people. They believed women were just as capable and able of being spiritual leaders and Perfecti.

They had many spiritual rites that differed from those of the Catholic Church's sacraments. They did not use baptism as a form of initiation, but instead were touched with hands of the initiator. They practiced the *consolamentum*, which was the rite where perfection was obtained. They then became the *Parfait* or the *Perfect;* This is similar to rituals it appears that Jesus and Mary practiced, promoting perfection by union with the Holy Spirit, or perhaps when the different demons went from them, and they became perfect. The consolamentum was usually done privately, as it was a secret tradition of initiation. The initiator may have even spoken in ecstatic tongues, which was a practice that was considered witchcraft by the Catholic Church. Upon achieving the Parfait status, they would then spend their time traveling and teaching Cathar practices.

One of the most well known massacres of the Albigensian Crusade took place at Béziers where, according to a letter to the pope, an astonishing 20,000 people were killed. Papal legate Arnaud Amalric led the crusaders to the city and demanded that the Catholics come out and the Cathars surrender. Neither group obeyed orders. When a soldier asked Almaric how to know the difference between Cathar and Catholic, he said, "Kill them all, God will know his own!" Every man, woman, and child was slaughtered. The city burned to the ground. The next place to fall to

236

the crusaders was the walled city of Carcassonne. The inhabitants were forced to leave all of their clothing and depart the city naked, ashamed, and with nothing.

Nearly 15 years later there was the *Siege of Montsegur.* Montsegur was a Cathar haven, where up to 500 Cathars were living. Sénéchal Hugues des Arcis led about 10,000 royal troops to the base of the mountain in May of 1243. Their strategy was initially to wait until the Cathars starved and surrendered, but the people were far more prepared than the French forces thought. They were able to hold out until March of 1244, likely because they had secret routes up and down the mountain, maybe even tunnels that allowed them to come and go and bring in supplies.

Surrender conditions were made in March of 1244. All that renounced the Cathar beliefs could leave the castle unharmed. Many chose not to renounce their faith, most of them being Perfecti. On March 16, 1255, somewhere between 210-215 Cathar believers were escorted down to the pyre by Bishop Bertrand Marty. They were not bound by rope to the stake. No, in fact, the Cathars voluntarily mounted the pyre, and burned without fear nor protest.

There are many stories about a few Perfecti escaping to recover or transport some treasure that was either hidden at Montsegur or buried nearby. The treasure was supposedly texts or relics that the Cathars were trying to protect. Supposedly the treasure made its way to the Cathar Church in Italy. The esoteric French writer Joséphin Péladanhave in 1906 even proposed that it could have been the Holy Grail itself. He argued that Montsegur was the Munsalväsche (or Montsalvat) of Wolfram von Eschenbach's *Parzival* written in the 13th century. Other stories say that the Knights Templar came to their aid and the treasure was passed on to them. Interestingly, the Knights Templar found excuses not to participate in the Albigensian Crusade, probably because they shared many similar beliefs and traditions with the Cathar people.

Chapter 15
The Knights Templar

One group of men that over the course of 900 years have gained popularity as one of the most mysterious orders to ever exist, right next to the Illuminati, is the Knights Templar; but who were they? We have heard of them in recent Grail lore, *The Da Vinci Code*, and similar stories. The question remains, what is fact and what is fiction?

The origin of Templarism itself has many mysterious aspects. The order can be traced back to the white-robe-wearing Cistercian monk, Bernard of Clairvaux. He was responsible for establishing several Cistercian monasteries; 68 to be exact. One of those churches happened to be in Seborga, Italy. Ancient documents tell of the "Great Secret of Seborga." It was here in 1113 that two men, who later became two of the first nine Knights Templar, were asked to come and guard the Great Secret. These men were known by the names of Gondemar and Rossal. At the time, there was a man in charge of this church, both Prince of Seborga and Abbot of Seborga, Edward. Christopher Columbus was born just outside of Seborga—interestingly, he had known Templar connections.

15.1 Bernard Clairvaux and His Devotion to the Goddess

Bernard of Clairvaux was born in a small town not far from Troyes, France in 1090. At the age of 23 he joined the Cistercian order, and not just Bernard, but he and 32 of his own family members. A tad strange, unless there was something a bit more to the story. At the age of 25 in 1115, he was sent to found Clairvaux Abbey. The land which this abbey resided on was actually donated by Hugh, Count of Champagne. Bernard appeared to be closely related to many of these aristocratic families as he came from a Burgundian aristocratic family that owned land in the regions of Montbard, Alise St. Reine and Dijon. Bernard's mother was actually the daughter of the Lord who presided over Montbard.

A very bizarre story emerged: the monk was said to be praying to a statue of the Virgin Mary when it suddenly came to life with baby Jesus in one hand and the other squeezing an exposed breast. The breast squirted out milk directly into the mouth of Bernard. At least, this is the story that has been passed on. The artwork depicting this is called "The Lactation of St. Bernard." To me,

Alonso Cano, The Lactation of Saint Bernard, 1650, Madrid.

this seems rather erotic for a 12th century monk, but nonetheless, there it was. *A miracle* it was called. This was said to take place at Speyer Cathedral in the year of 1146, at which time Bernard would have been 56 years old.

While breastfeeding remains a touchy subject in the modern era, it was entirely normal and natural in medieval times. Medieval people believed breast milk was the mother's blood turned into milk for the baby. Mary, the "Mother of God" per se, then would be feeding Bernard with the Wisdom of the Holy Mother, but also one could argue this was a symbol of drinking from the blood of Christ as Christians would have you do in church when taking communion. This would be the a nearly alchemical transformation, much like how Christianity teaches that when we consume the wine at communion, it transforms into the blood of Jesus.

Bernard himself had a certain fascination with the Queen of Heaven, a title that was an ancient one of the mother goddesses, but also of Venus in the heavens. This title naturally was absorbed by Christianity's own goddess, the Virgin Mary, Mother of God. He was said to have had a vision of the "Queen of Heaven" at a young age that stuck with him for the rest of his life, and inspired him to write many works about Mary. All Cistercian churches tend to be dedicated to the Virgin Mary. Later on, almost all Templar chapels and Templar related cathedrals also became dedicated to the goddess—*Our Lady.*

Understanding Bernard and his position within the medieval world will better help us understand the Templars and their original foundation. As you will see, Bernard played a very important part in the Knights Templar Order. The foundation date of the order is a little bit foggy, as the official sanction date of the Knights Templar came 10 years after its supposed founding, at the Council of Troyes in 1129, which was presided over by the one and only: Bernard of Clairvaux.

15.2 The Beginning and the End, or Was It?

In 1118, a man named Hugh de Payens from the Champagne region brought together a group of eight other knights, all somehow related. These nine knights were: Hugh de Payens, Godfroi de St. Omer, Rossal (or) Roral (Cistercian priest and cousin of Bernard),

Gundemar (Cistercian priest and cousin of Bernard), Godfrey Bisol, Payens de Montidier, Archambaud de St. Aman, Hugh I Count of Champagne, and Andre de Montbard (uncle of Bernard).

These men went to the Holy Land in 1118, and appeared before the King of Jerusalem, Baldwin II, cousin of Godfrey of Bouillion. Baldwin II was descended from some of the same noble families in France that these founding knights hailed from. Is that any coincidence? Furthermore, after only being king for a few weeks, Baldwin II granted approval to a new order founded by these nine knights; the "Poor Fellow Soldiers of Jesus Christ" and were formally recognized as "Knighthood of the Temple of Solomon." Upon the founding of this order in the Holy Land, King Baldwin II allowed them to take up residence in one of the wings of the palace, the Temple of Solomon. The first Grand Master of the Knights Templar was none other than Hugh de Payens.

This was not, however, Hugh's first visit to the East. Hugh had made multiple visits to the Holy Land alongside Hugh, Count of Champagne. Hugh accompanied the Count once during the period of 1104-1107 and a second time in 1114-1116. It was during Hugh's second visit to the Holy Land in 1114 that the Bishop of Chartres wrote a letter to him berating him for his behaviors. The accused behaviors included abandoning his wife and taking vows to the Knighthood of Christ. Is this a reference to the order that had not yet "officially" been founded? Could this indicate the conspiracy to create this order was many years in the making?

One element of this story I have not yet mentioned is the idea of the Holy Bloodline and its place in this Templar order. Many researchers suggest that these knights were all descended from specific bloodlines going all the way back to the house of David. This is not at all unlikely. In fact many of these noble families *can* trace their bloodline back this far. Could they have been descendants of the royal bloodline of Jesus? Or going back further, David, Solomon, and the Egyptian pharaohs?

Was Hugh de Payens here on multiple occasions to look for something, or someone specifically? What were the treasures the knights were so adamantly seeking beneath the Temple Mount? But also, *how* did they know there was even something to look for, and where to look? These secrets must have been preserved in an ancient family tradition for over a thousand years.

The Council of Nablus proved to recognize the order on a slightly more official level in January of 1120. It was here that they received recognition from the Patriarch of Jerusalem, Warmund, yet another distant cousin of Bernard of Clairvaux. An official insignia was given to the newly founded order: the Cross of Lorraine, the double-barred cross. The Cross of Lorraine was long associated with the Duke of Lorraine's coat of arms. The family of the House of Lorraine had many intimate connections with the Knights Templar and Jerusalem. It was Godfrey of Bouillon, Duke of Lorraine, who conquered Jerusalem and was offered the kingship. He denied it, and instead was called the "defender of Jerusalem" for only a year before his death in Acre. He ruled over Jerusalem until his death, after which his brother, Baldwin I, picked up the crown of Jerusalem. Baldwin II, the king to approve of the Templar foundation, was the cousin of Baldwin I, the throne staying within the family of the Royal Blood.

Hugh, Count of Champagne, interestingly quit his life in Champagne to return to the Holy Land once more to join these Templar knights, but this time swearing allegiance to his own vassal, Hugh de Payens in 1125. This is the same Count of Champagne who donated land to the Cistercian order, the land that became Clairvaux Abbey, founded by our rather popular St. Bernard. The Bishop of Chartres wrote him a letter too, reminding him of his duty to his wife and family after he joined the Templar order in 1125. The Bishop of Chartres seemed quite obsessed with marriage and discouraging these men from joining the Templar order. Had the Roman Catholic Church always had it out for these men? Was it because what lay beneath Solomon's Temple may have posed a threat to the Catholic Church's legitimacy?

About 10 years after the Patriarch of Jerusalem recognized the Knights Templar, the Council of Troyes convened on January 13, 1129, presided over by Bernard of Clairvaux himself. Hugh de Payens had petitioned the Church and wanted the order to become a recognized entity in the eyes of the pope. It was Bernard that wrote the charter for the order, and argued its purpose and legitimacy at the Council.

A curious requirement that Bernard made for those joining

the order was *obedience to Bethany and the House of Mary and Martha.* Without any shame, Bernard made it obvious that the Knights Templar must honor and obey the family of Mary and Martha, as if these women were God[dess] themselves. Bernard specifically named Mary who was more than likely the Magdalene and Her sister Martha. Note: Bernard did not name Jesus, James, Joseph, Mary mother of Jesus, or any other disciples within the order's charter. He made specific reference to the family of the woman who anointed Jesus. Bernard obviously had a reason to revere Mary Magdalene, and even Her sister. What did he know then that we don't today? Is it possible that all of the cathedrals built with Templar funds were actually dedicated to "Our Lady" Mary Magdalene, and the statues depicting Mary holding a baby are actually depictions of Mary Magdalene and Her child?

Why did it take 10 years for Hugh to finally seek recognition from the pope? Was it because they spent many years seeking, and finally found whatever treasure it was they were looking for beneath the Temple Mount? Whatever they found and brought back to Europe with them obviously held enough importance to demand official recognition by the Catholic Church. Bernard, being related to many of the original Knights Templar and Hugh himself, must have been aware of whatever it was that these knights were up to and supported their cause, even if it threatened the Catholic Church.

Was Bernard outwardly Catholic, but secretly venerating the goddess, and outwardly venerating Her as the Virgin Mary? His obsession with the Queen of Heaven was made no secret. Is it so shocking that all Templar chapels were founded in the honor of the Virgin Mary or Mary Magdalene? The declared patron saint of the order was the Virgin Mary. These Templars may outwardly have seemed Catholic as did Bernard, but perhaps this was just a smokescreen for the true tradition they followed. Not to mention the fact that the order was sanctioned on the 13th day of the year 1129.

Hugh of Payens, the Count of Champagne, and many of the other founding members had visited the Holy Land long before the public creation of the order. Once Hugh of Payens gathered up the eight knights—making nine including himself, obviously the number of months of human gestation—they went to the Holy Land and stayed there for nearly a decade. Up until 1128, it was only these original knights, therefore the idea that the order was created to protect the pilgrims en route to the Holy Land, their stated purpose, lacks credibility. How could only nine knights protect thousands of pilgrims all across Europe? They could not. There were no new knights added until after the Catholic Church admitted their legitimacy. Why?

Clearly the Templars had something the Catholic Church feared. They gave them legitimate recognition to keep them on their good side. The Templars used this to do many things that gained them even *more* power, such as create the first ever credit card banking system. The Templars set up banks all across the old world and began accepting deposits of pilgrims so that they could travel without fear of being robbed. Somewhere down the road, the pilgrim could show the Templars a "credit card" that had encrypted writing on it, to withdraw money.

The Knights Templar were geniuses. Not only did they have an elusive leverage over the Catholic Church, they controlled money all over the continent, and they had the ultimate power. Unlike other religious orders, the Templars did not answer to kings or any monarchy. They only answered to the pope, the alleged "source of God's power on Earth." The only way this could happen is if these mysterious knights had something in their possession that somehow equaled the *source of God's power on Earth.* What could possibly rival the legitimacy of the pope?

These "warrior monks" may have appeared to be the elite army of the pope, but their fealty was indeed to something much more ancient and threatening than the Roman Catholic Church. Their duty was to a tradition that survived for thousands of years, a tradition that has long been covered up. And on Friday the 13th, 1307, orders were opened simultaneously across France to arrest all Knights Templar. They were brought to Paris for the Inquisition. It must be noted that many of the Templars of the higher degrees were aware of what was taking place, and it was even admitted during the Inquisition that some escaped because they were tipped off.

The Templars were accused of several different heresies,

among them sodomy, spitting on the cross, and worshiping false idols. Many of them were likely just made up—it appeared that King Phillip used these charges to implicate many of his enemies such as King Boniface VIII just months prior to the trial of the Templars. Later the Cathars were met with the same charges. One heresy of the Templars in particular was worshiping a bearded head. The head was said to be called *Baphomet*.

What exactly was the *Baphomet?* There are many different theories on the matter, one of the most popular being that it actually was a derivative of *Muhammad*. Raymond of Aguilers, a chronicler of the First Crusade, wrote that the troubadours used Baphomet in place of Muhammad. Later scholars agree that this was a common Old French corruption of Muhammad, likely coming from *Mahomet*.

Pierre Klossowski in *Le Baphomet* proposes that, "The Baphomet has diverse etymologies... the three phonemes that constitute the denomination are also said to signify, in coded fashion, **Ba**sileus philoso**pho**rum **met**aloricum: the sovereign of metallurgical philosophers, that is, of the alchemical laboratories that were supposedly established in various chapters of the Temple. The androgynous nature of the figure apparently goes back to the Adam Kadmon of the Chaldeans, which one finds in the Zohar."[1]

The 18th century saw a reemergence of Freemasonry, Templarism, and the connections between such esoteric orders to Gnosticism. Andrew Michael Ramsay, a Scottish-born writer and tutor to the Bonnie Prince Charlie, gave Ramsay's Oration, a famous speech linking Freemasonry to the Knights Templar. Christoph Friedrich Nicolai (1733–1811), a Freemason, bookseller, and Illuminatus, claimed that Baphomet was made up of the Greek words βαφη μητ8ς, baphe metous, meaning Taufe der Weisheit, "Baptism of Wisdom."

Another theory proposes that the Baphomet was actually the veiled worship of the sacred feminine, of *Sophia, Goddess of Wisdom.* As early as 500 BC, a substitution cipher was used known as the Atbash Cipher. It was primarily used with the Hebrew alphabet, but could be applied to any alphabet that was in a particular order. It was used multiple times in the biblical book

---

[1] Klossowski, Pierre, and Michel Foucault. *The Baphomet*. Marsilio, 1998.

of Jeremiah. There were many texts from the Dead Sea Scrolls that had curious words that scholars could not decipher.

Dr. Hugh Schonfield applied the Atbash Cipher to some of these words, such as "hagu" which then became the Hebrew word for test, "tsaraph." Dr. Schonfield was especially fascinated by the Knights Templar, the enigma of the Baphomet, and decided that he might apply the Atbash cipher to the word. Though written in Hebrew, it translates to the Greek word *Sophia.* Is this any coincidence? Sophia is not only the Mother of Wisdom, but also the wife and mother of god. Just as the mother of Jesus was according to the dynastic god-king tradition, and just as Mary Magdalene would have been if She was the wife of Jesus and the mother of his children.

Shortly after the Templar arrests in Paris in 1307, interrogations began yielding interesting findings. One such finding from the Paris Temple was a silver reliquary in the shape of a *woman's* head. Inside were two small female head bones wrapped in white linen, and another in red. A label was attached bearing the inscription Caput LVIIIm: head 58m. The number 58 has yet to be understood to have any specific meaning, but if you add 5 and 8 together you get 13—the number of the goddess, but also the aeon in which Sophia the Goddess of Wisdom dwelled in the cosmology Jesus taught.[2] The "m" could very likely have been a symbol of the constellation Virgo, not exactly an m, but an m with the vesica

piscis fish symbol, hanging down from the right side. The first use of somewhat modern glyphs appears in 10th century manuscripts that could be traced to 6th century astrologer Rhetorius. However, the sign for Virgo in this manuscript was slightly different. We can assume it was between the 900s and the early 1300s that this symbol shifted into what we know as Virgo today—if it was in fact the

Virgo glyph.

---

[2] Found in the *Secret Book of John* and in the *Pistis Sophia.*

symbol shown on the label of Head 58.

The constellation Virgo has always been associated with a feminine deity. M was a symbol that represented the goddess from the beginning times. Why? When a woman has her legs up in the birth giving position, her legs form an M. For example, take a look at the Akkadian to Old Babylonian relief, from between 2500 BC and 2000 BC. It is obvious that from early times the natural birthing position would appear to make the letter "M." Is it by any accident that the M is the 13th letter in the English alphabet? Was it any coincidence that "Ma" was one of the very first words to mean mother and womb, dating back to Egypt?

The fish symbol that came to adorn the lower right side of the M in the Virgo glyph is likely representative of the vesica piscis shape that you saw representing the vagina and birth canal in 13.6. It could also be a reference to the Messianic tradition, and perhaps Jesus. The M could represent the goddess, the *mother of god,* and

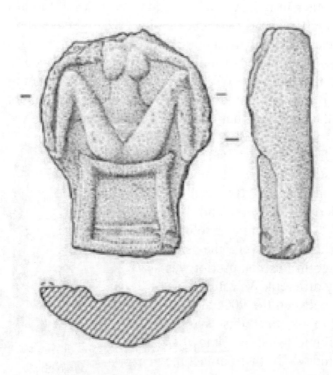

Akkadian to Old Babylonian relief, c. 2500-2000 BC.

the fish symbol could represent Jesus. It is possible the M was linked to both the mother of Jesus, Mary, and Mary Magdalene. Both women would have connections to Jesus and responsibility for carrying on a Messianic lineage. It is a symbol the Knights Templar would have seen as extremely sacred.

A knight, during the Inquisition's interrogations, specified that the silver female head was not at all connected to the bearded head used in Templar ritual. So what was the bearded head all about? One obvious connection is to that of an iconic biblical character who was beheaded: John the Baptist. It should be pointed out that Freemasonry's patron saints are the Holy Saints named John: John the Baptist and John the Evangelist. John the Evangelist experienced Jesus post resurrection, and learned of the Gnostic creation story from Jesus, who was indeed still whole and alive. This can be found in the *Secret Book of John*. Were the Templars Johannites? Did they see John the Baptist as the true prophet? Was there something more to it?

The severed head has stood as a symbol within esotericism for quite some time. It is possible that the use of the severed head in ritual could pertain to a phase in alchemy known as the Caput Mortuum—the "Dead Head" or the "Blackening." This occurred just before the precipitation of the philosopher's stone. In some traditions the severed head represents the souls, or spirit's, detachment from the body, from earthly and material pleasures. The idea of using a severed head in ritual was not new to the medieval Knights Templar, in fact it was something that began long before.

Vedic Hindu ritual texts written between 1200 BC and 1500 BC tell of "the head of the sacrifice" being rites that involve the severing and restoration of the severed head. There are two different heads that appear to be worshiped, one being the *Kirtimukha,* literally meaning the face of glory. The Kirtimukha was a representation of the god Shiva, the counterpart of the divine feminine cosmic creator Shakti.

To this day, the head of a goddess is still worshiped in India. The head is said to be of metal, vermilion, or stone.[3] The destroyer goddess Kali is also often depicted slaying demons and evil beings

[3] Dange, Sindhu S. "The Severed Head In Myth And Ritual" *Annals of the Bhandarkar Oriental Research Institute*, vol. 72/73, no. 1/4, 1991, pp. 487–96.

by decapitation. The Hindu goddess Chhinnamasta is the goddess of self-sacrifice, and is the goddess with the severed head. She severed Her own head in the spirit of self-sacrifice. In Tibetan Buddhism she is also found as Chinnamunda-Vajravarahi, the goddess with the severed head. The concept of a severed head being somehow central to ritual and spirituality was not something that began with the Templars, but rather was continued by them.

The Knights Templar were not committing many of the crimes they were accused of; rather the French king was broke—owing a large debt to the Paris Temple, and knowing he would not have the funds to repay it. He was in need of more money, and had heard legends of a great treasure lying within the Temple. King Phillip also seemed to be somewhat aware of the fact that the Templars were not the good Catholics everyone made them out to be, as he and the new "puppet pope," Clement V, ordered the Knights Templar to be arrested on a Friday, the day honoring the goddess Venus, and the 13th at that, a number central to the veneration of the sacred feminine. It was by no accident. Pope Boniface VIII seemed to be quite close to the Knights Templar, him being the pope to build the golden reliquary for the supposed remains of Mary Magdalene in France. It was when he did not agree to persecute the Templars, and attempted to protect them, that the king had him brutally attacked, and essentially killed. The pope remained in poor condition for nearly a month after the assault. He died two days before the arrest of the Knights Templar.

The Grand Master of the Knights Templar, Jacques de Molay, was tortured for seven years after the initial arrests in 1307. In 1314, he was greased up and roasted and burned alive. It was at this time that the Grand Master called out what was later to be deemed a curse. He claimed that the innocence of the Templar order would be known, and just months later, Pope Clement V, the puppet pope of King Philip, along with Philip himself, had died. Was this mere coincidence, or karmic justice balancing out the scales?

15.3 The Templars in Scotland After 1307

As we have seen, the king of France, Philip IV, owed the Templars a large amount of money, as they lent to him time and

250

time again. He knew that the Knights Templar had returned from the Holy Land with a great treasure, and that they were storing it in the Paris Temple. By arresting the Templars, he would be able to storm the Paris Temple and seize whatever treasure and money they were storing there. Unfortunately, when French soldiers entered the Temple, the treasure and any money were long gone.

Where did this treasure go? It likely escaped on the 18 galleon ships that left the Templar port at La Rochelle. We know these galleon ships escaped as Knight Jean de Châlon admitted during the Templar trials that the Templars had been tipped off about the scheduled arrest. The orders for the arrest of the Templars had been sent out on September 14. There was nearly a month for this intel to fall into Templar hands, which it clearly did. The knight specifically said that, "Gerard de Villiers, the Paris Preceptor, had escaped with 50 horses and 18 ships."

The Templars were always one step ahead. So then where would they have gone next? There was one nearby place where the Roman Catholic Church did not have authority. A place where the king himself had been recently excommunicated only a year earlier, in 1306. That place was Scotland.

The ports were well guarded all around Scotland. Michael Baigent and Richard Leigh, in their book *The Temple and the Lodge,* that there was only one route to Scotland that would have proven quiet and navigable without meeting the English Navy:

> Edward's fleet, based on the east coast of England, effectively blocked the established trade routes between Flanders and Scottish ports such as Aberdeen and Inverness. Templar ships, moving northwards from La Rochelle or from the mouth of the Seine, could not have risked negotiating the Channel and the North Sea. Neither could they have proceeded through the Irish Sea, which was also effectively blocked by the English naval vessel based at Ayer and at Carrickfergus in Belfast Lough.[4]

With this proposed route, it would have taken the Templars round the west coast of Scotland, which appears to be what at least

---

[4] Baignet and Leigh, *The Temple and the Lodge,* p. 65.

some of these Templars did. In an enchanting little country town called Kilmartin, there are Templar grave slabs that can be found dating back to the 14th century.

Did 18 galleons all go to the same place? Did some go to Scotland, and some elsewhere? There is no telling exactly what happened, but what we do know is there is some archaeological evidence to point to one specific location on the east coast of Scotland: Wemyss Caves. These 12 caves are situated on the Firth of Forth's coastline, just beneath MacDuff Castle. Many carvings fill the cave, some as old as 3,500 years. One cave in particular, one that is only accessible by crawling in, is home to a symbol that is inextricably linked with the Knights Templar. This is the most easily guarded cave of them all due to the small entryway. This symbol is a triple-barred cross, also known as the "Cross of Salem."

The Cross of Salem was the seal of the grand master of the Knights Templar, and still is used today within Freemasonry. The only other use of this cross was by the pope himself for ceremonial purposes. Could this suggest that the pope and the Grandmaster of the order were equals?

The original seal of the grand master was the Cross of Salem directly in the middle of the vesica piscis, the symbol we know to

Triple-Barred Cross in Wemyss Caves, courtesy of Fife Today.

represent the sacred feminine. What did the cross actually mean? There are various interpretation, for example, the holy trinity, or the three-fold concept of a leader's responsibilities: ecclesiastical, civil, and judicial supremacy. The pope is seen as sovereign priest, supreme judge and sole legislator. As was the grand master of the Knights Templar, bearing this symbol.

Save Wemyss Ancient Caves Society (SWACS) vice-chair Moira Cook said, "The latest finds appear to be Medieval although they cannot be totally discounted as a Templar symbol, as it is possible there were crusaders from this area." Is this the only evidence that suggests that the Templars hid out here? There is possibly further evidence to back up this theory. A hoard of journals was found in a basement by Diana Muir whilst visiting a distant relative. The journals detail many journeys made from Scotland to North America, Templar secret traditions, as well as the activities of the Templars in Scotland after Friday the 13th, 1307.

Diana's book is based on the journals that she found and her interpretations. We read in her book, *The Lost Templar Journals of Prince Henry Sinclair Book 1 - 1353-1395,* under the date of 2 February, 1383: "I have met with the Templari near the cliffs of Wemyss and have delivered provisions to them for the rest of the winter. They seem in good spirits and make good use of their time."

This would be 76 years after 1307. Were there "Templari" living here in the caves for nearly eight decades? These would likely now be the descendants of the original Templars. Just above is MacDuff Castle, which was built and inhabited by the Wemyss family (descended from the MacDuffs) until 1421, when Sir Michael Wemyss had Wemyss Castle built just a few miles down the coastline. To this day Wemyss Castle is still the seat of Clan Wemyss and remains their family home. Local tradition holds that in the back of Well Cave once stood a spiral staircase descending from the castle above. If this were the case, it is possible that these Templars and their descendants were able to survive here for many years being able to receive unnoticed care from those in the castle. The caves are large and could easily give shelter to several families.

There were a total of nine caves here prior to the 19th century.

The Bringer of Life

Two caves unfortunately are no longer accessible. One of those two is called the Glass Cave which contained Christian carvings and Pictish symbols. Sadly this cave collapsed due to subsidence caused by mining activity in the late 19th century (Guttmann 2002, 112). Perhaps if we were able to study that cave today we would have a bit more evidence to support the claims of the journals in Diana's book.

We can, however, examine other evidence that may support this theory. Historians and archaeologists alike contend the caves were used for Christian rituals and practices throughout the early Christian era to the medieval era. These rituals could have been led by monks, and why could they not have been conducted by warrior monks who wore white tunics with red crosses? It appears that there is *another* man-made feature constructed in the 1300s that can tie this site to the Templars.

The *Northlight Heritage Conservation Plan Wemyss Caves* when discussing Well Cave said, "Walkover survey has also identified a small but substantial masonry pier supporting the ceiling on the eastern side of the inner chamber." Why is this significant? What does this have to do with the Templars? Within Freemasonic lodges, the Master of the Lodge always sits in the East. The East is significant because of its connection to the Goddess in the heavens, the planet Venus. Within Chrisitianity Mother Mary or Mary Magdalene would have been one and the same with Venus, Queen of Heaven. This will be explained more in depth in Chapter 16 in relation to Freemasonry.

What we do know with certainty based on archaeological findings is that there was a significant medieval inhabitation of the caves. Inside the Well Cave medieval pottery was found, which is where an unsuccessful attempt to locate the passageway to the castle was made. Between Jonathan's Cave and Gasworks Cave there was a massive medieval shell deposit found spread out over 80 meters.

There is evidence that also suggests there was a "church" at East Wemyss as early as the 14th century that was known as *St. Mary's by the Sea*. This appears on Gordon's 1642 map of Fyfe Shire, and in 1654 on Gordon and Blaeu's Fifae Vicecomitatus, The Sherifdome of Fyfe, as "Cavehead." Was this *church* actually inside the cave? Was it a tradition that was born due to Templar use in the 14th century? All Templars dedicated their chapels to St. Mary; is this any coincidence?

The use of the cave as a ritual space is evident with the masonry found in the East, and proves that there was a gnostic sect of Christians there carrying out specific rituals. Whether they were the Knights Templar escaping persecution post October 13, 1307, we cannot say for sure. There are many rumors that the Templars did come here from Europe, as it was essentially a safe haven from any Catholic rule. Did all 18 ships go to Scotland? Did just a few? Were there just some stowaways that made it here? Did some Templars go east to Wemyss Caves, and others to the west coast? Scottish lore suggests that Templars hid treasure at Kilwinning Abbey, which by no coincidence, is where the Mother Lodge of Scotland reigns as Lodge 0. As noted, Templar grave slabs can also be found in Kilmartin.

Approximately 85 miles up the coastline from Wemyss Caves is the city of Aberdeen. The mouth of the River Dee opens wide to the North Sea, and it is an important port city. The port was first established in 1136, and early on served to be a strategic location for the warrior monks clad in white. Eight miles downstream they set up house along the River Dee at what became Maryculter House. The Templars' patron saint was Mary—be it Mother Mary or Mary Magdalene. The two ultimately became interchangeable. Between 1221 and 1236, Maryculter House was founded and built. It became one of two official Knights Templar preceptories in Scotland. The other was located near Rosslyn in Midlothian, on lands belonging to the St. Clairs.

Could any of the 18 missing galleons have gone to the preceptory of Maryculter House? Or did the refugees not trust their fellow Knights? Did they prefer to seek solace in secret? There are no records of an influx of men at Maryculter House post October 13, 1307 that I can locate. One problem, according to author Robert Ferguson's *The Knights Templar and Scotland,* is that the Templars would not have been able to sail up the northeast coast of Scotland due to English warships guarding the seaports.

Maybe some did appear, but were quietly absorbed into everyday routine. Or maybe, whatever these Templars escaped

The Fallopian Cross, Kings Cave, Isle of Arran.

from France with was so valuable that they did not trust anybody else to guard their precious secrets? Could this be why many of these soldiers chose to live their days out in a cave on the east coast of Scotland? Did some escape to the wild west of Scotland, the Scottish highlands, where they would never be seen again?

There is much speculation about where they went and what they did after that fateful day in 1307. Some say that the 18 ships hightailed it across the Atlantic ocean to what is now the United States of America. Others argue the knights merged into other monastic orders around Europe, such as the Poor Knights of Christ in Portugal. A country that was said to be founded around being the "Port du Gral" or *Port of the Grail.* Is this where Portugal got its name? A mystical concept, the Grail?

In May of 2022, Scott Wolter and I visited some caves on the Isle of Arran in Scotland that appeared to have some ritual significance. After a hike down to Kings Caves along the coastline, we entered a few different caverns. Different carvings were

The Grand Hailing Sign of Distress, Kings Cave, Isle of Arran.

around. In one small cave was a carving of a delta symbol, but it was the large cave that yielded the most intriguing carvings. Upon entering the cave, you notice it has a very high ceiling, a long passageway in, and then straight ahead, you come face to face with a wall that has two large unique carvings. They are not like the typical Pictish symbols you find in most caves in Scotland; no, these symbols are completely unique, likely medieval or later, and completely esoteric.

The first symbol on the left is a cross, but make no mistake—this is not a typical Christian cross. At the base of this cross you see what appears to be a basic representation of the birth canal and fallopian tubes (see diagram in 4.2): the female reproductive system. Who do we know that venerated the sacred feminine in the guise of good Catholic soldier-monks? This symbol alone was striking, as I have never seen any other cross carved quite this way. How do we know for certain it was Templar? It was the symbol next to the fallopian cross that sealed the deal for me: a human with their elbows raised at a 90 degree angle, hands up. The symbol that is known as the Grand Hailing Sign of Distress in Freemasonry.

One intriguing theory that I cannot seem to shake is that they fought by the side of one of Scotland's most iconic figures: *Robert the Bruce,* who might I add, visited the Isle of Arran in the early part of 1307. Coincidence? Was he perhaps scouting safe locations for the Templars to initially land, and hide certain money, treasure, and artifacts?

Seven years after the order was hunted down in France, Robert the Bruce won Scotland's independence from England, in the most peculiar of circumstances. The story itself almost does not make sense when you take away the potential for the Templars fighting side by side, as you will notice when we dive into the Bannockburn narrative.

15.4 The Battle of Bannockburn

On June 23 and 24, 1314, Robert the Bruce led the Scots into battle against the English. This battle started off just the same as many of the Bruce's previous battles. The chances the Scots had were by no means great, considering that the English army harbored over 13,000 infantrymen, along with 3,000 cavalrymen and some Welsh archers. Robert the Bruce had a group of men that comprised 7,000 infantrymen and some cavalrymen as well. The English boasted over twice the number of men that Bruce had, and these were *trained* soldiers. Bruce mustered up many brave Scots, but they lacked training. The Bruce did have full Scottish support, as there were no more strongholds that were loyal to the English King Edward II. There was one castle that was still besieged by the English, and that was Stirling Castle. The men holding Stirling threatened to surrender to the Scots if the English did not bring in reinforcements by June 24.

Keep in mind that prior to 1307, Robert the Bruce had a very rough time trying to maintain his status. It was only a year before the Templar persecution that he was defeated at the Battle of Dail Righ in Ayrshire by John MacDougall of Lorn. By the spring of 1308, the Bruce had been victorious at the Battle of Inverurie in Aberdeenshire, and later in Argyll at the Pass of Brander. Within that past year, somehow Bruce became wealthy in victories, but also appeared to gain more money—because somehow he was able to provide his troops food and weaponry, which he wasn't able to do previously. Perhaps the funding came from an exiled order of monks who escaped Europe with considerable wealth. Would it be so far-fetched to propose that Bruce made a deal with the Templars, veterans of war who clearly know how to fight, to help defend Scotland in exchange for a new homeland?

Coincidentally, June 24 is the Feast Day of St. John the Baptist, whom the Knights Templar were accused of worshiping in the form of a severed silver head. All Masonic lodges today are dedicated to the holy St. John. It was on this second day of the Battle of Bannockburn that the Templars supposedly joined the Bruce in battle. This very obviously would have been a sacred day to the warrior monks, and how better to spend it than fighting for freedom for a country Jesus and Mary Magdalene themselves likely traversed and deemed sacred? The Templars knew what it was to be persecuted, to have to fight for freedom, and so they very likely could have aided the Bruce in fighting for Scotland.

Sir Henry St. Clair, 7th Baron of Rosslyn, along with his two sons John and William, fought alongside Robert the Bruce at

Bannockburn. William was purportedly a Knight Templar. Whether he was deemed Knight Templar before or after Bannockburn is unknown. Is there a chance he could have been initiated in the caves beneath MacDuff Castle in East Wemyss? Was he a Knight Templar at Bannockburn?

Sir Michael Wemyss of MacDuff Castle had once been a supporter of King Edward II, but for some reason, the tide had turned. He became a loyal supporter of Robert the Bruce, and even led his clan to Bannockburn. Their associations with the St. Clairs go back many decades before Bannockburn. The two families were consistently intermarrying, and both claimed descent from the House of David in Jerusalem.

If these two prominent Scottish families who supported the Bruce and fought at Bannockburn were aiding the Knights Templar and offering them shelter in Wemyss Caves, is it really so unlikely that the Templars also fought at Bannockburn? It was on the second day of battle that Robert the Bruce's *secret weapon* helped change the outcome not just of the battle, but of Scotland's future.

The soldiers who had fought on the first day of battle were extremely exhausted, and the second day proved to be even more taxing. Thankfully, the Bruce had a few tricks up his sleeve. The cavalry that was led by Sir Robert Keith had been held back until Bruce ordered them to attack the English army's Welsh archers. They quickly disbanded amongst the chaos. It was the next charge from the Scottish side that struck an unparalleled sense of fear into the English. This final charge that determined the fate of the battle has been the source of much academic debate. Right over the hill from where the battle was taking place is where this charge stemmed from. Some say it was just the small folk, the *ghillies,* who were made up of roughed up servants and cooks, that came cascading down the hill, weak and starved but with the patriotic spirit of Scotland within them.

But would this sight truly have caused the English to panic and flee in a matter of seconds? Likely not. Who or what could possibly appear to be so frightening to the English that it would cause them to break up and retreat in fear as they did? I propose there was truly only one thing: the elite special forces of the medieval era, men who were trained for war. Men that knew battle tactics like the back of their hand. Men who would have called themselves the Knights Templar. Could they have come just after Keith's cavalry? Another group of men, galloping over the hilltop or perhaps on foot, carrying weapons and using specific strategies used only in the Holy Land by the Knights Templar and the Saracens?

Robert the Bruce ended up claiming victory on the Feast Day of St. John the Baptist, as did Scotland gain Her freedom. Where the Templars were before, during, and after Bannockburn is something we are still trying to piece together. Whoever it was that came across the hill that day struck terror amongst the English, that much we know.

The second book of Sinclair journals,[5] yields an entry that confirms the Templars fought at Bannockburn, if in fact the journals can be authenticated. The journal entry is dated May 1, 1395. Whilst discussing their preparations for their journey across the Atlantic to what is now America, Henry writes, "Our goal is to find a better route to the empires of China further south than the ice covered lakes, and suitable land for settlement beyond the boundaries of Groenland which we visit on our journey. We also travel with 120 remaining Knights Templars, descendants of those at Bannockburn under my grandfather's rule in search of a free Templar state. We search for suitable places to transfer the Templar treasure hidden in Scotland."

If these journals can someday be authenticated, could this be proof that not only did the Sinclairs make multiple voyages to the New World before Columbus, but that the Knights Templar did, indeed fight at Bannockburn?

---

[5] Muir, Diana. *The Journals of Prince Henry Sinclair Vol. 2*, Books 2-10.

The Bringer of Life

Chapter 16
Roslin Chapel and
the Grail

With a chapel made famous by the movie *The Da Vinci Code*, Roslin is a small town just outside the capital city of Edinburgh. Roslin is decorated with myth and legend; some will say Merlin the magician wandered the woods here, others tell tales of modern children who lost several hours, even a day, of time in Roslin Glen, so many hours that a search party was sent out for them. Then. ideas that the Holy Grail may be hidden here, or the body of Mary Magdalene Herself emerged within the last half century; or were there earlier references to such great tales?

16.1 Templar and Masonic Connections

There are real Knights Templar and Masonic connections here, and much information pointing to Roslin Castle having been a reliquary of sacred ancient texts and perhaps other artifacts. The castle was said to house a scriptorium, which was beneath the castle and supposedly connected to several tunnels that are rumored to lead to the chapel. The building of the chapel began in 1446 by the Earl William St. Clair on what is known as a Shekhinah, Venus and Mercury rising together, which is when he placed the cornerstone. Not too much later a devastating fire struck the castle in 1452. While everyone was being evacuated from the castle, William was more concerned with evacuating several books and chests by frantically hurling them out the window. They must have been rather valuable considering that it wasn't his family he was hurling out the window!

August 2019 was my first visit to Roslin Chapel and Castle; I just so happened to be renting Roslin Castle, and had it all to myself. I managed to go down into the older part of the castle after unlocking a combination lock meant to keep kids and pets from venturing down to the lower un-lived in levels. Once down there the damp and cool air swirled around me. Dust and cobwebs were in every direction. What I can confirm is that on the lowest level were old rooms where likely the servants and monks stayed. There was a walled up doorway, sealed shut. Then another curious door that was locked, and there was no way I was getting that open without a key.

While walking through the glen, I made it to the exact spot where the kids allegedly spent an entire day and night, thinking it was merely a few hours. Right along the river there was a little carved out rock shelter spot, just big enough for a few kids to climb down into. While it was too muddy and I wasn't sure I wanted to risk losing so much time, I investigated the area from the banks of the river. I noticed the telltale sign that I was in the right place—ancient rock art on the opposite side of the river. Timeless symbols like spirals and star markings were carved and well weathered on the rocky riverside. This rock art was around 3,000-5,000 years old, which was a pretty good indication that something has been luring people to Roslin for quite some time. Some have suggested

Roslin Chapel with the Engrailed Cross of the St. Clairs.

Baron of Roslin, William St. Clair became the Grand Master of Scotland in 1737.

that Roslin is a portal of some kind, which I would not write off. There is something special about the place that is ancient and powerful that I don't think anyone can really put into words yet.

One of the most interesting things that I saw inside Roslin Castle was a 16th century tapestry in the library room. This tapestry happened to have an iconic image on it: *the Birth of Venus*. There is Venus, looking entirely like Mary Magdalene with Her flowing red locks of hair, standing proudly on the clamshell, another symbol of the goddess. Did the St. Clairs revere the sacred feminine, I wondered? Or was it really a veiled reference to their alleged ancestor, Mary Magdalene? Later that same year I read the Sinclair journals for the first time.

The first book of the Sinclair journals confirms that the Sinclairs were outwardly good Catholics, while privately they worshiped the goddess in Her many different facets. She was worshiped as many different goddesses, and as many different elements, but at the root of all of it was the one *Great Goddess,* just as God is called by many names today. Following are entries from the journals.

May 21, 1354

Today we celebrated the Bright Mother Goddess Day with our new friends. They too celebrate the Great Goddess who brings life to them throughout the year. We have many similarities.

Note: This entry is referring to Henry's interaction with the indigenous people in the Americas. This could have been some kind of holiday related to a planetary alignment, the celebration of St. Brigid, or the celebration of the birth anniversary of the Goddess Sita who is an emanation of the Goddess Lakshmi. Or potentially this could be an old Pagan holiday that we do not know about.

Sep 16, 1354

Today we celebrate the Greek festival of [the goddess] Demeter. I wish I were old enough to participate in the rituals but am happy my father includes me in the festival.

Note: The festival in question is Thesmophoria. It was one of the most widespread Greek festivals in the Old World. Demeter was heavily associated with the constellation Virgo the Virgin.

Mar 9, 1357

Today my mother participated in the festival to honor all Mother Goddesses along with my sister Margaret. Father Dominic is teaching me about the old religion and is also teaching me Greek. It is difficult and I much prefer Latin.

Note: Early March was rife with celebrations of the goddess. March 8 was the celebration of the Greek goddess Artemis. March 9 was the celebration of Aphrodite and her Divine Union/Hieros Gamos with Adonis. On March 10 the old goddess Anna Perenna was honored. No wonder he says *all* Mother goddesses!

Sep 29, 1364

Today we celebrated Michaelmas which my expectant bride has enjoyed very much. She is happy and well and looks forward to becoming a mother. Tomorrow I must ride to the nearby villages where they celebrate the Feast day of Saint Sophia. She is the mother of Faith, Hope and Charity and is known as the Goddess of Wisdom. I pray that she grants me wisdom in becoming a father and a good Lord to my people.

Note: Sophia is the gnostic goddess of Wisdom and Creation. She is the mother and the wife of God. Her feast day is September 30th, which Henry was going to attend.

Aug 3, 1365

Today we celebrate the festival of Artemis the Goddess of the Hunt and of the Moon.

Note: The festival of Artemis took place this day. The Romans celebrated Her too, but to them She was known as Diana or Diana Lucifera—*Diana the Bringer of Light.*

May 31, 1368

We have arrived in Norway in time for the Feast of the Triple Goddess. I give thanks to the Great Goddess and ask her to bless me in my life that I may fulfill her will. We meet in the morning with King Magnus and his court.

Note: May 31 is indeed the Feast Day of the Triple Goddess where the Spring Maiden becomes the Bountiful Mother. Also on this day is the ancient Roman Festival of Persephone.

These journals, if they can be verified, once again will provide lots of insight into who the Sinclairs were, and what secret and mysterious traditions they practiced. The journal entries certainly point towards a family who practices the old ways as well as the new religion of the era: Catholicism.

Debate surrounding the Templar connections to Roslin Chapel has arisen, but as always the truth prevails. In fact there *are* legitimate Templar links to the chapel and the Sinclairs. A certain William St. Clair, son of Henry St. Clair, 7th Baron of Roslin, was tasked with taking the heart of King Robert the Bruce to the Church of the Holy Sepulchre in the Holy Land, along with his brother John, Sir James Douglas and Sir Robert Logan of Restalrig. While crossing through Spain in 1330, they were set upon by Moors. They never made it to their destination. William, his brother John, and Douglas were killed. An effigy to William de St. Claire with a marker "Knight Templar" remains in Roslin Chapel. There are no documents that mention when he was initiated into the Brotherhood of the Knights Templar, whether it was before or after the Battle of Bannockburn in 1314, where the Templars were said to be the secret weapon of Robert the Bruce. We know with certainty that Henry, 7th Baron of Roslin, was by the side of Robert the Bruce, along with his two sons William and John, at Bannockburn.

The year 1441 yielded a new honor bestowed upon William St. Clair the builder— he was appointed by King James II the Patron and Protector of the Masons of Scotland. This became a hereditary position, and a few hundred years later, another Baron of Roslin named William St. Clair became Grand Master in Scotland in 1737. It becomes blatantly obvious that though an official organization of "Freemasonry" was not perhaps established, there was some type of significance to the craftmasons of the day. To make the St. Clairs hereditary grand masters and protectors of the craft indicate that there was something special about their family, what they believed, and perhaps what they knew.

The St. Clairs of Roslin clearly have a long history with Freemasonry and the Knights Templar, that is no longer in question. Knowing that protecting certain Masonic traditions, which we know stem from very ancient practices, was something of a hereditary duty of the family, would it really be shocking to think that Roslin Chapel is in possession of certain ancient texts, knowledge, and artifacts? Were the prized possessions removed during the fire at Roslin Castle brought to the chapel? Chances are the answer is *yes.*

16.2 The Battle of Roslin

On my first visit to Roslin, when I stayed at the castle, I experienced something eerie in the night. The woman who had checked me in had told me to listen for the White Lady who guards the treasure of Roslin Castle, as she was meant to make her debut at midnight. I never heard the White Lady, but I heard something else. Spending the night in a castle on your own is a bit intimidating, but I took comfort in knowing that I was at least locked in behind some very thick walls. No one was getting in, nor getting out.

I had been laying awake, waiting to hear the ghostly song floating through the castle, but instead I heard shouting, screaming, clanking of metal, that sounded as if it were coming from outside. I did not dare go outside to investigate. Instead, I tried to ignore the sounds that obviously sounded like fighting taking place beneath the castle down in the glen. Were there just kids getting drunk and fighting down in the glen? What was I hearing? I had goosebumps, as I imagined it sounded quite like a battle occurring, and for some reason I felt I was experiencing something that wasn't meant for me. Or was it?

After the first night alone in the castle, I did not hear anymore nightly activity. No White Lady. No fighting down in the glen. I brushed it off. That is until I was on my flight back to Texas, many days later. While on the long haul flight, a small voice inside me said *why don't you see if there is any connection between the Ramsays and the St. Clairs of Roslin?* I began searching for connections between the two prominent families.

My ancestors, the Ramsays, the Earls of Dalhousie, resided in Dalhousie Castle just down the road from the St. Clairs. They would have *surely* known each other right? Right. The first thing that appeared on my Internet search was the "Battle of Roslin." Chills ran down my spine. There was a Lady Margaret Ramsay of Dalhousie Castle, one of my Ramsay ancestors, who had caught the eye of two young men: the English lieutenant of King Edward I, the knight John de Segrave, and the dashing Scottish Henry St. Clair of Roslin, who was to be Lord of Roslin. According to the legend, Segrave often used to wine and dine Margaret and her family at Dalhousie. He was always out to impress her. However, it was at Henry's knighting at Roslin Castle in 1297 where he appointed Margaret to do the honors as his queen of the day, that they announced their betrothal. Sir Symon Fraser, a Scottish noble, knighted Henry. Many other nobles were present, including William Wallace, the guardian of Scotland.

The news of the happy couple and their marriage in 1302 got back to the not so happy Segrave in the early part of 1303. He was furious, as he intended to marry the Lady Margaret but also because this marriage could further cement the strong ties the St. Clairs had to France. France then was an imposing threat against English rule of Scotland. If France armed and supported the Scots, they could become a country free from the tyrannical rule of the English crown.

When Segrave found out he immediately wrote to King Edward, and asked for permission to march on Scotland to wage war. An army of approximately 30,000 English soldiers gathered in the Scottish borders, where Segrave had them split into three smaller groups. One group headed to Borthwick Castle, another to the home of Lady Margaret herself: Dalhousie Castle, and a third army went to Roslin to eliminate the Lord of Roslin, Henry St. Clair.

The eve before the battle, the Scottish army under John Comyn set up camp in the woods. Early the next morning during the dark hours, on February 24, 1303, Comyn's men launched a surprise attack on Segrave's forces who slept by the River Esk. This is the river that both Dalhousie and Roslin sit upon. A total slaughter ensued. The English soldiers who managed to escape were picked off by other Scots in the area; there was no mercy shown for these men. Next, Comyn's troops moved to Dalhousie Castle, which had been laid under siege by Sir Ralph de Confrey, the second army of Segrave. Confrey ordered his men to march towards the Scots near the summit of Langhill. Comyn's archers and pikemen left no survivors.

With battle still left to do, the Scots looked to the west to the Pentland Hills where they saw a saltire cross set on fire. Cistercian monks led by Prior Abernethy, who very likely was a retired Knight Templar, had set the cross ablaze in order to rile the Scots' spirits for their third battle—if they had won two battles, it was God's will they win all three. Men were mustered, including the Knights Hospitaller in West Lothian from Torphichen Preceptory.

The English and Scottish forces met above the Esk River. With the knowledge of the glen, the terrain, and the English not familiar with the territory, the Scots successfully ambushed the English by closing in on them after forming a crescent formation. There were approximately 8,000 Scots, while the English had an army of 30,000, of which only 2,000 English soldiers survived by the end of it all. Segrave was captured and imprisoned by Henry St. Clair before he was ransomed back to the English crown. Henry St. Clair went on to sign the Declaration of Arbroath in 1320. As far as we know, Lady Margaret and Lord Henry lived happily ever after. Today, a small token of the connection between the Ramsays of Dalhousie and the St. Clairs of Roslin can be found in Dalhousie Castle's chapel: a modern replica of one of the small statues of Roslin Chapel bearing the engrailed cross.

16.3 The Grail Families

There are many different legends about the origin of the St. Clairs of Roslin. Where did they come from? Who are they? Are they really the descendants of Jesus and Mary Magdalene as many modern writers suggest? While Roslin Chapel is full of symbolism, are there any symbols that allude to the Holy Grail, or a royal bloodline?

Inside Roslin Chapel, the ceilings are adorned with a section of five-pointed stars (representing Venus), lilies, and roses. The flowers, five-pointed stars, and roses are all symbols of the goddess. The roses tend to play a paramount role in this chapel considering that the name of the chapel and town is *Roslin*. There are many debates about the origin of the name—some argue it is named after the nearby waterfall, or *linne* in Scots Gaelic. Others argue it stemmed from the name Rosalind, which in Latin was *rosa linda,* or "lovely rose."

The rose has long been a symbol of secrecy, but also of the goddess. In ancient Roman mythology, Cupid gave the god Harpocrates a rose so that he would not reveal the secrets of the goddess Venus. Harpocrates was the god of silence and secrecy, an adaptation of the Egyptian god Horus, who also presided over secrecy and mystery. The phrase "sub rosa" or beneath the rose, has been indicative of keeping a secret for a very long time, beginning in Rome. Roses were offered to the goddess Venus in Porta Collina rites from as early as 500 BC. The Iliad tells of Aphrodite protecting the body of Hector using the "immortal oil of the rose." In Egyptian mythology, the rose was a symbol of Isis, and was often depicted next to Her within her temples at Thebes. Isis was a goddess associated with the afterlife and resurrection. The rose was a symbol of this as it bloomed, died, and then bloomed once again. The rose was associated with Astarte, Ishtar, and Inanna as well. It was always a symbol for the sacred feminine.

Dan Brown of *The Da Vinci Code*, asserts in his novel that the site was named after the *rose line* which was connected to the Paris Meridian. The rose line, then, actually pointed to the *bloodline* that "hid beneath the rose" at Roslin Chapel. Many argue that Roslin is in fact on a ley line, a line of concentrated earth energy that the ancients built monuments on. Prior to the St. Clairs' arrival in Roslin, it was said that the site where the chapel stands now was originally a Pagan temple. People inhabited Roslin Glen for thousands of years, clearly seeing the place having some spiritual significance. Maybe it is indeed a portal as many have suggested. Roslin Chapel literature even mentions that geomancers claim that two ley lines intersect in the northeast part of the chapel, a place where a vortex is said to be present.[1]

Mother Mary was often called *Mary of the Rose.* Why? There are biblical references from the Song of Solomon: "I am the Rose of Sharon, the lily of the valley." Here is Solomon speaking to his bride, saying that the rose or the lily has some kind of connection

---

[1] https://www.Roslinchapel.com/wp-content/uploads/2020/02/256_Roslin_Article_Ley_Lines_and_Roslin_Chapel.pdf

to his own family, or lineage, which later Jesus would be a part of. Isaiah 11:1 mentions that, "a shoot shall sprout from the stump of Jesse, and from his roots a bud shall blossom."

A poem called "Rosa Mystica" was written in 1875 by Gerard Manley Hopkins in devotion to Mother Mary. One line reads, "Mary the Virgin, well the heart knows, She is the mystery, She is that rose." If it was carrying on royal bloodlines that deemed Her a rose, Mary Magdalene is also a rose. If there was a bloodline that continued beyond Jesus and Magdalene, where did that family go?

A book appeared in 1982 that stirred up controversy all over the world: *The Holy Blood and the Holy Grail* by the authors Henry Lincoln, Michael Baigent, and Richard Leigh. In this book, many different secretive societies were discussed in relation to their part in concealing a larger than life secret: the royal bloodline of Jesus, or the Holy Grail. They proclaim that upon Mary Magdalene's flight to France after the crucifixion She gave birth to a child there. That child rooted a new dynasty in France called the *Merovingians*.

Is there any evidence to support this? Going back to the beginning of their dynasty, the first king of the line to give them their infamous name was King Merovech, also known as Merovius. He was allegedly the son of Chlodio, King of Franks, who was born around 390 AD near the Rhine. King Chlodio was likely descended from Salian Franks, who began settling the Belgium area as early as the 300s AD.

According to the *Chronicles of Fredegar*, Chlodio married a woman who fell pregnant in 410 AD, but not with his own child. Chlodio's wife went for a swim in the North Sea. She was attacked and impregnated by a "beast of Neptune" or a sea monster—really. The sea creature was said to have horns and resemble a quinotaur. The quinotaur is a mythical five-horned bull-like sea creature. Could this have been more of a symbolic way of telling a story of origin?

Was this so odd a story in antiquity? I would suggest, *no,* in fact there are many creation stories of ancient times that suggest life sprang from the "primordial waters." The Egyptians taught that the world emerged from an infinite and lifeless sea (who was Nun/Naunet, goddess of the primordial waters, or sometimes her consort Nu) when suddenly the Sun rose for the very first time.

This is often called zp tpj (Zep Tepi), which translates to "the first occasion." Interestingly the primordial waters, Nun, was also associated with *chaos* similar to the Gnostic creation story that Jesus taught. It was from this dark and primeval abyss that the original mound of land rose.

There was an Egyptian deity who was born from the primordial waters and also happened to be a sea beast called "Heryshaf." His name literally meant "He Who is on His Lake" or even "Lord of the Waters/Lake." Heryshaf was a half-ram deity that likely reflected the age of Aries. He was associated with Ra and Osiris in ancient Egyptian tradition, as well as Dionysus or Heracles in the Greek tradition.

The ancient Egyptian kingly line claimed descent from the original gods of creation, but specifically Horus, which is why the pharaoh ritually embodied Horus, god on Earth. Therefore, would not all pharaohs of this royal line be descended from the "sea beasts" of the primordial waters? Could this be the basis for a connection between the Merovingian bloodline and the Egyptian lineage of the pharaohs?

Many different religions and traditions hold that there is some kind of "lake" or even "fiery lake" that has some relationship to judgment after death, not at all dissimilar to the Christian idea of Judgment Day. In the Egyptian Book of the Dead, they often reference the "Lake of Fire." In the "fifth hour" (in their cosmology of a day) depicts the lake in the *Amduat*. The Amduat is a funerary text also known as "Text of the Hidden Chamber Which is in the Underworld" that was reserved only for pharaohs in the New Kingdom. It gave names to certain gods, demons, and more, that only the king-high priest should know. Duat, which is the realm of the dead, is represented by the pentagram—the symbol of Venus. This connection between the Egyptian Underworld and Venus likely stems from Venus's time beneath the horizon during Her synodic cycle, which the ancients equated with the Underworld.

It is in the lake in Egyptian cosmology that there is a pyramid which is connected to Isis, and beneath this pyramid is the tomb of Osiris. During the sixth hour in Egyptian cosmology, the "ba" or the spirit/body of Osiris reunites with the soul of the king/pharaoh. It is at the sixth hour of Jesus's appearance on the cross that he

274

"dies" and is removed from the cross.

The book of Revelation also refers to a fiery lake, and the first beast to make an appearance is coincidentally the "beast of the sea." Revelation says that the "great whore" or the "Whore of Babylon" sits upon the beast. Revelation 17 says, "Come hither; I will shew unto thee the judgment of the great whore that sitteth upon many waters. With whom the kings of the earth have committed fornication, and the inhabitants of the earth have been made drunk with the wine of Her fornication."

It is obvious the connection the "whore" has to the waters and the sea beast. The Holy Spirit is also said to sit on the "face of the waters" of the Earth in Genesis. However, it would appear that the whore in this case is associated with the old ways of the goddess worshiping societies, which were deemed wrong throughout the bible; on multiple occasions the women were called out for worshiping the Queen of Heaven and not Yahweh. Revelation goes on to tell us that She has a secret name written on Her forehead, a great mystery was her name. It is much like how the Jews were not allowed to say the name of Yahweh; only the high priest was permitted to invoke his name in the temple.

I find the parallel between Revelation's whore upon the sea beast and the story of how Chlodio was conceived—his mother being raped by a sea beast—most intriguing. Was Merovech actually literally sired by a sea beast? No, probably not, but to tell this story would show something special about their lineage, giving them legitimacy to rule. There is always the possibility they told this story because it is one that has been passed down through many early cultures, like the Egyptian pharaohs descending from the gods of the primordial waters. If the Merovingians were descended from them, would it not make perfect sense for them to claim a connection to this story to honor their ancestry?

Obviously Jesus's ministry was heavily centered around the ocean, as he and his followers were "fishers of men" and performed baptism using water, beneath the astrological Age of Pisces. Jesus, who likely descended from Egyptian and Mesopotamian kings, probably was familiar with the story of the miraculous conception of baby Horus by Isis, whose husband was dead. The idea of a miraculous or somehow extraordinary conception within a royal

275

lineage is an age-old concept. Perhaps this is why he too was said to be conceived by some awesome and divine means.

The Mesopotamian goddess of the primordial waters was called Nammu, who arose from the sea. She was known as "She who gave birth to the heavens and the earth" as well as "She has given birth to the great gods." The storyline is not limited to one culture, but appears to go back much further. Do these connections prove that the Merovingians were descended from the ancient royal lines of the Mesopotamians or Egyptians? No, but it does show there were common themes that absolutely line up, many centuries apart.

Another take on the legend of Merovech's mother being impregnated by the sea creature is that it could be an allegory for whatever bloodline was contributed by her own ancestry. Certain traditions, such as Judaism, are passed down through the maternal line: you are only Jewish if your mother carries Jewish blood. Perhaps she carried a bloodline that in some way had connections to the ocean, the god Neptune, etc.

The Holy Blood and the Holy Grail (let us say *HBGB* for short) mentions the supernatural elements of the Merovingians, in saying, "Merovingian monarchs were occult adepts, initiates in arcane sciences, practitioners of esoteric arts—worthy rivals of Merlin, their fabulous near-contemporary. They were often called 'the sorcerer kings' or 'thaumaturge kings'. By virtue of some miraculous property in their blood they could allegedly heal by laying on of hands...

"They all supposedly bore a distinctive birthmark, which distinguished them from all other men, which rendered them immediately identifiable and which attested to their semi-divine or sacred blood. This birthmark reputedly took the form of a red cross, either over the heart—a curious anticipation of the Templar blazon—or between the shoulder blades."

The Merovingians claimed descent from the biblical Noah, and likely because of this birthmark. Deuteronomy 33:12 reads of the blessing Moses bestowed upon the forefathers of the twelve tribes of Israel. Of Benjamin, Moses says, "The beloved of the Lord shall dwell in safety by him; and the Lord shall cover him all the day long, and he shall dwell between his shoulders." Did the Benjamites carry the same birthmark between their shoulder blades? Could Noah's alleged ark and surviving the flood have anything to do with the famed sea creature? One proposed lineage of Mary Magdalene also has her descending from the tribe of Benjamin, a Benjamite princess. Is this another tie between the Merovingians and Mary Magdalene? The Benjamites were known for worshiping the Golden Calf in ritual, which in turn could be associated with worship of the Mother Goddess. Could the bull aspect of the sea beast be connected to the Benjamite lineage? Is it possible that this tradition began during the Age of Taurus, and continued for thousands of years into the Age of Pisces during Jesus's ministry? Or is it all completely unrelated? For now we don't know for certain, but we can speculate.

Further, the Merovingians were known for their long hair which also had magical properties. Mary Magdalene is always shown with her long flowing and uncovered hair. The Nazirites of biblical times also kept long hair, which during their vow they were not allowed to cut; take Samson for example. The Nazirites were not too different from the Essenes, both being mystical Jewish sects. In the year 754 AD, Childeric III was deposed and imprisoned. The pope then ordered his hair to be shorn as an insult to his spirituality, lineage, and power.

The link between their spiritual prowess and kingship is undeniably similar to that of the early priest-kings of Judah, and before that of the pharaohs of Egypt. Once more, in *HBGB* it is pointed out that, "Skulls found of Merovingian monarchs, for example, bear what appears to be a ritual incision or hole in the crown. Similar incisions can be found in the skulls of high priests of early Tibetan Buddhism—to allow the soul to escape on death, and to open direct contact with the divine." If this is true, it could perhaps link specific Tibetan traditions with the Merovingians, and I must point out that evidence has suggested that Jesus spent time in Tibet, which might draw another connection.

A later Merovingian king, Clovis, made a pact with the Roman Catholic Church after converting. It was then that he was made what was referred to as the "new Constantine" governing over the west as emperor, but maintaining a strong bond with the other leading power of the era, the pope.

Later, after a series of unfortunate events, Merovingian prince Dagobert II, was kidnapped and shipped off to Ireland; there he married a Celtic princess named Mathilde. She died giving birth to their third child, and Dagobert returned to Europe and took a second wife. He aligned himself with another royal family by marrying Giselle de Razes, daughter of the count of Razes and niece of the king of the Visigoths. Giselle's home was the infamous Rennes-le-Chateau in southern France, whose chapel is dedicated to none other than Mary Magdalene. It's said they were even married in this very chapel. He had a son and was able to claim kingship once more.

The continuance of the Merovingian bloodline has not been proven, but it likely lives on in many people of today's world. The word itself has etymological origins meaning both "mother" and "sea" which is precisely what the name Mary/Maria can be linked to. The second half of the word being *vin* or vine. Could this be even seen as "the vine of Mary" or perhaps "the vine of the Mother" inferring that the Merovingians were of royal descent by way of a special or divine ancestral mother?

The Da Vinci Code purports that the St. Clairs of Roslin were in fact descendants of the Merovingians, truly descendants of Jesus and Magdalene. Tales of antiquity tell of Mary Magdalene fleeing to France and taking with her the Holy Grail. Other legends tell of Joseph of Arimathea taking the Grail to Britain. Is there any real connection between the St. Clairs of Roslin Chapel and the Merovingian dynasty?

The family crest of the St. Clairs from about 1500 onwards into the 17th century showed the engrailed cross beneath what appears to be a representation of the female reproductive system: the fallopian tubes, ovaries, and the womb. Sitting above is the dove—a symbol of the goddess for thousands of years, and later to be a symbol of the Holy Spirit, or Holy Sophia.

To the left of the cross is the griffin. Griffins were notoriously used as a symbol of Wisdom, but also of protection. In mythological legends, griffins were guardians of a treasure hoard that they would hide high up in the mountains. Does this symbol on their coat of arms imply that the St. Clairs could have been guarding a great treasure? Are they still?

278

The St. Clair Coat of Arms, sculpted c. 1500.

To the right of the cross you'll find a mermaid, which was a symbol that was condemned by the Catholic Church, which is a bit odd considering the St. Clairs were a prominent Catholic family. The mermaid symbol has always represented rebirth, fertility, sexuality, and the mother of the sea. The Catholic Church always saw it as an evil symbol of lust and temptation, because the Catholic Church hates anything that gives power to the feminine, and anything sexual in general. The mermaid is the *goddess* of the sea, which is why sailors began to fasten figures of them to the front of their ships for protection in the 1500s. The goddess of the

279

sea, was capable of both protection and destruction, which is why sailors had Her guarding their ship.

She holds in one hand seaweed, which represents the deeper mysteries, "what lies beneath the surface" and appears to be hidden from someone outside of the water. It can represent the unconscious aspect of self, but also a secret. She holds the seaweed, the secret in Her hand. In the other hand She carries a torch to navigate the dark depths of the abyss. The torch is an obvious symbol for light, or enlightenment.

It must be pointed out that the mermaid too is a sea creature, and one could even argue that She represents the beginning of creation since many cultures attributed creation to the primordial waters, and to the feminine. Half fish, half goddess. Could this be a link to the Merovingian dynasty? Believing that their origin was also of the sea? The mother of Merovech would have been human, but her womb filled with the seed of a sea creature. She would have embodied both the goddess and sea creature aspects.

Is this a symbol of the St. Clair's family origins? Do they guard a great secret? The coat of arms is almost entirely made up of symbolism of the goddess—it is clear that She was important to the family. Could this be part of a royal bloodline that stems back thousands of years through different cultures? Could it be a more recent tradition? Beginning perhaps with Mary Magdalene? A tradition remembered and passed down through each generation? Why is it that the female reproductive system makes an appearance in the family coat of arms? What significance does the female womb have to the St. Clairs, and so much so that it is on the coat of arms for everyone to see? Was something passed down through a maternal line, or from a divine ancestress? This coat of arms can be seen upon the ceiling of the old withdrawing room/dining room in Roslin Castle.

In the year 1546 Mary of Guise, wife of James V and mother of Mary Queen of Scots, had visited Roslin Chapel on its 100th anniversary to meet with Sir William St. Clair, grandson of William the Builder. During this time Mary of Guise was acting as Queen Regent since Mary Queen of Scots was just four years old. During her visit she must have been shown something rather important, as she writes in a letter after her visit: "We bind and oblige us to the said Sir William, and shall be a loyal and true mistress to him. His counsel and secret shown to us we shall keep secret, and in all matters give to him the best and truest counsel we can, as we shall be required thereto."

This letter is rather strange, considering that Mary is the acting queen of Scotland, yet her attitude appears quite subservient to William St. Clair. What was it that was so important that she would pledge loyalty, protection, and secrecy to her own vassal? Not only did she do that, but she also gave him a yearly pension of 300 merks, which does not sound like a lot, but it is about £54,900 in today's economy. That is a lot of money for the crown to be giving out, all because of this "secret" she was shown at Roslin Chapel. Mary herself was the granddaughter of René II of Anjou and Lorraine. Both Renés had inherited the title "King of Jerusalem" which descended from Godfrey of Bouillon's brother, Baldwin. Her own lineage was special, coming from these prominent families, which have been speculated to be a part of the "Grail" lineage.

What was this secret that she was shown at Roslin exactly? Was it the vault where the St. Clair knights lay buried? Was it a treasure? Was it the Holy Rood and the crown jewels from Holyrood Palace that the St. Clairs had been entrusted with a few years earlier? Was it artifacts and old texts? Was it a bloodline? The grail itself?

Are there other families that carry these traditions as well? A closely related lineage stems from another prominent family who lived just down the road from the St. Clairs of Roslin. The Ramsays of Dalhousie. The link between the two families was made clear in the section on the Battle of Roslin. For many centuries the two families made marriage alliances with each other, but also within a small circle of other prominent Scottish nobility. Was there anything particularly special about the Ramsay ancestry? We cannot be sure, just as we cannot be entirely sure about the St. Clair lineage; all we can do is investigate and hypothesize until further evidence comes forward.

One of the few things we are able to investigate regarding the Ramsays are the legends and lore behind the origin of the clan. As early as 1066, it was said a pirate, the progenitor of the Ramsay clan, followed William the Conqueror to Britain. In the year of 1124 a knight of Norman descent named Symon de Ramesie accompanied the Earl of Huntingdon, who became King David I, to Scotland and saw him installed as king. King David saw fit to gift him with the lands of Dalhousie, then called Dalwolsey. The original castle here was first constructed by Symon. His last name tells us he came likely from the area of Ramsey in England, which was a town built up around the Ramsey Abbey which had been established in 969 AD by Oswald, Bishop of Worcester on land donated by Æthelwine, Ealdorman of East Anglia (Earl Ailwyn).

Prior to the official establishment of the abbey, there had already been a small wooden chapel built. The hermitage had been decided by the fateful actions and indications of a bull.[2] Before the bull, the island had been inhabited by nothing other than natural vegetation and one single animal, specifically a single *ram*. The site itself was actually a small island that rose up in the middle of a marshy lake area, making it difficult to get to until a causeway had been built, hence the name coming from "ram's island." The body of water surrounding the island was known as the Ramsey-Mere, mer being the root word for sea in many old languages including French, but also the French word mère meaning *mother*. As we know, the sea and the goddess (or mother) are inextricably linked. The Ramsey Chronicler tells us that nearby was a sandy shore where many local people fished and was known as Mersham. Sham/Shem is a Hebrew word meaning *divine*. It is important to remember that the early Egyptian title of God's wife that later became a popular name was *Miriam,* beloved of Amen. It is odd that the Hebrew word "sham/shem" should have been in use by the local Anglo people at this time unless there was some type of Hebrew influence.

The name of the beachy area could be interpreted as the "divine mother" but also as the "divine sea" as it was teeming with marine life which provided food and sustenance to the people. The ram was clearly a sacred symbol of the island, being that it existed there prior to anyone else, and on its own at that. The ram was a very important symbol, but not just to the abbey. It was the symbol of the primordial Egyptian god Amen, but also of the Egyptian

---

[2] https://ramseyabbey.co.uk/founding/

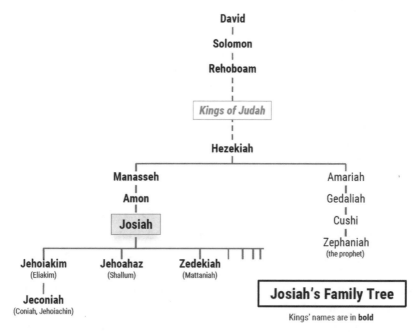

David
|
Solomon
|
Rehoboam
|
Kings of Judah
|
Hezekiah

Manasseh — Amariah
Amon — Gedaliah
Josiah — Cushi
— Zephaniah (the prophet)

Jehoiakim (Eliakim) — **Jehoahaz** (Shallum) — **Zedekiah** (Mattaniah)

Jeconiah (Coniah, Jehoiachin)

Josiah's Family Tree

Kings' names are in **bold**

Josiah's Family Tree.

god Heryshaf we mentioned earlier, being "Lord of the Lake." The ram on the island here almost fulfills this story of the gods being born from the primordial waters and rising up on a mound of earth from these primordial waters. It is nearly identical to Egyptian creation myth.

Was there really a single ram seen grazing on this island? Or was it all allegory? Is it possible there was an existing Egyptian tradition in the area? Did Egyptians perhaps travel here, or followers of the Egyptian traditions, and leave behind their own stories of creation? I must also mention that the name is awfully similar to the Egyptian *Ramses*, which was a dynastic name in ancient Egypt. The establishment of this dynasty came following Ahkenaten's attempt to convert the Egyptian people to worshiping a single deity, Aten. Ramses I restored the original religion of Amen—the god represented by the ram, amongst many of the other gods and goddesses. Amen was a mystery god, one who only shared his mysteries with the worthy initiates, much the same as Jesus.

Another Old World connection to the name Ramsay can be found in the Arabic language. Still to this day a popular Arabic boy's name is *Ramzi*. The name has a couple of different meanings. In the Quran, the word ramz meant a secret code, gesture, or symbol. It is used in the Quran verse 3:41 when it says, "He said, 'My Lord, grant me a sign.' The angel said, 'Your sign is that you will not be able to speak to people for three days except by *signs*." The boy's name *Ramzi* literally means "he who keeps secrets." Jesus also did not speak to people for three days as he went through ritual death and resurrection; he instead underwent a period of personal contemplation and reflection.

The Ramsey Abbey crest contains three ram's heads, the ram being a distinct symbol of the abbey. William Dugdale in his 1836 publication *Monasticon Anglicanum: A History of the Abbies and Other Monasteries and Cathedral and Collegiate Churches in England and Wales, Volume 2* mentioned that documented was an abbot whose seal contained a *ram in the sea*, but it is not clear when or for whom this seal originated. A ram rising from the sea seems in essence Egyptian, following right along with the stories of Heryshaf and Amen.

A beautiful artifact remains from Ramsey Abbey known as the Ramsey Abbey Incense Boat. It was made around 1350, and was found in the 19th century about seven to eight miles from Ramsey Abbey in Whittlesea Mere after it had been drained. The incense boat has a ram's head rising from the water adorning each end of the object. It likely ended up being hidden in Whittlesea Mere after the dissolution of the monasteries across Britain—one of few valuable artifacts from the abbey that survive today. The origin of the Ramsay clan and of the abbey are steeped in mystery that seem to have rather mysterious ties to old Egyptian and Hebrew tradition.

The clan crest contains the clan's motto which is "Pray and work" or in Latin: *Ora et labora*. This is interestingly the *same* motto of the Cistercian monks, the same white-robed monks that founded the Knights Templar. Again, this is why the Templars wore white tunics. In the center of the crest the unicorn is also seen, providing another mystical intrigue which ties the family to the most famous royal lineage of Scotland.

The Stuarts are another family I could write about for ages, but I will keep this bit limited to what is really significant. The House of Stuart is often known as the *House of the Unicorn* because it was the dynasty to adopt the unicorn as the national animal of Scotland. Indeed it is a mythical beast, the unicorn, but it held substantial significance to the Stuart family. Sometimes the unicorn was used as an allegory for Christ in the medieval era, but even earlier than that the unicorn was seen to have a horn that held healing properties. The accounts of a unicorn go back to 400 BC, and there are even more primitive accounts before that of a similar creature. They were first mentioned being in India, Tibet, and the Himalayas[3] which is one of the regions that Jesus allegedly made an appearance in.

The unicorn was very much a symbol for the Stuart line, but one could also argue it was a symbol for Jesus's bloodline as well. In the 3rd century AD, St. Basil refers to Jesus as the "Son of Unicorns" because he too was irresistible in might and unsubjected to man. The unicorn in this sense can be equated with the lineage of "god-kings" or "priest-kings" established in ancient Judah.

Is there any evidence that the Stuarts could be a part of a more ancient royal bloodline, tying it to Judah, and to King David himself? What is their claim to royal fame exactly? The Stuart bloodline can be traced back through Banquo, Thane of Lochaber, who was descended from Kenneth MacAlpin, and even from Áedán mac Gabráin, father of the supposed King Arthur (Arthur mac Aedan). Following this line back, it takes us to the High Kings of Ireland.

In 586 BC Nebuchadnezzar, king of Babylon, conquered Jerusalem. The biblical prophet Jeremiah fled to Egypt with his scribe Baruch and the princess of Judah, daughter of the King of Judah, Zedekiah. There the Pharaoh Hophra allowed the group to stay at one of his palaces, and looked after Teia as his own daughter. The palace, although now in ruins at Tel Defneh, is known today as "Quasr Bint el Jehudi" which means "Palace of the Daughter of Judah." From here Jeremiah took the princess to Ireland. Supposedly he is the one who brought the Stone of Destiny to Ireland, but that conflicts with the tradition that Scota and Gaythelos brought it nearly one thousand years earlier. Could both stories be true, could there have been multiple stones that Jacob slept on? "...He took of the *stones* of that place, and put

---

[3] *Indica.*

them for his *pillows,* and lay down in that place to sleep." (Genesis 28:11-12)

Going back to the princess of Judah and her escape to Ireland, Jeremiah made sure they were going to be well taken care of. With their ancestral seat of Jerusalem being taken over by Babylon, there needed to be another way to establish the Judaic royal lineage elsewhere, somewhere far enough away that the bloodline could be protected. Ireland seemed a good solution, and Jeremiah had the Princess Teia Tephi married to Eochaidh, the High King of Ireland. This instilled the Davidian bloodline into the High Kings of Ireland that later became the Kings of Dalriada and Scotland, the same kings that the Stuarts claim descent from.

There are many other families that have ties and connections to mythological beginnings, but I will save those for a later time. One could argue that these ties to the Scottish families are simply conjecture, but there appear to be more connections and coincidences than not. It could be that none of this is significant, but it could also be that it is. That is up to you as the reader to decide for yourself.

The King's Knot, Stirling, UK.

Chapter 17
Traditions of the Goddess Preserved

There would seem to be a very primordial connection to certain words, a connection that seems to span across the entire planet. Why is that? Are all humans at some basic level connected in thought process, or in evolution?

17.1 The Goddess Etymology

Have you ever wondered why the first word out of most babies' lips is "ma-ma?" This is universal, and not just in English speaking countries. According to Russian linguist Roman Jakobson, the easiest vocalizations for babies to make are open mouthed vowel sounds. Also according to Jakobson, babies tend towards the "m" consonant sound because this is easiest to make with their mouth around their mothers' breast when feeding. It is interesting how the sound "ma" is a worldwide linguistic phenomenon, and how it is interconnected to so many different concepts. For example, "Ma" is the root for "Mary" or "Maria."

The Egyptian word for mother was simply "ma" while in Hebrew the word "mah" literally means *the womb*.[1] The Egyptian goddess "Ma'at" is the goddess of truth, justice, and cosmic harmony.

Earlier we mentioned that Miriam is ancient Egyptian for "Beloved of Amen." In Christianity, we invoke the Egyptian God every time we close a prayer and say, amen. So where does the connection between Miriam and Mary come? In Chapter 5, when discussing Mediterranean goddesses, we saw that it appears that the cult of the Mother Goddess in the forms of Cybele and Rhea were rather significant in Rome in the early centuries AD. The name "Magna Mater" or Great Mother is synonymous with

---

[1] Massey, Gerald. *A Book of the Beginnings*. Williams and Norgate, 1881.

The Bringer of Life

Cybele and Rhea. In Merlin Stone's brilliant book (*When God Was a Woman*), Stone suggests that Rhea may have even been known as "Ma Rhea" in some regions. Could "Ma Rhea" be the origins of the seemingly anglicized "Maria?" While Ma Rhea would descend from the Greek language, it still holds that divine implication, just as Miriam in the Egyptian language does.

We know that Cybele and Rhea were worshiped openly and regularly in Rome until 268 AD—and that a lot of these old ways were interwoven into the new Christian traditions. In the same work by Stone, she claims that, "Roman reports of the rituals of the Cybele record that the son, this time as an effigy, was first tied to a tree and then buried. Three days later a light was said to appear in the burial tomb, whereupon Attis rose from the dead, bringing salvation with him in his rebirth." This tradition existing hundreds of years prior to the birth of Jesus the Christ provides evidence that the story told about his alleged resurrection in scripture was in fact stolen from earlier rites.

This brings up many questions. Did the Church use this ancient story to try to appeal to Pagans in order to convert them? Was Jesus ever really in the tomb, and if so, did he actually die? Since Mary Magdalene was the first to appear to him after the alleged resurrection, would she represent the Goddess [Ma] Rhea? Was this simply a tradition, reenacted by Jesus and Mary Magdalene that was passed down from his ancestors? Does this mean that Jesus himself, a Jew, practiced the old religion of the Goddess? How does this tie Judaism to the Goddess? What we do know with certainty, is that this tradition has been linked with Goddess worship for thousands of years, and existed prior to the birth of Christianity.

The primordial cosmic energy known as Shakti has many different names in India, one being *Mariamman*. The etymology of the name is quite intriguing, as *Mari* means rain or water, which is not at all surprising. *Amman* actually meant "mother." This is an interesting concept as it is nearly identical to the Egyptian mystery god, "Amen." Is the core center of Amen actually Shakti, the goddess? Is the goddess in the center of all gods? It is quite possible, considering that in Egyptian the name Amen translates to "the hidden" or the "hiddenness of divinity." In Chapter 1 we

288

discussed that Shakti is that unseen inconceivable creation energy, therefore *She is the hiddenness of divinity*, wouldn't you say?

Coming back around to the "Ma" phenomenon, we now have seen that it is associated with the archetypal mother, but also with Mother Goddess. It is at the root of many words, especially concerning water. In French the word for sea is mer. In Spanish it is literally mar as in Maria. The ancient Egyptian word for water was mo. There is a universal connection to motherhood, and water as Her life force. It is intriguing that even in the Hebrew language, the word for water is mayim which sounds awfully similar to the Egyptian name Miriam.

17.2 The Goddess In Hebrew

How could She be found in a religion like Judaism, where women are considered nothing more than property of their husbands? In 1 Timothy 2:13-15, Paul says, "Let your women keep silence in the churches: for it is not permitted unto them to speak... And if they learn anything, let them ask their husbands at home." Women are not even allowed to speak in church at this time according to Paul, but we find this conflicting with how Jesus himself interacted with women.

For example, we know based on many texts that Jesus treated women with kindness, and even traveled with them as well. Based on the Gospel of Philip, it is clear Jesus had a special relationship with Mary Magdalene, but what about the other women who traveled with them?

There are two other women who were major contributors to Jesus's cause. In Luke 8:2-4, we read that, "Also, some women were with him. They had been cured from evil spirits and various illnesses. These women were Mary, also called Magdalene, from whom seven demons had gone out; Joanna, whose husband Chusa was Herod's administrator; Susanna; and many other women. They provided financial support for Jesus and his disciples." Provided financial support. These women obviously were of wealth, and aided the Jesus mission with their own money. Does it not seem controversial for the time, that these women would have been traveling alone with a group of male disciples and Jesus himself? In fact it was. Joanna had run off with this young prophet and his disciples and left her life behind. The passage in Luke alludes to many other women who were part of the discipleship as well— could these other women potentially be partners of Jesus's male followers?

The identity of all the female followers aside, there is a certain element to the Hebrew and Aramaic languages that can be identified with male and female, much like with any language. A word can either be feminine or masculine in nature. In reference to what the Holy Spirit or Holy Ghost is, we find that it is called by the Aramaic word: *ruach*. We will come back to this shortly.

Throughout the Old Testament, we are presented with passages that mention the Holy Spirit quite often. Genesis 1:2 "And the earth was without form, and void; and darkness was upon the face of the deep. And the Holy Spirit moved upon the face of the waters." The connection between water and the Holy Spirit is made, which is an age-old concept of water being a feminine element. In the previous chapter, we made mention of the Hebrew word for water being "mayim."

In one of the gospels of the Nag Hammadi collection (The Gospel of Phillip) Phillip the Apostle even says: "when did a woman ever conceive of another woman?" which is a clear reference to the Ruach or Holy Spirit. This is the one time in the Christian scriptures where the Holy Ghost is referred to clearly and directly as "Woman." It is no wonder that Phillip's gospel is excluded from the patriarchal canon, of course organized by the Pauline School.

The Aramaic word "Ruach," which is the word used by Jesus to refer to the Spirit and Breath (meant to be the same as the first breath a newborn breathes after exiting the water-filled womb), it's feminine in the Aramaic language and is translated as the Holy Spirit or Holy Ghost in English, which came through Latin as the Spiritus Sanctus which the Pauline influenced Roman Catholic Church has made masculine. We know Paul was not particularly fond of women and their importance in religion, and believed them to be solely under the power of their husbands, as especially in 1 Corinthians 11:7: "For a man indeed ought not to cover his head, forasmuch as he is the image and glory of God: but the woman is the glory of the man." Do not forget, women were not, and are not

290

still, allowed to achieve a clerical position in the Roman Catholic Church, but Jesus and his family were members of the Nazarite tradition which gave women the ability to be priestesses or even bishops.

Isaiah 11:2 says, "The Spirit of the Lord will rest on him— the Spirit of wisdom and of understanding, the Spirit of counsel and of might, the Spirit of the knowledge and fear of the Lord..." There are many clear references to the Holy Spirit as Wisdom. Sophia, in Gnostic tradition, was the Goddess of Wisdom. And Proverbs 4:6 says, "Do not forsake Wisdom, and She will protect you; love Her, and She will watch over you."

The "ruach" when perceived as meaning "to breathe" or breath, is interesting when you compare it to a Gaelic word *ruanaich*, which means "to say" or "to speak." There is a settlement on the Isle of Iona in Scotland named Ruanaich, which happens to have very close ties to Jesus and Mary Magdalene. There are numerous legends about the couple and their presence on the islands of Scotland. It was said they visited Iona with their son, whom they intended to be educated by the priestesses at the Mystery School on the island. There are other stories that speak of the body of Mary Magdalene being buried in one of the caves on the island. The name Iona itself is Hebrew, which means dove. Considering the island appears to be in the shape of a dove, it is quite suitable. But why Hebrew...?

17.3 Jesus, Mary Magdalene, & Scotland

An article by Barry Dunford[2] tells us of the many connections of Jesus, Mary Magdalene, and their children to the highlands and islands of Scotland:

The Scottish literary writer, William Sharp (using the pseudonym Fiona MacLeod) in his essay Iona (1900) refers to "the old prophecy that Christ shall come again upon Iona." This presupposes that Christ had already visited Iona according to an ancient oral tradition. Curiously, just 80 miles due north of Iona is to be found another small Hebridean island, located in Dunvegan Bay, off the west coast of the Scottish Isle of Skye. It is called Eilean Isa (currently spelt Isay) which translates from the gaelic as the "Island of Jesus". Isa is the Middle Eastern Arabic name for Jesus, whereas His name in gaelic is Iosa. So why do we find the appellation of this island with the arabic spelling rather than the gaelic?

Interestingly, there are no religious sites on Eilean Isa or anything to suggest that it's name was conceived from a religious dedication. During the early centuries A. D. a placename was often given to record the actual presence and sanctification of a specific place by the early Celtic Christian monastic saints who were seen as holy men and women. So it could be conjectured that the "Island of Jesus" was so named as a result of it being sanctified by the presence of Jesus Himself.

While visiting the Scottish Hebridean Islands in 1895, Henry Jenner, a former keeper of the manuscripts department at the British Museum in London, came across an intriguing oral tradition. In an article published in The Western Morning News in 1933, Jenner wrote "I was staying on South Uist, in the Catholic part of the outer Hebrides, and found there a whole set of legends of the wanderings of the Holy Mother and Son in those Islands." Taking the foregoing associative elements into account the idea that Jesus (Isa) may actually have visited Iona may not be as far-fetched as might at first appear to be the case.

Furthermore, according to Christine Hartley, in her classic work *The Western Mystery Tradition* (1968): "There is a legend too that Mary Magdalene lies buried in Iona." Writing about Mary Magdalene's legendary association with Scotland, Hartley further says, "Wandering the hills of Scotland, she came to Knoydart." Knoydart is a peninsula located on the west coast of Scotland adjacent to the Isle of Skye which, as we have seen, has a possible association with Jesus. Some ten miles or so, south of Knoydart, can be found another west coast peninsula named Moidart where, on old maps, can be seen the placename Essa Hill, which may relate to the presence of Jesus/Isa there.

Pertinently, during the 1st century A. D. Jesus was known in the Egyptian Christian Coptic Church as Essa, which is the phonetic pronunciation of Isa. It is intriguing to note that legends and place names appear to link both Jesus and Mary Magdalene to the hebridean western isles and the west coast of Scotland.

It is likely that Christine Hartley's source for this intriguing legend was the Scottish writer William Sharp who, in his essay on Iona, remarks: "A Tiree man, whom I met some time ago on the boat that was taking us both to the west, told me there's a story that Mary Magdalene lies in a cave in Iona. Perhaps an islesman had heard a strange legend about Mary Magdalene.. In Mingulay, one of the south isles of the Hebrides, in South Uist, and in Iona, I have heard a practically identical tale told with striking variations." This would suggest there was an oral tradition current among the western isles of Scotland which placed Mary Magdalene there. Could there be some truth in this? Professor Hugh Montgomery in his treatise The God-Kings of Europe: The Descendants of Jesus traced through the Odonic and Davidic Dynasties (2006) provides the interesting information, "John Martinus was believed in the early Christian Period to be the last son of Jesus by Mary Magdalene. In some versions he was born on Iona." Curiously, as Christine Hartley has pointed out, the holy isle of Iona was also known as the Isle of John. Could this relate to the presence of the child of Christ, John Martinus, on Iona?

The Rev. J. F. S. Gordon in his book *Iona*, published in 1885, comments on "Cladh-an-Diseart, 'Burial-ground of the Highest God' called sometimes Cladh-Iain, 'John's burial-ground.' It is situated some distance to the north-east of the Cathedral, in the low ground towards the water-edge, and near it on the south is Port-an-Diseart, 'Port of the Highest God'." It would appear this John association with Iona was of some spiritual significance. Another possibly pertinent gaelic place name is noted by the Rev. Edward C. Trenholme: "Eilean Maolmhartainn (Maelmartin's

Island) is near the south-west corner of Iona. Maelmartin (Devotee or Servant of Martin) may have been one of the ancient Celtic monks of Iona." (*The Story of Iona*, 1909)

On the tombstone of Anna MacLean, the last Prioress of the Nunnery on Iona, who died in 1543, is an effigy of a woman and child with an inscribed dedication to "St. Maria." The presumption would be that this relates to Mary, the Mother of Jesus and the Christ child. However, this woman is portrayed with long hair and is flanked by twin towers, both medieval symbols to denote St. Mary Magdalene. Margaret Starbird refers to "the lore of the Mary called Magdalen, who dried the feet of Jesus with her [long] hair and whose epithet means 'tower' in Hebrew." (*The Woman with the Alabastar Jar*, 1993) Is it possible that this tombstone actually depicts Mary Magdalene with the child of Christ, John Martinus, allegedly born on the holy isle of Iona? If so, this would suggest that Anna MacLean knew about this legend.

Expanding upon the prophecy of Jesus coming again on Iona, mentioned by William Sharp in his essay, it is plainly obvious there is some connection to the sacred feminine. He says, "When I think of Iona I think often, too, of a prophecy once connected with Iona... the old prophecy that Christ shall come again upon Iona, and of that later and obscure prophecy which foretells, now as the Bride of Christ, now as the Daughter of God, now as the Divine Spirit embodied through mortal birth in a Woman, as once through mortal birth in a man, the coming of a new Presence and Power: and dream that this may be upon Iona, so that the little Gaelic island may become as the little Syrian Bethlehem... A young Hebridean priest once told me how, 'as our forefathers and elders believed and still believe, that Holy Spirit shall come again which once was mortally born among us as the Son of God, but, then, shall be the Daughter of God. The Divine Spirit shall come again as a Woman. Then for the first time the world will know peace." There is a strong sense of dualism here that I find incredibly righteous. For Jesus himself gave instruction to a woman to carry on his teachings, so why couldn't the Christ-Sophia energy reincarnate as the "daughter of God" this time around?

The original Gaelic name of Iona was Innis-nam Druidbneach, *Island of the Druids*. Before St. Columba's arrival in the 6th century, it was a large Druidic center of pilgrimage. Many generations have found it a sacred place, sacred enough for four Irish kings, eight Norwegian kings, forty-eight Scottish kings including MacBeth and the Lords of the Isles to be buried there.

There are many questions raised by the content of Dunford's article. Could it be true that Jesus survived the crucifixion? Would Jesus and Mary Magdalene actually voyage so far to Scotland? We know with utmost certainty that Mary Magdalene's presence was significant in the south of France. Some local stories in the south of France also tell of Jesus being there as well. How and why did they manage to get to France? Local legends say that Mary Magdalene, Mary Salome, Mary Jacobi, Lazarus (brother of Magdalene), Cedonius, St. Maximin, a servant girl named Sarah (or was she perhaps the daughter of Jesus and Mary?), and perhaps even Jesus washed ashore in France after being recognized at a port in the Middle East. When the Roman soldiers recognized them, they were allegedly pushed adrift to sea, with no way to control the boat. There are some theories that perhaps Jesus posed as somebody else, as Maximin or Lazarus, to avoid questioning by the Romans.

The first question that probably comes to your mind is, *what about Jesus's death at the crucifixion?* Historically speaking, many people were crucified, but it was never an act that caused rapid death. At one point, Jesus said, "I thirst" (John 19:28). The Roman soldiers gave Jesus a sponge soaked full of wine and vinegar mixed with a drug that was to help dull the senses. This drug very likely helped him endure the pain and helped him ease into a deep sleep which could appear to resemble death. While we know that death by crucifixion could take up to three days or even longer, Jesus only suffered on the cross for *six* hours, at which point he was removed from the cross. There are many pieces of artwork depicting Mary Magdalene in red/orange and green, weeping at his feet—reminiscent of her bathing his feet in her tears and oils earlier on. Joseph of Arimathea, who according to the initiated author Laurence Gardner, was in fact the brother James of Jesus, was the one to ask to remove Jesus from the cross. Pilate granted his permission, which seems odd considering Jesus was not on the cross for nearly as long as others who were condemned to the crucifix. Was there some kind of secret deal between Pilate and Joseph of Arimathea/James? In ancient Jewish custom, only a family member could touch the body of the dead, therefore if Joseph of Arimathea was not a close family member, he would not have petitioned for the removal of Jesus's body. He then takes Jesus to what is referred to as "his family's tomb."

According to the controversial Gospel of Barnabas, Jesus himself claimed, "I confess before heaven, and call to witness everything that dwells upon the earth, that I am a stranger to all that men have said of me, that I am more than man... For I am a man, born of a woman, subject to the judgment of God; that live here like as other men, subject to the common miseries." Also in this controversial text, is the claim that it was not Jesus that died on the cross, but Judas Iscariot.

Another intriguing suggestion that Jesus survived the crucifixion or was never crucified, is that he allegedly appeared post-crucifixion to the apostles. Jesus was supposedly crucified at 9 am, which is the hour of the Goddess. He appeared on at least eight occasions within 40 days before the "ascension to heaven." The more likely of scenarios, since no human being has ever been *resurrected* or beamed up into heaven, is that Jesus was never really dead after the crucifixion. A more probable suggestion is that he was allegorically killed, like in the ancient Egyptian then turned Masonic legend and ritual of Hiram Abiff. This was because he was being initiated into High Priesthood, and must exit material society to enter the Kingdom of Heaven, or the Holy of Holies within the tabernacle, where only the High Priest was permitted to enter. This was also where God was said to appear to the High Priest. Jesus says how he must ascend to his father, prior to his ascension, which would fall in line with his entering High Priesthood.

Post-crucifixion, Mary Magdalene goes to his tomb with her oils. The next level of initiation has come, and Mary Magdalene goes to fulfill her duty as the wife-priestess of Jesus. She goes to anoint the Priest King to prepare him to be *raised up* as a high priest. We are aware already that Jesus refers to Magdalene as the Holy Spirit, and has given her initiatory powers. When Jesus cries out to her not to touch him, it is because he is considered "unclean" while he is still supposed to be dead. This is in the morning on the third day of the allegorical death. Jesus should have ritually remained dead until sunset that day, therefore his absence from the tomb was alarming.

Regardless of the events immediately following the crucifixion, somehow there was reason to believe that Jesus and Mary Magdalene both made it to France, and then to Scotland with their son. It remains evident and clear that they had a significant influence throughout the highlands and islands of Scotland, and it should not be surprising that they were aware of Scotland. Joseph of Arimathea in fact, was a tin trader, and often traded in the British Isles.

At Glastonbury Abbey remains a thorn tree that he was said to have planted, that he brought with him from the Middle East. As a tin trader, he would have been very familiar with the territory, and as a spiritual man, he would have been aware of the Celts in Britain who had many close connections to the Celts in France, and their ancient roots of Egypt. Records even place thousands of Celtic mercenaries in Egypt between 283-246 BC assisting to overthrow Ptolemy II. This leads us even further back to relations between the Scots, the Celts, and the Egyptians.

17.4 Egyptian Queen of Scots, the Stone of Destiny, and King Arthur

Egypt and Scotland, what countries could seem more different? Could it be that there was an Egyptian influence in the founding of Scotland, and even Ireland? That it was due to a runaway Egyptian princess and her lover that the Gaelic language developed? And what about the Stone of Destiny, also known as the Stone of Scone, that became *the* stone that all Scottish kings were required to be crowned on? How does this one rock relate to Egypt?

An article featured on Undiscovered Scotland, "Scota,"[3] explains the varied theories and stories of the first queen of

---

[3] https://www.undiscoveredscotland.co.uk/usbiography/s/scota.html#:~:text=Sco-ta%20is%20the%20name%20of,out%20in%20our%20Historical%20Timeline.

Scotland who was said to exist around the centuries of 1400 BC:

There are several variations on the basic story, but according to the early Irish chronicle Lebor Gabála Érenn or "The Book of the Taking of Ireland", Scota was the daughter of an Egyptian Pharaoh named Cingris. She married Niul, son of Fenius Farsaid, a Babylonian. They had a son, Goídel Glas, who gave his name to the race he founded, the Gaels. He also created the Gaelic language by combining the best features of the 72 languages then in existence.

The modern Scottish version of the story dates back to John of Fordun's five volume Chronica Gentis Scotorum, published in about 1360. This first complete history of Scotland drew heavily on myth and legend in its early volumes, and Fordun seems to have rationalised several versions of the story of Scota found in Irish mythology into something that sounded right to him. According to Fordun, it was Goídel Glas (who he calls Gaythelos) who married a Pharaoh's daughter called Scota. Goídel Glas and Scota were subsequently exiled from Egypt (accounts differ as to the reason). After wandering for many years they eventually settled in the north-west corner of what is now called Spain, near the modern city of A Coruña.

Having settled in Spain, they had a son, Míl Espáine. Here things get a little complicated because by some accounts Míl Espáine married another woman called Scota who, coincidentally, was also the daughter of an Egyptian Pharaoh. This suggests that, depending on the source you believe, Scota was either the wife, the mother, or the grandmother of Míl Espáine. In some ways it doesn't actually matter, because the key purpose of this creation myth was to tie the regal authority of the Kings of Ireland (and, subsequently, Scotland) back to a source of power that would never be questioned. An Egyptian Pharaoh served the purpose admirably, whatever the details of the actual chain of relationships.

The story continues that Scota and Míl Espáine had a

number of children. Two of their sons, Eber Finn and Érimón, later launched the "Milesian" invasion of Ireland (named after the "sons of Mil"), and after defeating the resident Tuatha Dé Danann or "peoples of the goddess Danu", divided the island of Ireland between them. Over time, some of the residents of the island came to call themselves Scoti, after Scota, as did the residents of Dalriada in western Scotland, who, under Kenneth I, went on to form what is now Scotland. As a final twist, among the possessions carried from Egypt by Scota was a 152kg sandstone block which had been used as a pillow by Jacob when he had the dream reported in Genesis about Jacob's Ladder. This became Scotland's Stone of Scone or Stone of Destiny.

If the Egyptian princess Scota knew about Scotland and Ireland in about 1400 BC, then the Celtic people made it to Egypt in 283 BC, I think it is pretty clear it is very probable Jesus and Mary Magdalene were able to make it there in the mid first century AD. Iona has been said to have been a home to ancient priestesses of the goddess Isis, and that there was said to have been a great Mystery School—a school teaching mysteries much like Jesus and Mary grew up being initiated into.

The Stone of Destiny has many names: Stone of Scone, Coronation Stone, Jacob's Pillow... It is a stone claimed to be the same stone Jacob lay his head upon in the book of Genesis, over 3,700 years ago. Jacob lived somewhere around 1600-1700 BC—making this stone a rather ancient biblical artifact. If the story of Queen Scota is true, she would have brought this stone over with her only a couple hundred years later. It would not be surprising if she had brought priestesses of Isis with her. Coincidentally, or perhaps not so coincidentally, the Stone of Destiny was brought to Scone Abbey from the *Isle of Iona* around 841 AD by the Dalriada, Pictish, and Scottish King Kenneth MacAlpin. The English forcefully removed it in 1296, at least what they thought was the real stone. Many believe the monks of Scone hid the real Stone of Destiny, as older descriptions do not at all match the current "Stone of Scone." In 1996 this stone was returned to Scotland where it remains on display in Edinburgh Castle.

There are theories that could potentially tie the Stone to the Knights Templar. In 1950, some students stole the stone from England and brought it back to Scotland. A shocking twist to this story was revealed in 1999 when a claim was made that the Knights Templar were in possession of the *real* Stone. In an online article found by *The Scotsman*[4] the intriguing story is told:

Two men have spoken exclusively for the first time about their role in the secretion of what many believe is the "real" Stone of Destiny. And if what the pair say is correct, the genuine article may still be hidden at a secret location somewhere in Scotland.

Charles Henderson, now 72, a retired engineer of Auchtermuchty, was working his way around the country photographing castles in the early 1990s when he befriended David Eaton, now 73, of Meigle, who was at that time custodian of Dunfermline Abbey.

In 1991, Charles was asked by David, who was a chevalier with the Knights Templar, if he would help him move the "real" Stone of Destiny from the former St Columba's Church in Dundee. Locked inside an iron cage, it had been on display in the Lochee church since 1972 under the care of the Rev Dr John MacKay Nimmo.

A Scottish nationalist organisation, the 1320 Club, claimed it was the genuine stone stolen from Westminster Abbey by four students in 1950 and never returned, whereas the one sent back to Westminster was a replica, made by a Glasgow stonemason. Charles' involvement in the scheme came entirely by chance.

"I was asked to help because I had a Peugeot 305 diesel van," he said.

"According to the late Rev Nimmo, after the stone was stolen from Westminister in 1950, the one placed on the high altar at Arbroath Abbey in April 1951 and returned to London, was actually a copy.

"The real one was kept and moved around secret

[4] Ascroft, Cath. "Is the Stone of Destiny a Fake?" *The Scotsman*, 25 Mar. 2016, https://www.scotsman.com/regions/dundee-and-tayside/stone-destiny-fake-2463764.

locations under the guard of the Knights Templar...
"Rev Nimmo certainly believed it to be the real stone. He was a man of the cloth and he had no doubt in his mind whatsoever that this was the real stone we were moving."

There are many important connections to note within this story. The Kingdom of Dalriada became home to the legendary but also very real Scottish "King Arthur." The father of the Scottish Arthur was a King of Dalriada from 576-609 AD named Áedán mac Gabráin. Some have even suggested that Iona was the true Avalon. This kingdom of Dalriada was primarily the Argyll and Bute areas of the Scottish highlands.

The eldest son of Áedán mac Gabráin, Artuir mac Áedáin, could very well be the inspiration for King Arthur. The sacred place where kings were crowned in Dalriada was a place called Dunadd Fort. Here there is a rocky hill, with symbols carved all around, including a carved footprint. This footprint was where Artuir famously placed his foot, knelt down with his sword ceremoniously, and then rose as king. To the onlookers below the rocky hill-top, it would appear that he miraculously drew his sword from the stone, and thus a legend was born.

Artuir's family burial plot rests on the Isle of Iona, the same place where Jesus and Mary Magdalene purportedly visited, and where according to local legend Mary Magdalene is also buried. Is it a coincidence that King Arthur and his family are buried on the same island that Jesus and Magdalene have such strong connections to? Could it be that the blood that ran through King Arthur's veins was the same as Jesus and Mary's? If you were to call the royal bloodline of Jesus, that was carried by Mary in her womb, the Holy Grail, would it be wrong to believe that the Grail *was* in fact brought to Scotland?

It was said that Arthur fought 12 battles, which may be historically accurate, but in an esoteric light it could have some kind of connection to the 12 zodiac signs. One of these battles was fought near Stirling, and seemed to hold some kind of significance to King Arthur, as he was said to have built his round table here.

Some archaeologists and researchers believe the search for the legendary table is over. The site in question rests just beneath the iconic Stirling Castle in the royal gardens. Vast intricate earthworks cover the grounds. The one particular area that lends itself to the possibility of being the round table is known as the "Kings Knot." While it's believed that the present earthworks were constructed around 1620, geophysical technology tells us that the current earthworks were constructed on top of a much older site. This central circular ditch and mound beneath the surface yields multi-period construction dates as early as the Iron Age. Many historical documents confirm that King Arthur's round table was known to be in the area. In 1375, Scottish poet John Barbour claimed that "the round table" was south of Stirling Castle, and in 1478 William of Worcester told how "King Arthur kept the Round Table at Stirling Castle."

The supposed origin of the inspiration for the *round table* comes from an earlier tradition of Joseph of Arimathea's "Grail Table." It too was a round table, made to honor the infamous Last Supper. Joseph's table was made of silver, and was used by he and his followers after a divine vision of Jesus. There are two different stories as to whom the Round Table came from. One story tells that it was Queen Guinivere's father who bestowed the Round Table upon Artuir. Another story says that it was Artuir's father, known as Uther Pendragon, who built this Round Table by instruction of Merlin, to resemble the Grail Table built by Joseph of Arimathea. This table had 13 total seats, 12 seats, and one empty—representing Judas' seat. It is not meant to be filled until a knight achieves the Grail. According to legend, Joseph took this Grail Table to the Isle of Avalon, aka the Isle of Iona. What can one believe, knowing that the family burial plot of King Arthur is on Iona, and the alleged Grail Table, is also there, on the same island that Jesus and Mary traversed?

Woven into the stories and legends of King Arthur is an important theme not to be overlooked: the sacred feminine. In Arthurian legend, She is known as the *Lady of the Lake*. Perhaps She could be based on an ancient goddess of the lands, or perhaps She embodies the Mother Goddess aspects seen throughout so many different cultures and ages. The Goddess springs forth from the water, like a newborn springs forth from its mother's water-filled dark womb. Her name in these tales is Nimueh, not so far off from Nammu, the Sumerian creation goddess, who herself rose from the sea and gave birth to heaven. Nammu, remember, was the Sumerian goddess of the sea, the primordial waters of creation.

As the story goes, She lives in a lake near the Isle of Avalon, which we can safely assume is Iona. This brings about an interesting connection between the goddess, the supposed burial of Magdalene on Iona, and the family burial plot of Artuir. It seems to be that the creator goddess of the old world now appears to guard the Isle of Iona, and the royal blood of those buried there.

Nimueh plays many roles throughout the different stories. Firstly, She is the one who gifts Arthur with the sword responsible for proving his worth in the story: Excalibur. The sword becomes a symbol of his strength but also of his worthiness, and his being the chosen one. She raised Lancelot from the time he was a baby, and was also called the mother of Mabuz, or better known as the Celtic goddess Mabon associated with the autumn equinox. The Lady of the Lake assists in the capture of Merlin, and then helps take the dying King Arthur home to Avalon…Iona.

Le Morte d'Arthur or *The Death of Arthur* is a tale that was more appropriately originally titled The Whole Book of King Arthur and of His Noble Knights of the Round Table. It is in this book that the stories of the knights and their noble quest for the grail can be tied to King Arthur. The Knights of the Round Table were bound by a strict code of chivalry, and were meant to protect the kingdom of Arthur, as well as the women of the area. Later, they also embarked on quests for the Holy Grail, much like the later Knights Templar were said to have done.

There came to be 150 Knights of the Round Table according to the legends, and allegedly there existed a table that could fit all of them. Considering we know the Round Table was built to seat 13 people, this theory is unlikely. What else could this have actually meant? I propose that the 150 *Knights of the Round Table* could in fact be a fraternity (if there were even in fact that many in reality) that was created with many purposes in mind, but the chief one being to preserve certain traditions and knowledge, perhaps locate certain artifacts as the medieval Templars came to do. The possibilities are endless.

Within half a century from the time of Arthur, the order of the

Knights Templar came to be, with many similarities. These same Knights Templar also came to seek refuge in Scotland after 1307, fought by the side of Robert the Bruce at Bannockburn, and likely brought with them their treasures and secrets. A few hundred years later, the first Masonic Lodge appeared in Scotland.

Freemasonry was born of Egyptian root, mingled with the blood deep bond of brotherhood shared between the Knights Templar. What better place for the very first Masonic lodge, than in a country whose name was birthed by that of an Egyptian queen?

17.5 Was Jesus a Mason?

The origin of Freemasonry is a cloudy beginning, there is no official time or place that we can pinpoint as being the birth of certain traditions or rituals. The more you look into these traditions, the further back in time you go. The Bible tells us that Jesus was a *carpenter.* But is this truly an accurate translation? Let us go back to the original language that the book of Mark was written in: Greek.

The word used for carpenter in Greek is *tekton. Tekton* literally means *craftsman.* This is referring to anyone of the trade guilds— be it a stoneworker (mason), an ironworker, or even architect. Within Freemasonry the supreme being is most often referred to as the *Grand Architect of the Universe.* Jesus himself being a stonemason, or architect, a craftsman at the very least, tells us that he was a member of the guild. Builders, tradesmen, typically stuck together. They traveled where the Work took them, as Jesus also traveled lots through his life and ministry. Maybe it is possible that Jesus worked with chisels, hammers, *squares, and compasses,* and not carpentry tools.

Being that the landscape around Israel is not nearly as rich in wood as it is in stone, it is far more likely that he worked stone and not wood. Almost all the homes in Israel, as well as temples, were built from stone and not wood. Hebraic scholar James W. Fleming explains that, "Jesus and Joseph would have formed and made nine out of ten projects from stone either by chiseling or carving the stone or stacking building blocks."[5]

Jesus tends to tie in many of his lessons with allegories of

---

[5] Fleming, W. James. *The Jewish Background of Jesus.* 2004.

stone. In Luke 20:17-18 he makes a comparison to a cornerstone when he says, "Then what is the meaning of that which is written: The stone the builders rejected has become the cornerstone? Everyone who falls on that stone will be broken to pieces; anyone on whom it falls will be crushed." After Jesus turns tables over in the temple in John 2, angry because people are using the temple as a marketplace, he says, "Destroy this temple, and I will raise it again in three days." John 2 goes onto say that Jesus is actually comparing his body to the stone temple. Jesus says in Matthew 16:18, "I tell you that you are Peter, and on this rock I will build my church, and the gates of Death will not overcome it." Jesus says that his church will be founded upon rock, upon stone. If Jesus was raised by Joseph who was a stonemason, would it be any surprise how often Jesus makes these comparisons?

In Mark 6:2-3 we hear him referenced as a *tekton* when it says, "'Where did this man get these things?" they asked. "What's this Wisdom that has been given him? What are these remarkable miracles he is performing? Is this not the *stonemason,* son of Mary? Isn't this Mary's son and the brother of James, Joseph, Judas and Simon? Aren't his sisters here with us?' And they took offense at him."

In this passage many took offense at Jesus as he was teaching in the synagogue on Sabbath. The people know that he walks with Wisdom, and shares this Wisdom with those who "have the ears to hear." This is a phrase that Jesus uses on several occasions throughout his ministry, and typically just before he has a prophetic teaching to deliver. Within Freemasonry today, the Fellow Craft Degree's "staircase lecture" teaches of the five senses and how they are relevant to the Mason. Hearing is one of the principle senses because hearing allows the Mason to hear the ritual and the words that would identify one Mason to another.

Jesus makes a reference to the cornerstone in the Gospel of Thomas, which traditionally is the first stone to be laid, a concept familiar to all stonemasons, when he says, "Show me the stone which the builders have rejected. That one is the cornerstone." However, this is not the first time it was said. The phrase can be found in earlier scripture that was written likely a thousand years before Jesus, by his own ancestor, King David, son of King

Solomon, in Psalms 118. Perhaps the tradition of stonemasonry was something passed down, be it an actual trade or maybe even part of an esoteric tradition as Freemasonry is today. Many of the traditions of Freemasonry stem from legends of Solomon's Temple, so is this really so far-fetched? The early origins of Freemasonry appear to predate Jesus, and very well could go back thousands of years.

There could potentially be another link to Jesus within the third degree that is tied to an age-old story of the building of Solomon's Temple: the story of Hiram Abiff, the son of a widow. Hiram is the chief architect of the temple, and holds all of the secret passwords. Three ruffians assault him when he refuses to give up the secret passwords, and they end up murdering him with a Masonic tool, which varies within Masonic jurisdictions.

Tim Wallace-Murphy and his wife Cindi propose in their book, *Rex Deus,* that:

> Freemasonic traditions and ritual profess that the craft emerged from the time of Hiram Abif, who was killed by a blow to the temple for his refusal to betray a secret. This produces an inescapable parallel with the documented details of the death of James the Just [brother of Jesus]. Hiram Abif was killed immediately before the completion of Solomon's Temple and nearly 1,000 years later, when work on the Herodian Temple was nearing completion, building was brought to a temporary standstill as a mark of respect for James, the brother of Jesus, who had been ritually murdered. Chris Knight and Robert Lomas conclude that the tradition concerning the death of Hiram Abif is used as an allegory to mask the ritual commemoration of the murder of James the Just. Therefore, when Freemasons celebrate the ritual death of Hiram, they are commemorating one of the founders of Rex Deus.

Could it be that the story of Hiram Abiff within Freemasonry is an allusion to James the Just's death? If not, is there some other kind of connection present? Is that all just mere coincidence?

Jesus was supposedly crucified on April 3, 33 AD and reportedly

306

died at 3 pm. There are 33 degrees of Scottish Rite Freemasonry. Was the crucifixion set specifically for this time, day, and year due to the numerological significance? Could this have been some type of initiation or degree that Jesus was undergoing physically to "ascend" to the next degree? Earlier groups, such as those who were initiated into the Dionysian Mysteries practiced ritual death and resurrection as well. Jesus appeared to have styled himself and his teachings after many Dionysian traditions.

The number 33 would seem to be important in many different areas around the world. Humans are born with 33 vertebrae, and on average have 32 vertebrae after growth, making the 33rd the Mystery, or the Third Eye, the Crown chakra. This could heavily be influenced by the kundalini energy, the Shakti energy of the divine feminine that runs through the chakras, up and down the spine. Did the ancient people know this? Is this why 33 has always been so important to them? If we place Jesus's birth at 0, which it likely was not, but just for figurative purposes, he would have been 33 at the time of the crucifixion.

Was Jesus in fact a stonemason and not a carpenter, a brother of the craft...?

17.6 The Goddess in the Cathedrals

Awe inspiring cathedrals began to surface all over Europe in the medieval era, with some of the most incredible architectural feats. But who built these cathedrals, and why? Many of the cathedrals were financed by none other than the Knights Templar, therefore the builders of the cathedrals would be under the orders of the Templars. The Knights Templar had seen beautiful buildings whilst in the Holy Land, and brought back some of the architectural phenomena they witnessed there.

A well known example is Notre Dame Cathedral, in Paris France. Construction began here in 1163, but this was not the first temple to exist on that exact spot. Prior to it being a cathedral, it was a temple dedicated to a Pagan god, Jupiter. It is possible the temple to Jupiter was erected as early as 52 BC, following the Roman occupation of the city.

The front of Notre Dame Cathedral is an iconic image: two tall towers reigning high above its rose window, and the intimidating gargoyles that guard the entrance. What could a cathedral built by the Knights Templar have to do with the goddess, you may wonder? As you approach the cathedral, you will enter through the doors beneath the rose window.

Upon entering the cathedral, you are allegorically entering into the womb of God[dess]. Does one not enter the church in order to be born again? The two towers represent a woman with

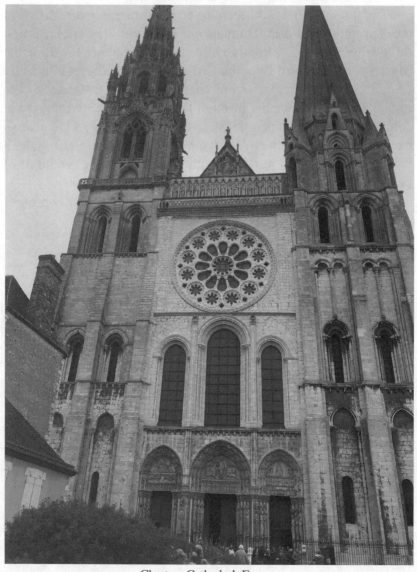

Chartres Cathedral, France.

her legs up in the birth giving position, as mentioned in section 4.1. The rose window appears to be in the place of the clitoris. The doorway would be the vaginal entrance to the birth canal. There are figurines that have been found from all over the world showing the mother goddess in such a position. For example, the Lajja Gauri icon dating from the 6th century, found in Madhya Pradesh, India, shows the goddess as if She is giving birth. On

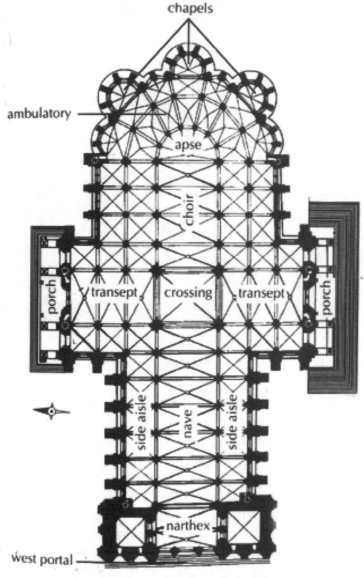

The layout of Chartres Cathedral.

6th-century AD Lajja Gauri icon, India. Courtesy of Carol Radcliff Bolon.

the other side of the world in Mexico, the Aztec people were also creating similar figurines.

Why would the Knights Templar build cathedrals to honor the goddess? Well, because they revered Her. The Templar tradition was far more ancient than anyone truly gave them credit for, and though their patron saint may have been Mary, She represented something far older and far more ancient.

Another beautiful example of this is found at Chartres Cathedral, with the two towers. The actual layout of Chartres Cathedral is nearly identical to the layout of the stone chamber at Newgrange in Ireland built thousands of years earlier; it resembles the female reproductive system. Did the Templars style their architecture after

A Black Madonna at Chartres Cathedral. Photo by Elena Dijour.

these ancient stone chambers, or was it just a universal understanding of the sanctity of the sacred feminine and Her womb?

While exploring the inside of the cathedral, I found many pieces of art alluding to the goddess, one being a statue of a very pregnant woman. It was not labeled, but I immediately thought: Mary Magdalene. The statue holds a grail cup in one hand and points to it with the other. Could this indicate that She was carrying the Holy Grail, the royal blood of Jesus? One could certainly argue that this is the pregnant mother of Jesus, and not the Magdalene. However the Knights Templar in France held a special affinity for the Magdalene, and She was who many of their churches were dedicated to. Next to the statue there was a rectangular stone work showing what looked like flowers or leaves making up the uterus, fallopian tubes, and birth canal. Unfortunately I cannot find my photo of it nor find one online, but it was absolutely beautiful.

Many of the cathedrals in France were built up around the Black Madonnas that were brought back from the Holy Land by the Templars, but some locals argue the Black Madonnas were in France hundreds of years before. An 11th century Black Madonna consecrated the cathedral, but unfortunately it was replaced by a newer one. More recently, during the restoration of Chartres Cathedral, the Black Madonna was made white. Surrounding the Madonna you will notice many five-pointed stars, symbol of Venus, Queen of Heaven, just as Mary was called. It is only fitting, considering that before it was a cathedral it was also a Pagan temple dedicated to the mother goddess.

311

Adorning the floor of the cathedral is a labyrinth. A labyrinth is another Pagan tradition, originating in Greek mythology. It was used in sacred dance and ritual. While walking, the labyrinth takes the initiate close to the innermost part of the labyrinth, and then out to the edge again. The idea is to trust the path that you are on, and to know that it will lead you to where you are meant to be. In the labyrinth, one is never lost.

When I was visiting France in 2019, there was a specific sculpture that I was dying to see. As I arrived at the Basilica of Saint Remi, I noticed what appeared to be the engrailed cross as seen on the coat of arms of the St. Clairs of Roslin just above the door. There is debate about when this carving dates to, so one cannot be sure.

Upon entering, I eagerly looked around for the sculpture that I was there to see. There it was. A sculpture depicting eight figures: Jesus laying on the slab, Nicodemus, Mary of Cleophas, the Virgin Mary bent down in mourning, the apostle John, a very pregnant Mary Magdalene, next to her is Mary Salome whose stomach

The Five-Pointed Star in Amiens Cathedral.

The sculpture of Jesus lying on a slab surrounded by figures.

appears rather flat in contrast, and lastly is Joseph of Arimathea. The plaque dedicated to the sculpture reads as follows: *This sepulcher, made in 1531 and transferred here from the Temple in 1803, has been given to the Church of St. Remi by M. Lemoine-Doriot, who adorned the chapel in 1814.*

What is interesting about the Magdalene here, aside from her robust belly, is her hands. She has thrown her hands up in distress, much like the symbolic arm gesture one Mason makes to another when he is in distress. Earlier in section 5.5 we also saw that Tanit, the Moon goddess is often shown with Her hands up in the same manner. Whoever created the sculpture may have been trying to convey a scene of distress of an expecting mother and Jesus's closest friends and family.

The same symbol is depicted in Royston Cave in England. The cave is notorious for its Knights Templar and Masonic symbols carved into it, and very well could have been either an initiation cave or a hiding place. There are many shadowy legends and stories that surround it, but what is obvious to me is the Masonic connection—at least with this specific carving.

Down in the south of France is an iconic chapel called "Rennes-le-Chateau" which was dedicated to none other than Mary Magdalene. There are strange stories that surround the chapel, the Merovingian dynasty, and connections made to legends of the

Mason in distress carving, Royston Cave, England. Courtesy of Andrew Gough.

Grail, of the royal bloodline of Jesus and Mary Magdalene. Some of these theories are explored in *The Holy Blood and the Holy Grail.*[6] The south of France is a magical area, rich in mythical lore. It was also the area that Mary Magdalene supposedly came to post-crucifixion.

One cathedral in particular is of interest: Amiens Cathedral. The cathedral houses the skull of St. John the Baptist, and not only is the skull of St. John the Baptist there, but so is a symbol of the goddess. In the north transept rose window is a downward facing five pointed star, a symbol the Catholic church came to demonize as a Satanic symbol. So why is it found in a Roman Catholic Cathedral? Probably because the construction and design of the cathedral was set in place by the medieval Knights Templar who also financed its building. The symbol of Venus guards over the severed head, the skull of John the Baptist.

All across Europe you can find hints of ancient stories depicted in architecture, art, and local tales. The goddess, in the form of the archetypal mother goddess, or in the form of Mary, is all over. She is found in churches, ancient tombs, and more. Behind almost every Mystery, intrigue, and controversy, there is usually *Goddess* awaiting to once again be restored to Her rightful place: *Queen of Heaven.*

---

[6] Henry Lincoln, Michael Baigent, Richard Leigh.

Chapter 18
The Goddess In the Lodge

So this leaves us with the question: Where is the goddess today? Is She still here? Or has She been completely erased and forgotten in our modern world?

18.1 The Goddess Nation

The sacred feminine has been carefully veiled within institutions both ancient and new. Within one of the new institutions She is hidden in plain sight. What is the new institution? Some say that it is the most powerful country in the world: the United States of America. What is one of the most iconic symbols of America? The Statue of Liberty. What many do not know is that Liberty is in fact a goddess. She is the Roman goddess: Libertas.

She stands symbolically guarding the city that served as the first capital of the United States, New York City, from 1785-1790. While Her statue appeared nearly a century later, the symbolism remained strong. It was placed in NYC because of the continuous use of New York as a passenger and merchant port. The statue stood with a blazing torch of Light to guide and to welcome all incoming immigrants, reminding them that they have now reached a free nation, shorelines that promised, once met, their bondage and slavery have ended.

Libertas was first built a temple on the Aventine Hill over 2,000 years ago, in 238 BC. In 46 BC, the Roman senate voted to build a temple to Libertas in honor of Julius Caesar, but the temple was never built. In place of the temple, a statue of Libertas was erected in the iconic Forum. Libertas was often depicted with a conical hat that freed slaves, men and women alike, wore. She was strongly invoked by those seeking freedom, and revered by those who had been granted freedom from their slave owners.

After the French Revolution in 1792, a new republic was formed and so were a new seal and new coins. In 1848 this became the Great Seal of France. It was designed depicting the Liberty that we all know and love today as the American symbol. The man responsible for its creation was a man named Jaques Jean Barre. Just like the Statue of Liberty, there are also seven points on Her crown.

The Great Seal of France.

What is the meaning of seven here? The answer from the National Parks Service is that it represents the seven continents and the seven seas. The number seven is significant for so many reasons, but one that has always stood out to be can be found in Luke 8. It is said that Jesus cast seven demons from Mary Magdalene. There are many different interpretations floating around out there, some being that it was the seven deadly sins that were cast out of her. In the book *The Jesus Secret: the Unknown Life of Jesus* Dr. Robert Siblerud says, "Prior to marriage, Mary was under the authority of the chief scribe, who was Judas Iscariot. Judas was known as the Demon Priest Number 7. It was a name given to him by the Zealot party. Judas held the position once held by Gabriel, which included authority and supervision over celibate women, before and after marriage. The new testament calls Mary the woman from whom seven demons had gone out. This means that she was under the authority of the demon priest, and she was released from the Essene arrangement by Judas Iscariot... Jesus' marriage to Mary was required to fulfill the rule of his dynastic order."

The number seven is also associated with perfection, as God was said to have created the Earth in seven days. There are seven sacraments, and the White Buffalo Calf Woman comes to the Lakota and teaches the seven sacred rites. The number seven can be found in many intriguing places throughout history. Now, seven spikes can be seen on the iconic Statue of Liberty. The statue of the Roman goddess was commissioned in 1865 by none other than a Freemason, Edouard de Laboulaye. The sculptor he employed to build the monument was also a Freemason named Frederic Auguste Bartholdi. What exactly is the significance to the goddess within Freemasonry? And how does She play a part in the founding of America?

Masonic Compass and Square.

The United States is one of the youngest countries out there, and was established to escape the tyranny of the Church and monarchy. The country was founded by men who were part of the secretive fraternal order known as Freemasons: George Washington, Benjamin Franklin, John Hancock, George Mason, William Ball, just to name a few.

The American flag itself has the goddess written all over it—fifty of the five-pointed stars that represent Venus, along with 13 red and white stripes. Thirteen is the number of Venus years it takes to complete that cycle. The Capitol in Washington DC even has the goddess standing proudly, gazing out over our nation. She is called "Freedom" and has a five-pointed star on her helmet. The city of Washington DC was laid out by George Washington and his boundary markers, in the shape of a diamond. Why could that be? Where did the inspiration for this shape come from? It can be seen in an iconic symbol. The compass and square of Freemasonry. Now what is at the center of the Masonic symbol? That is up for debate, but a very possible explanation is rather simple. The upward pointing triangle would represent the masculine, the downward pointing triangle would represent the feminine. And together, they are the sacred life-producing union of male and female. At the center of the compass and square is the letter G. It it often debated over what the G stands for—God, Goddess, or Geometry?

The Pentagon is another structure that has been born of a goddess symbol. When you draw a five-pointed star, what is in the center of the star? Nothing other than the pentagon. And what is housed in the Pentagon? Arguably some of the most classified

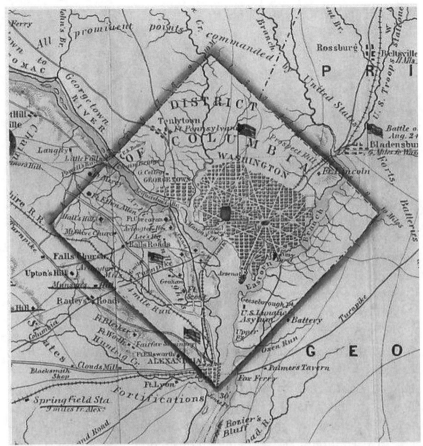

Map of the original boundaries of Washington DC.

secrets of our nation. Protected by Her.

Another symbol of the goddess in DC was mentioned in Chapter 13, the Washington Monument, which sits right inside the vesica piscis, another union of male and female. The goddess is all over the Capital, watching over the nation that was initially presided over by brethren. And now, we will examine Her influence within the brotherhood.

18.2 The Three Great Pillars of Freemasonry

There are considered to be the "Three Great Pillars of Freemasonry." What are these pillars and what do they represent? They are: Strength, Beauty, and Wisdom.

Strength is what gives us the ability to dive into the deeper meanings and mysteries of life. These deeper meanings and mysteries often lead to uncomfortable realizations and answers—which is often why people would rather believe what they are told and have "faith" than seek Light for themselves. It takes strength to tread uncharted waters, and this is something that Freemasonry asks its initiates to do.

Beauty is seen not as a physical appeal, but rather an inner appeal. Beauty in this sense is found within someone who has an open, loving and selfless heart, someone who does good work for the greater good of humanity, for example, as the bible says: *loving thy neighbor.*

Wisdom is something that comes with time, we call upon Her, asking for Wisdom to grace us with the understanding and perspective to be better and more prepared. Wisdom requires patience, because it is not something that can be learned or taught overnight. Wisdom also requires humility, the willingness to adapt and learn. To achieve Wisdom, one must admit that they know nothing in the grand scheme of things. Wisdom is extremely intriguing being one of the Three Great Pillars, as she is the head of this trinity, the one who has an ancient basis as being considered goddess—Sophia, Mother of Wisdom. Proverbs 4:6-7: "Do not forsake Wisdom, and She will protect you; love Her, and She will watch over you. Wisdom is supreme; therefore get Wisdom. Though it cost all you have, get understanding."

18.3 The Three Lesser Lights

Within Freemasonry are what are known as the "Three Lesser Lights." These are described as being: Sun, Moon, and the Worshipful Master [Master of the Lodge]. The Master of the lodge sits in the East, which as we know has long been identified with Venus because She rises in the east as the Morning Star. While some Masons, such as Albert Pike, will argue that the Worshipful Master is more appropriately identified with Mercury, I argue that this is not the case. Albert Pike once said, "They are still the Three Lights of a Masonic Lodge, except that for Mercury, the Master of the Lodge has been absurdly substituted." The *three brightest lights* of the sky would be the Sun, the Moon, and Venus. She is the third brightest object in the sky. Beyond that, the next brightest object in the sky is usually Jupiter and sometimes Mars, but not Mercury. Mercury was associated with the underworld, and some Masons argue that the Worshipful Master governed his people "below" in the earthly realm while the Sun and the Moon governed above in the heavens.

Even if this is the case in point, Venus would make far more sense as the Worshipful Master because She too, governs the underworld during part of her astronomical journey as seen from Earth. Recall that in Chapter 13 we discussed Her routine: 263 days as a morning star, 50 days below in the allegorical "underworld" as Queen of the Dead, missing from the sky, and then raised up once again but this time as the evening star for another 263 days, only to disappear once again from the sky for a further eight days before beginning the cycle over again. This entire cycle takes 584 days, which when reduced down numerically, gives us the number 17—and then eight. Eight is the number which comes after seven, and biblically seven was seen as the number of perfection. Eight would be beyond natural perfection, therefore encompassing divine perfection attainable through only divine means. Do not forget that it is also *eight Earth years* and 13 Venus years that it takes to complete the Pentacle of Venus in the heavens, the five-pointed star.

It is argued that Jesus was resurrected on the eighth day, the day after the seventh day, the Sabbath, and that eight therefore should represent resurrection and new creation. St. Augustine makes this argument when he says, "Christ suffered voluntarily, and so could choose His own time for suffering and for resurrection, He brought it about that His body rested from all its works on Sabbath in the tomb, and that His resurrection on the third day, which we call the Lord's day, the day after the Sabbath, and therefore the eighth..." We must not forget that the first person to appear to him upon his resurrection is indeed Mary Magdalene, the Venus Herself. She has come to anoint him, to raise him to the next degree. Jesus is raised on the eighth day, just as Venus goes below the horizon and emerges again as the morning star on the eighth day to begin Her new cycle. Mary is the one to bring him the anointment, or the *new life* he is to begin after his allegorical death.

There is a Sumerian story written in the form of a poem, titled

"The Descent of Inanna." Inanna, Queen of Heaven, always seen as one and the same with Venus, goes down to the underworld to see her sister, Ereshkigal, who is Queen of the Dead. Ereshkigal proceeds to make Her sister enter through the seven gates, and to strip off a piece of clothing or jewelry at each gate until She comes to the throne room. When Inanna asks why She is stripped of her crown and all garments, the gatekeeper Neti says to her, "Quiet, Inanna, the ways of the underworld are perfect. They may not be questioned."

Once Inanna makes it to the throne room, She is naked and shamed, much like Jesus. Judgment is passed upon Her and Ereshkigal sets the Eye of Death on Her. She is struck and killed by Her sister. It is after six days of Her death that the sister feels pain and regret for what she has done. Inanna is then fed the food and water of life, and She is resurrected on the eighth day. If Inanna is only dead for six days, how could her resurrection be the eighth? Inanna descended upon Day 1, and is not seen. The next day presumably She is dead, and for a further five days. On Day 8, She rises from the underworld, back to her position as morning star (in the synodic cycle) and as Queen of Heaven.

Jesus also compares himself to the morning star in Revelation 22:16 when he says, "I am the Root and the Offspring of David, and the bright Morning Star." He calls himself the bright morning star as he has risen as She does, on the eighth day of Her transitional phase between *evening* and *morning* star. Jesus too, is going through his transition between phases of his life, going from just a prophet who walks the streets, to High Priest, the Fisher King, the priest-king of Jerusalem.

Venus/Inanna goes down willingly to the underworld, is shamed, humbled, and struck (just as a Masonic initiate is). Then She is raised up, and takes back her place in heaven, as Jesus took his in the allegorical heaven of his church. When She rises, She is the bright morning star. Not only does Jesus rise on the eighth day like Venus, but he brings with him knowledge, or in esoteric tradition, *light*.

Venus being both one who will bravely venture into the underworld and rise up yet again would be a perfect candidate to be Master of the Lodge, more perfect than Mercury, as She is

Stele depicting King Meli-Shipak II beneath the Star of Ishtar, Louvre.

the third brightest light in the heavens. A beautiful depiction of the eight-pointed star of Venus can be seen on a relief carving found in the Louvre. The art dates back to the 12th century BC, and shows the King Meli-Shipak II sitting on his throne, master of his kingdom, beneath none other than Venus. Also in the sky are the Sun and the Moon. This art is extremely reminiscent of the depictions of the Three Lesser Lights. Isn't it interesting that these ancient people put Venus as the *light* overhead their king, their master? Instead of the Sun, the Moon, Sirius (which was the heavenly manifestation of the goddess Isis who was also been suggested as the third), or "Mercury?"

18.4 The Umbilical Cord of the Lodge

Within the lodge, a Mason does not walk between the Worshipful Master in the East and the altar, because the Master needs to keep an unbroken connection between himself and the Three Great Lights. The Three Great Lights provide the Master with Wisdom, Truth, and Light. The Three Great Lights themselves are the book of sacred law (usually the Bible), the compass, and

322

the square.

Upon learning of this rule of etiquette, it occurred to me that this is much the same as in Native American sweat lodge ceremonies. There is a stone umbilical cord that leads to the altar, or sometimes the fire pit with the stones. The umbilical cord must not be walked across by anyone but the leader of the sweat lodge, the medicine man or woman. Is this not the same thing?

The evidence to connect Masonic, and even earlier Templar, ritual with that of the indigenous people of the Americas appears blatantly obvious. The ritual of sweat lodge has been taking place amongst the Lakota people for nearly 2,000 years, since the first coming of White Buffalo Calf Woman, according to their tradition. This is since the time of Jesus and Magdalene. You have to wonder, where did this tradition come from? Was this a more ancient concept, of an umbilical cord in a lodge, or in a temple, that predated even the time that Jesus walked the Earth? Freemasonry largely has its origin based on the legends of King Solomon and his temple. It was beneath the Temple Mount the Knights Templar went and reportedly recovered some kind of treasure, in the depths of the womb of the Temple. Was it here that there was some kind of unbroken energy exchange, between altar and high priest? Just like in the Masonic lodge, the altar in Solomon's Temple faced East.

The idea of building a temple to face the East, the rising of Venus, but also the rising of the Sun, the two heavenly bodies that represent the god and goddess, go back even before the building of Solomon's Temple. The earliest pyramid ever built in Egypt was completed during the reign of the Pharaoh Sneferu sometime between 2613-2589 BC. The pyramid's temple faced *East.*

Was the concept of the energetic umbilical cord considered in the lodge? Is this something Freemasons introduced into the lodge all on their own, or were they influenced by their indigenous brethren and their sweat lodge? When did this tradition within Freemasonry begin? Was this a Templar tradition before it was a Masonic one?

18.5 The Blazing Star & the Weeping Virgin

The apron of the famous American explorer Merriweather

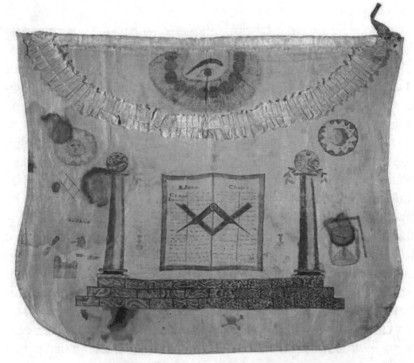

The Masonic Apron of Merriweather Lewis.

Lewis shows the Three Lesser Lights. The Sun, the Moon, and what in the middle? None other than the All Seeing Eye. Could the All Seeing Eye represent creator, or creatress? Venus, the Third Lesser Light? The Gnostic creation story tells us that it was Sophia, the Goddess of Wisdom who created Jehovah, the Demiurge God of the Material World. If Sophia is the Mother of All, would not the All Seeing Eye represent her omnipresence? Is it the divine feminine energy that is the creation energy of the dark energy, and dark matter?

In fact, within Freemasonry, the "Blazing Star" is associated with the All Seeing Eye. Many argue it also should be considered Mercury/Sirius, but the Blazing Star is clearly the five-pointed star, the ancient symbol of Venus. I came across a photo online of a Masonic coin, but could not find an origin, or any information about the coin in the picture.

Masonic coin.

324

What it certainly does show are the Three Lesser Lights, and the Venus symbol in a spot that is usually occupied by the letter G. Here the Venus star represents the Worshipful Master and harbors the letter G. Could this be because G stands for Goddess, as in the goddess in the heavens, Venus or even Sirius-Isis?

The Blazing Star, found in both the Fourth and the Ninth Degree of Scottish Rite Masonry, is considered the *star of direction*. The Blazing Star is meant to offer guidance to the initiate throughout their life. In the 28th Degree, the Freemason becomes the essence of the Blazing Star. The Mason "becomes like a blazing star, shining with brilliancy in the midst of darkness." Similar to how Jesus referred to himself as the bright Morning Star (Venus).

In February of 2022, my colleague and co-researcher, Scott Wolter, sent me photos of an interesting find he viewed in his own Masonic Lodge. This is a 19th century baldric.[1] At the bottom of the baldric is the Blazing Star with the G right in the middle once again.

She can be found in another American Masonic tradition, the *Broken Column* of the Third Degree. It is in this tradition that the story of the fall of one of the chief members of the Craft is taught. To the ancient Hebrews, the kings, princes and nobles were referred to as "pillars" of the nation. Mourning the symbolic death of the pillar is the *Weeping Virgin.* Who do we often see mourning at the foot of the cross? Mary Magdalene. She indeed is the one depicted as weeping at the feet of Jesus. This is reminiscent of an earlier initiation which was possibly part of their bridal chamber ritual, where she washes and anoints his feet with her oils.

The 1503 work by Cosimo Rosselli titled "The Crucifixion with the Madonna and Saints" depicts Mary Magdalene, who is often seen in red/orange and green, at the foot of the cross, like many other famous pieces of art. The mother Mary of Jesus is usually depicted in blue and red/pink. She is never the one at the foot of the cross, yet she is considered to be most intimate with Jesus being his mother, unless of course Jesus were to have a wife: Mary Magdalene.

Any crucifixion art will show the Magdalene weeping at her Master's feet, and Mary the Mother very near. The Weeping Virgin within Freemasonry also represents Magdalene, Venus, and Her position beneath the Sun at that time as we mentioned in an

[1] A belt for a sword or other piece of equipment, worn over one shoulder and reaching down to the opposite hip.

earlier chapter. The Broken Column is like the dying Sun God, or the life of Jesus the Master, which has been cut off too soon (allegorically). The dying Sun God throughout all religions and traditions is usually a younger man, like Jesus. This event is also witnessed in the heavens, for when Venus is an evening star, and shines Her Light (knowledge and Wisdom) in the Darkness, the Sun has already set, or has gone beneath the horizon and symbolically died. After the Sun has died, it is Venus who is bringing the Light, just like Mary Magdalene is instructed by Jesus after his allegorical death to continue his teachings.

The Weeping Virgin stands mourning over Her master, and Father Time stands behind Her. In the depictions of the Weeping Virgin, her long hair is displayed, just like Mary Magdalene's is always on display where She is seen in art. All of the other

The Crucifixion with the Madonna and Saints, Cosimo Rosselli, 1503.

The Weeping Virgin and Father Time.

women, including the Mother Mary, cover their hair, but Mary Magdalene's is always seen as being "disheveled." In the depictions, the Weeping Virgin's disheveled hair is being untangled by Father Time. This is an act of comfort, for many times when a young woman cries, her mother or father will brush her hair as a comforting gesture. It is interesting, because while this is an intimate act, it is not too intimate to interfere with grieving. As we have seen, long hair is also a symbol of power in many cultures, one of them being Nazarite, which Jesus and Magdalene both were. Later the Merovingians of France were said to have magic long hair, and Native American cultures believe long hair to be a symbol of Wisdom.

The Bringer of Life

In the artwork of Nicholas Flamel (1330-1418), Mary Magdalene is shown kneeling before the ictorious Lord with long blonde hair flowing down her back in the artwork found in Pomposa Abbey in Italy from between 1351-1360.

What is the significance of the objects the Weeping Virgin holds? In one hand, the Weeping Virgin holds an acacia sprig, an important Masonic symbol which represents immortality of the soul, and in another hand She holds an urn which would contain the cremated remains of the "broken column" or of Her master. Father Time stands behind Her; his presence reminds us that we are mortal, and only have so much time here on Earth. To the Weeping Virgin this may be both comforting, knowing Her soul is immortal and will once again meet with Her beloved deceased, but also scary, knowing Her time in the physical world is temporary.

It could almost be argued here that we are seeing the Holy Trinity: The Father (Time), the Son (Pillar/Sun), and the Holy Spirit (Mother/Goddess). Father Time has always seemed to be the model for which all art of the Christian god has been designed, so it is not surprising. However, these depictions could very well be symbolic for the grieving Isis over Her husband Osiris, and the resurrected Osiris standing behind Her comforting Her. In fact, it was labeled so in a picture that Scott Wolter shared with me from the Grand Lodge Library in New York.

The legend of Isis and Osiris, death and resurrection, are a monumental element of Freemasonry. It can even be seen in the Masonic phrase of distress, "Who would help the widow's son?" The widow most definitely being Isis, and the son of the widow being Horus. The tradition is played out through many ancient cultures, and specifically with Jesus.

18.6 The Not So Broken Pillar of Rosslyn Chapel, Scotland

Inside the chapel, there is a pillar with a story that is reminiscent of the Broken Column element of Freemasonry. This pillar is called the "Apprentice Pillar." Back during the medieval days of stonemasonry, boys trained many years as an apprentice beneath the Master Mason. They began typically at the age of 13, a number we know is very deeply tied to the sacred feminine, and were considered an apprentice until the age of 21. This is eight

328

years as an apprentice, and I cannot help but wonder if this has anything to do with the Venus cycle of the five-pointed star, which takes eight Earth years.

That being said, the story of the Apprentice Pillar has a gruesome side—it too is about a young man's life being cut short. Interestingly, it was once called the "Prince's Pillar" before it got the name Apprentice Pillar. Just like the Broken Column likely represents Jesus, who was a prince by birthright, and the Weeping Virgin the Magdalene.

Rosslyn Chapel's fact sheet about the pillar in question tells us the story:

> There was once a Master Mason in charge of building Rosslyn Chapel. This Master Mason had an idea of how marvellous the Chapel could be, and he planned to make a beautiful pillar decorated with all sorts of wondrous leaves and vines. But when his pillar was finished, he was dissatisfied. He knew it could have looked even better—more beautiful and more alive—but it was his own skill and craftsmanship that had fallen short. What he needed to do, he felt, was to travel abroad and see the amazing cathedrals of Europe. If he could study them, he would be able to come back with the knowledge needed to create the pillar of his dreams for Rosslyn Chapel.
>
> Sir William St Clair gave him permission to travel, and he left.
>
> He was gone a long time. Years, in fact. And while he was gone, a lowly apprentice boy had a vision, in which he realised how this amazing pillar could be made. He set to work, and created the feat of stone carving that you see today—the famous 'Apprentice Pillar'.
>
> When the Master Mason returned, he felt he finally had it in him to create the pillar he wanted. Into Rosslyn he came, full of ambition and plans. Imagine his feelings, when he saw the Apprentice Pillar, standing there already in all its glory! And then imagine his anger when he discovered that it was not even a craftsman of high status who had made it, but a lowly apprentice! He flew into a

rage of jealousy, picked up his mason's mallet, and struck the young apprentice on the head, killing him outright. His fellow craftsmen and Sir William were appalled.

The Mason was taken to trial for the murder and was hanged according to the law of the time, but the other masons felt this punishment was not enough. They created an image of the young apprentice's head, with the gash on his forehead, and placed it on the Chapel wall as a memorial. And they made an image of Master Mason as well, and placed it where his gaze would rest on the Apprentice Pillar for eternity.

Not only was it the Master Mason and the Apprentice who have been carved into the walls of the Chapel, but the "Weeping Mother" of the apprentice as well. This is the Rosslyn Chapel's version of the Weeping Virgin. The intricate work of the pillar is stunning, including the bottom portion which shows *eight* dragons guarding the pillar. Speculations have been made that the pillar was said to have represented the Tree of Life. Norse mythology reveals that their version of the tree is called Yggdrasil, and there is a dragon underneath called Niðhöggr which is trying to destroy all life by gnawing through the tree's roots. The Apprentice Pillar is one of 13 columns which support the chapel. Coincidence? The Apprentice Pillar, the Prince's Pillar, is found closest to the high altar of the Virgin Mary, the Lady Chapel, which is two steps higher than the ground. The Apprentice Pillar also stands tall next to the staircase that descends 22 steps down into the crypt.

Is there truly any treasure that lies at Rosslyn? What is this treasure? Is it coin, artifact, or knowledge? Whatever it may be, it appears to be safely guarded over by the goddess.

18.7 The Goddess and the Ionic Capital

Within the Fellowcraft Degree, the initiate learns of five different orders of architecture: Tuscan, Doric, Ionic, Corinthian, and Composite. There is one specific capital we must look at: the Ionic. Now the word Ionic is already interesting to us as we already know that Iona is a Hebrew word meaning dove, and that there is an isle in Scotland named for its shape of the dove. This is

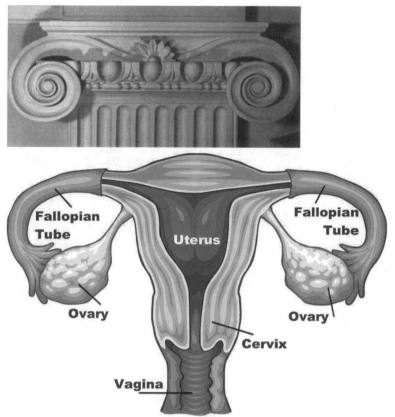

The Ionic Capital next to the Reproductive System.

the same isle that is rumored to be the burial place of Magdalene and her last son with Jesus, John Martinus. We have also already seen the use of the dove as a symbol of reverence of the goddess. With this in mind, let us take a look at the Ionic Capital.

The shape is undoubtedly similar to that of primitive depictions of the female reproductive system. One could argue it is not intended to depict the fallopian tubes and ovaries, but how could you support that argument? What *else* does the Ionic Capital look like to you? Knowing that the word Iona is Hebrew in origin and means dove, a symbol of the goddess, this seems to be far too many coincidences.

The Ionic order stems from an older form of classical architecture: the Aeolic order. This capital is slightly different as it appears *more* feminine in nature. In this capital, a palmette or what appears to be a clamshell in some cases rises between the two

Aeolic capital.

spirals, which would appear to be symbolic of the womb. A long time symbol of Venus is the clamshell, or scallop shell in fact. This depiction here was found on the Temple of Athena in Old Smyrna. An Aeolic capital on a temple dedicated to a *goddess* of old, how am I not surprised?

18.8 The Goddess and the Grand Hailing Sign of Distress

Earlier in section 5.5 (see photos), I pointed out that Scott Wolter proposed that the Tanit symbol was actually a representation of the constellation Virgo above. Both Tanit and Virgo show us a feminine icon with their hands up in much the same fashion as the *Grand Hailing Sign of Distress* found in the third degree of Blue Lodge.

When a Mason calls out to another brother in distress, his hands go up in the exact same position. Why? Where did the symbol originate? Was it to mirror the constellation Virgo in the heavens? When a Mason throws his hands up in this manner, is he really calling upon the goddess in the heavens for help?

The ancient Jews used to pray in this fashion, with their hands up. This was part of the "Priestly Blessing" performed by the Kohanim (priests descended from Aaron). Later, early Christians adopted this posture for their own prayer. It is referred to as the "orant." Orant is a medieval Latin word that translates literally to "one who is praying (or) pleading."

This symbol can even be found in ancient Egypt. The depiction on page 70 shows Isis flanked by two birds: a hawk on the left which served as a guardian of the earth, and a vulture on the right, representing death, specifically the death of Osiris, Isis with Her hands up signaling Her distress. You cannot forget that in section 17.6 we described the statue of a very pregnant Magdalene with Her hands up also, mourning the dead Jesus. In this depiction of Isis I must note that She too is wearing the colors of the Magdalene, green and orange/red.

The Grand Hailing Sign of distress is a tradition associated with a "widow" and the sacred feminine going back to ancient Egypt, and likely long before. Was it because they were mirroring the constellation Virgo, the goddess in the heavens, praying to Her? Did this tradition of invoking the goddess carry on into Judaism in the same fashion?

As above, so below...

18.9 The Mother Lodge

Freemasonry ultimately was born in Scotland, stemming from other ancient traditions, many of the legends and rites being strikingly Egyptian. Is it any surprise, considering there are many old ties to Egypt in Scotland, from Queen Scota to Freemasonry? There are arguments over which lodge came first, The Lodge of Edinburgh: Mary's Chapel, or the so-called Mother Lodge of Scotland, Kilwinning Lodge.

Robert the Bruce was said to have founded an order similar to Freemasonry. This order was said to have been founded at an

Venus guarding the door of the Mother Lodge of Scotland.

already existing Masonic Lodge. Thory, in the Acta Latomorum, gives the following chronicle: "Robert Bruce, King of Scotland, under the title of Robert I, created the Order of St. Andrew of Chardon, after the battle of Bannockburn, which was fought on the 24th of June, 1314. To this Order was afterwards united that of Herodem, for the sake of the Scotch Freemasons, who formed a part of the thirty thousand troops with whom he had fought an army of one hundred thousand Englishmen. King Robert reserved the title of Grand Master to himself and his successors forever, and founded the Royal Grand Lodge of Herodem at Kilwinning."

Alexander Lawrie, in his *The History of Freemasonry* (1804), argues that authentic documents have been presented proving that Kilwinning Lodge was in existence as early as the late 1400s, and likely even earlier. There was in fact a group that traveled mainland Europe and called themselves "Traveling Freemasons." According to records they may have traveled into Scotland as early as the 12th century, which is when activity in Kilwinning really begins. These men were very likely the architects of Kilwinning Abbey, which borders right against Kilwinning Lodge today.

The abbey was constructed in the late 1100s, and was dedicated to the Virgin Mary and Saint Winning. The monks that occupied the abbey were Tironensian Benedictine monks from Kelso Abbey

The East of the Mother Lodge of Scotland.

in the Scottish Borders. Around this time, there is evidence there was essentially a lodge on the property as well, functioning as a storage and meeting place for the architects of the abbey. Is it possible that these stonemasons were actually Freemasons? Or were they really just stonemasons? There are almost too many connections to deny. Kilwinning Abbey proceeded to have a very strong Templar presence. Kilwinning is located on the west coast of Scotland, situated on the Firth of Clyde. If the Templars had indeed fled to Scotland, it is very possible that they were to seek refuge here. There are also rumors that there was buried treasure beneath the abbey. Local residents have told tales of mysterious tunnels they came across as children, but unfortunately these tunnels have not been photographed or documented.

The Mother Lodge of Scotland, Kilwinning Lodge's website says, "The Lodge was founded in the chapter house within the Abbey and remained there until the reformation in 1560 when the Earl of Glencairn, a blood enemy of the Earls of Eglinton who hold a long tradition with the Lodge, sacked the Abbey." This proves there was a very early founding of the Kilwinning Lodge, and would point to this being the oldest Masonic Lodge in the world. Scott Wolter and I visited the Lodge in Kilwinning in December 2021. Upon arrival at the doorstep we found a beautiful floor mosaic depicting the Pentacle of Venus, surrounded by flowers.

While visiting, we made an exciting observation in the East. Up high in the East was the Masonic compass and square symbol, and just below this sat the symbol we have come to know so well in this book—the *five-pointed star.* The East was dedicated to Venus, to the goddess, within Freemasonry. Here it was: She guarded the door to the Mother Lodge, the very oldest Lodge in existence, and also could be found beaming in the East, above the Master of the Lodge. One of the Three Lesser Lights, indeed. This was not showing Her as the Blazing Star, but just as the plain old five-pointed star, reigning above the Master of the Lodge, and above all Masons. There She was—shining bright with all of Her Wisdom and Light. She is at the core structure of Freemasonry, Templarism, and so much more. She is known as Venus, the Blazing Star, Magdalene, Isis, Inanna/Ishtar, the Weeping Virgin, Lady Liberty, Queen of Heaven, and so many more names.

The goddess has never truly disappeared, She was only veiled, protected, as She is the Bringer of Life, creator of all, the cosmic mother of creation. The founding fathers of America knew this, and incorporated the sacred geometry to honor Her all over the capital city of the US.

The goddess has been hidden in plain sight for a long time. She has been suppressed, but She has never left us. No matter how hard the patriarchal societies of the modern world have tried to eradicate Her, She has prevailed, with a bright and shining strength. One day people will sing Her praise again, and tell the stories of old that have long since been passed down for thousands of years. She will return, just like many different cultures have prophesied. The Truth is She has always been there, but only if you knew where to look...

"Blessed are your eyes, for they see: and your ears, for they hear," once said Jesus (Matthew 13:16). With the eyes to see and the ears to hear, you will see Her everywhere.

Conclusions

Coming to the end of this chronological tale of the divine feminine throughout the course of history, I hope you begin to see that She is all around us, in everything that we do. In every spiritual, esoteric, and religious tradition we hold dear to our hearts, the Great Mother can be found. She is in Judaism, Christianity, and is not only the source of the *Messiah,* but the source of creation itself.

She is found in scientific beginnings, in the Big Bang as dark energy, the creation force that spurred every chaotic movement into motion that took billions of years and has brought you to reading this book. She was seen in Mother Earth, the breast from which all of life is sustained, the Mother of all Mothers. She offers her womb for us to bury our dead so they may be reborn. She provides us with water, shelter, natural medicine, and food. She has given us all we truly need. She is the pure embodiment of the soul that knows no such thing as materialism and greed; She only knows pure love, a Mother's love.

The indigenous people still honor Her today through their ceremonies, allowing men to have their own union in the womb of the Earth Mother to gain Her Wisdom since they do not bleed unto Her like women do. She is found above us in the Moon, who guides our menstrual cycles every month, bestowing Wisdom to the women that bleed with Her.

Ancient people around the world built stone monuments to Her, as passage tombs, dolmens, stone circles, and so much more for many thousands of years. At these monuments on Her feast days they sang and danced Her praise; rejoicing in Her infinite love. Hieros gamos rituals took place, looking to achieve union to be whole, perfect, and granted the Wisdom of the goddess.

The Messianic tradition was birthed by the acknowledgement that man may only be born of the Queen of Heaven, the cosmic creation force of the Dark Mother, Shakti, Isis, Venus, or whatever you choose to call Her. The ancient people looked to the heavens for their guidance and Wisdom; and they sought to do on earth as it was in heaven, thus honoring Her through the way of the Mashiach, making the queen the incarnation of the goddess who was literally giving birth to the god-kings. It was Her above all else that was revered. Somehow the ancients had some universal understanding of the creation of the cosmos, earth, and light. These were the same traditions that Mary, Mother of Jesus, and Her husband Joseph followed. Later, Jesus and Mary Magdalene followed in The Way of the Mystery, and Mary understood more than all of the disciples. She experienced Her own union with the Holy Sophia, the Holy Spirit.

The people began honoring Her through specific secret rituals thousands of years ago, which evolved into Mystery Traditions. In the medieval era the Knights Templar honored Her, keeping Her veiled to protect the ancient and natural ways, but preserved the sanctity of Her by building cathedrals in reverence to the Great Mother. They were named for the Christianized earthly version of the goddess, both Mother Mary and Mary Magdalene. She can be found in the modern Masonic lodges and degrees around the globe, reigning supreme in the East, being invoked when in distress. She maintains a flow of Wisdom from the altar to the Worshipful Master that may not be crossed by anyone but the Master, just as in indigenous sweat lodge ceremonies. The stream of Wisdom, in the case of the sweat lodge, is the stone built umbilical cord that may not be crossed by anyone but the leader of the sweat lodge.

The Founding Fathers who fought for freedom and liberty, fought also for a free state where they would not be persecuted for their own spirituality—for their own reverence of the goddess—as the Templars were in 1307. They looked to found a nation that allowed people to worship deity as they wished, because they knew that to find God-Goddess was to find yourself.

For so long women were suppressed, pushed down into the depths of the early patriarchy, where women became property, where they were meant to cover their heads and not speak their mind. What was it about the feminine spirit that scared men so much that they must literally cover them up, and silence them? The strength they had? The spiritual awareness, their interconnectedness to Source itself? With the fall of goddess worship and introduction of a single male god came the suppression of the feminine, the view that women were property to be owned by man, when prior to this women were revered as the goddess incarnate.

The Age of Aquarius, or the Age of the Grail Bearer, currently reigns over us. She is seen in the tarot deck as the Major Arcana card *The Star.* She brings balance, harmony, emotional understanding, and infinite Wisdom; to the Egyptians She was *Ma'at.* She is the constant stream of water, of love, and of Wisdom that flows into the Universe. This is what the world has been missing for far too long.

It is time for Her return.

GIANTS ON RECORD
By Jim Vieira and Hugh Newman
Over a 200-year period thousands of newspaper reports, town and county histories, letters, photos, diaries, and scientific journals have documented the existence of an ancient race of giants in North America. Extremely large skeletons ranging from 7 feet up to a staggering 18 feet tall have been reportedly uncovered in prehistoric mounds, burial chambers, caves, geometric earthworks, and ancient battlefields. Strange anatomic anomalies such as double rows of teeth, horned skulls, massive jaws that fit over a modern face, and elongated skulls have also been reported. Color Section.
420 pages. 6x9 Paperback. Illustrated. $19.95. Code: GOR

COVERT WARS & BREAKAWAY CIVILIZATIONS
By Joseph P. Farrell

Farrell delves into the creation of breakaway civilizations by the Nazis in South America and other parts of the world. He discusses the advanced technology that they took with them at the end of the war and the psychological war that they waged for decades on America and NATO. He investigates the secret space programs currently sponsored by the breakaway civilizations and the current militaries in control of planet Earth. Plenty of astounding accounts, documents and speculation on the incredible alternative history of hidden conflicts and secret space programs that began when World War II officially "ended."
292 Pages. 6x9 Paperback. Illustrated. $19.95. Code: BCCW

THE ENIGMA OF CRANIAL DEFORMATION
Elongated Skulls of the Ancients
By David Hatcher Childress and Brien Foerster
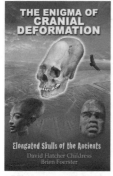
In a book filled with over a hundred astonishing photos and a color photo section, Childress and Foerster take us to Peru, Bolivia, Egypt, Malta, China, Mexico and other places in search of strange elongated skulls and other cranial deformation. The puzzle of why diverse ancient people—even on remote Pacific Islands—would use head-binding to create elongated heads is mystifying. Where did they even get this idea? Did some people naturally look this way—with long narrow heads? Were they some alien race? Were they an elite race that roamed the entire planet? Why do anthropologists rarely talk about cranial deformation and know so little about it? Color Section.
250 Pages. 6x9 Paperback. Illustrated. $19.95. Code: ECD

ARK OF GOD
The Incredible Power of the Ark of the Covenant
By David Hatcher Childress

Childress takes us on an incredible journey in search of the truth about (and science behind) the fantastic biblical artifact known as the Ark of the Covenant. This object made by Moses at Mount Sinai—part wooden-metal box and part golden statue—had the power to create "lightning" to kill people, and also to fly and lead people through the wilderness. The Ark of the Covenant suddenly disappears from the Bible record and what happened to it is not mentioned. Was it hidden in the underground passages of King Solomon's temple and later discovered by the Knights Templar? Was it taken through Egypt to Ethiopia as many Coptic Christians believe? Childress looks into hidden history, astonishing ancient technology, and a 3,000-year-old mystery that continues to fascinate millions of people today. Color section.
420 Pages. 6x9 Paperback. Illustrated. $22.00 Code: AOG

ANDROMEDA: THE SECRET FILES
The Flying Submarines of the SS
By David Hatcher Childress

Childress brings us the amazing story of the German Andromeda craft, designed and built during WWII. Along with flying discs, the Germans were making long, cylindrical airships that are commonly called motherships—large craft that house several smaller disc craft. It was not until 1989 that a German researcher named Ralf Ettl, living in London, received an anonymous packet of photographs and documents concerning the planning and development of at least three types of unusual craft—including the Andromeda. Chapters include: Gravity's Rainbow; The Motherships; The MJ-12, UFOs and the Korean War; The Strange Case of Reinhold Schmidt; Secret Cities of the Winged Serpent; The Green Fireballs; Submarines That Can Fly; The Breakaway Civilization; more. Includes a 16-page color section.
382 Pages. 6x9 Paperback. Illustrated. $22.00 Code: ASF

GODS AND SPACEMEN THROUGHOUT HISTORY
Did Ancient Aliens Visit Earth in the Past?
By W. Raymond Drake

From prehistory, flying saucers have been seen in our skies. As mankind sends probes beyond the fringes of our galaxy, we must ask ourselves: "Has all this happened before? Could extraterrestrials have landed on Earth centuries ago?" Drake spent many years digging through huge archives of material, looking for supposed anomalies that could support his scenarios of space aliens impacting human history. Chapters include: Spacemen; The Golden Age; Sons of the Gods; Lemuria; Atlantis; Ancient America; Aztecs and Incas; India; Tibet; China; Japan; Egypt; The Great Pyramid; Babylon; Israel; Greece; Italy; Ancient Rome; Scandinavia; Britain; Saxon Times; Norman Times; The Middle Ages; The Age of Reason; Today; Tomorrow; more.
280 Pages. 6x9 Paperback. Illustrated. $18.95. Code: GSTH

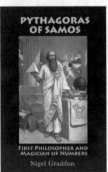

PYTHAGORAS OF SAMOS
First Philosopher and Magician of Numbers
By Nigel Graddon

This comprehensive account comprises both the historical and metaphysical aspects of Pythagoras' philosophy and teachings. In Part 1, the work draws on all known biographical sources as well as key extracts from the esoteric record to paint a fascinating picture of the Master's amazing life and work. Topics covered include the unique circumstances of Pythagoras' birth, his forty-year period of initiations into all the world's ancient mysteries, his remarkable meeting with a physician from the mysterious Etruscan community, Part 2 comprises, for the first time in a publicly available work, a metaphysical interpretation of Pythagoras' Science of Numbers.
294 Pages. 6x9 Paperback. Illustrated. $18.95. Code: PYOS

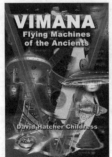

VIMANA:
Flying Machines of the Ancients
by David Hatcher Childress

According to early Sanskrit texts the ancients had several types of airships called vimanas. Like aircraft of today, vimanas were used to fly through the air from city to city; to conduct aerial surveys of uncharted lands; and as delivery vehicles for awesome weapons. David Hatcher Childress, popular *Lost Cities* author, takes us on an astounding investigation into tales of ancient flying machines. In his new book, packed with photos and diagrams, he consults ancient texts and modern stories and presents astonishing evidence that aircraft, similar to the ones we use today, were used thousands of years ago in India, Sumeria, China and other countries. Includes a 24-page color section.
408 Pages. 6x9 Paperback. Illustrated. $22.95. Code: VMA

THE LOST WORLD OF CHAM
The Trans-Pacific Voyages of the Champa
By David Hatcher Childress

The mysterious Cham, or Champa, peoples of Southeast Asia formed a megalith-building, seagoing empire that extended into Indonesia, Tonga, and beyond—a transoceanic power that reached Mexico and South America. The Champa maintained many ports in what is today Vietnam, Cambodia, and Indonesia and their ships plied the Indian Ocean and the Pacific, bringing Chinese, African and Indian traders to far off lands, including Olmec ports on the Pacific Coast of Central America. Topics include: Cham and Khem: Egyptian Influence on Cham; The Search for Metals; The Basalt City of Nan Madol; Elephants and Buddhists in North America; The Cham and Lake Titicaca; Easter Island and the Cham; the Magical Technology of the Cham; tons more. 24-page color section.
328 Pages. 6x9 Paperback. Illustrated. $22.00 Code: LPWC

ADVENTURES OF A HASHISH SMUGGLER
by Henri de Monfreid

Nobleman, writer, adventurer and inspiration for the swashbuckling gun runner in the *Adventures of Tintin*, Henri de Monfreid lived by his own account "a rich, restless, magnificent life" as one of the great travelers of his or any age. The son of a French artist who knew Paul Gaugin as a child, de Monfreid sought his fortune by becoming a collector and merchant of the fabled Persian Gulf pearls. He was then drawn into the shadowy world of arms trading, slavery, smuggling and drugs. Infamous as well as famous, his name is inextricably linked to the Red Sea and the raffish ports between Suez and Aden in the early years of the twentieth century. De Monfreid (1879 to 1974) had a long life of many adventures around the Horn of Africa where he dodged pirates as well as the authorities.
284 Pages. 6x9 Paperback. $16.95. Illustrated. Code AHS

NORTH CAUCASUS DOLMENS
In Search of Wonders
By Boris Loza, Ph.D.

Join Boris Loza as he travels to his ancestral homeland to uncover and explore dolmens firsthand. Throughout this journey, you will discover the often hidden, and surprisingly forbidden, perspective about the mysterious dolmens: their ancient powers of fertility, healing and spiritual connection. Chapters include: Ancient Mystic Megaliths; Who Built the Dolmens?; Why the Dolmens were Built; Asian Connection; Indian Connection; Greek Connection; Olmec and Maya Connection; Sun Worshippers; Dolmens and Archeoastronomy; Location of Dolmen Quarries; Hidden Power of Dolmens; and much more! Tons of Illustrations! A fascinating book of little-seen megaliths. Color section.
252 Pages. 5x9 Paperback. Illustrated. $24.00. Code NCD

GIANTS: MEN OF RENOWN
By Denver Michaels

Michaels runs down the many stories of giants around the world and testifies to the reality of their existence in the past. Chapters and subchapters on: Giants in the Bible; Texts; Tales from the Maya; Stories from the South Pacific; Giants of Ancient America; The Stonish Giants; Mescalero Tales; The Nahullo; Mastodons, Mammoths & Mound Builders; Pawnee Giants; The Si-Te-Cah; Tsul 'Kalu; The Titans & Olympians; The Hyperboreans; European Myths; The Giants of Britain & Ireland; Norse Giants; Myths from the Indian Subcontinent; Daityas, Rakshasas, & More; Jainism: Giants & Inconceivable Lifespans; The Conquistadors Meet the Sons of Anak; Cliff-Dwelling Giants; The Giants of the Channel Islands; Strange Tablets & Other Artifacts; more. Tons of illustrations with an 8-page color section.
320 Pages. 6x9 Paperback. Illustrated. $22.00. Code: GMOR

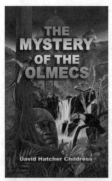

THE MYSTERY OF THE OLMECS
by David Hatcher Childress

The Olmecs were not acknowledged to have existed as a civilization until an international archeological meeting in Mexico City in 1942. Now, the Olmecs are slowly being recognized as the Mother Culture of Mesoamerica, having invented writing, the ball game and the "Mayan" Calendar. But who were the Olmecs? Where did they come from? What happened to them? How sophisticated was their culture? Why are many Olmec statues and figurines seemingly of foreign peoples such as Africans, Europeans and Chinese? Is there a link with Atlantis? In this heavily illustrated book, join Childress in search of the lost cities of the Olmecs! Chapters include: The Mystery of Quizuo; The Mystery of Transoceanic Trade; The Mystery of Cranial Deformation; more.
296 Pages. 6x9 Paperback. Illustrated. Bibliography. Color Section. $20.00. Code: MOLM

ABOMINABLE SNOWMEN: LEGEND COME TO LIFE
The Story of Sub-Humans on Six Continents from the Early Ice Age Until Today
by Ivan T. Sanderson

Do "Abominable Snowmen" exist? Prepare yourself for a shock. In the opinion of one of the world's leading naturalists, not one, but possibly four kinds, still walk the earth! Do they really live on the fringes of the towering Himalayas and the edge of myth-haunted Tibet? From how many areas in the world have factual reports of wild, strange, hairy men emanated? Reports of strange apemen have come in from every continent, except Antarctica.
525 pages. 6x9 Paperback. Illustrated. Bibliography. Index. $16.95. Code: ABML

LEY LINES OF THE UK AND USA
By David R. Cowan with Anne Silk

Chapters include: Megalithic Engineering; Burial Grounds across Scotland; Following a Straight Ley Line to its Source; Saint Columba and Iona; The Royal Triangle of Great Britain; The Strange Behavior of Ley Lines; The Dance of the Dragon; Ley Lines in the USA; The Secret Knowledge of the Freemasons; Spirit Paths; The Occult Knowledge of the Nazis; How to Use Divining Rods; The Amazing Power of the Maze; more. Tons of illustrations, all in color!
184 Pages. 7x9 Paperback. All Color. Profusely Illustrated. Index. $24.00. Code: LLUK

THE CHILDREN OF MU
By James Churchward

According to Churchward, the lost Pacific continent of Mu was the site of the Garden of Eden and the home of 64,000,000 inhabitants known as the Naacals. In this, his second book, first published in 1931, Churchward tells the story of the colonial expansion of Mu and the influence of the highly developed Mu culture on the rest of the world. Her first colonies were in North America and the Orient, while other colonies had been started in India, Egypt and Yucatan. Chapters include: The Origin of Man; The Eastern Lines; Ancient North America; Stone Tablets from the Valley of Mexico; South America; Atlantis; Western Europe; The Greeks; Egypt; The Western Lines; India; Southern India; The Great Uighur Empire; Babylonia; Intimate Hours with the Rishi; more. A fascinating book on the diffusion of mankind around the world—originating in a now lost continent in the Pacific! Tons of illustrations!
270 Pages. 6x9 Paperback. Illustrated. $19.95. Code: COMU

ANCIENT ALIENS ON THE MOON
By Mike Bara

What did NASA find in their explorations of the solar system that they may have kept from the general public? How ancient really are these ruins on the Moon? Using official NASA and Russian photos of the Moon, Bara looks at vast cityscapes and domes in the Sinus Medii region as well as glass domes in the Crisium region. Bara also takes a detailed look at the mission of Apollo 17 and the case that this was a salvage mission, primarily concerned with investigating an opening into a massive hexagonal ruin near the landing site. Chapters include: The History of Lunar Anomalies; The Early 20th Century; Sinus Medii; To the Moon Alice!; Mare Crisium; Yes, Virginia, We Really Went to the Moon; Apollo 17; more. Tons of photos of the Moon examined for possible structures and other anomalies. **248 Pages. 6x9 Paperback. Illustrated.. $19.95. Code: AAOM**

ANCIENT ALIENS ON MARS
By Mike Bara

Bara brings us this lavishly illustrated volume on alien structures on Mars. Was there once a vast, technologically advanced civilization on Mars, and did it leave evidence of its existence behind for humans to find eons later? Did these advanced extraterrestrial visitors vanish in a solar system wide cataclysm of their own making, only to make their way to Earth and start anew? Was Mars once as lush and green as the Earth, and teeming with life? Chapters include: War of the Worlds; The Mars Tidal Model; The Death of Mars; Cydonia and the Face on Mars; The Monuments of Mars; The Search for Life on Mars; The True Colors of Mars and The Pathfinder Sphinx; more. Color section. **252 Pages. 6x9 Paperback. Illustrated. $19.95. Code: AMAR**

ANCIENT ALIENS ON MARS II
By Mike Bara

Using data acquired from sophisticated new scientific instruments like the Mars Odyssey THEMIS infrared imager, Bara shows that the region of Cydonia overlays a vast underground city full of enormous structures and devices that may still be operating. He peels back the layers of mystery to show images of tunnel systems, temples and ruins, and exposes the sophisticated NASA conspiracy designed to hide them. Bara also tackles the enigma of Mars' hollowed out moon Phobos, and exposes evidence that it is artificial. Long-held myths about Mars, including claims that it is protected by a sophisticated UFO defense system, are examined. Data from the Mars rovers Spirit, Opportunity and Curiosity are examined; everything from fossilized plants to mechanical debris is exposed in images taken directly from NASA's own archives. **294 Pages. 6x9 Paperback. Illustrated. $19.95. Code: AAM2**

ANCIENT TECHNOLOGY IN PERU & BOLIVIA
By David Hatcher Childress

Childress speculates on the existence of a sunken city in Lake Titicaca and reveals new evidence that the Sumerians may have arrived in South America 4,000 years ago. He demonstrates that the use of "keystone cuts" with metal clamps poured into them to secure megalithic construction was an advanced technology used all over the world, from the Andes to Egypt, Greece and Southeast Asia. He maintains that only power tools could have made the intricate articulation and drill holes found in extremely hard granite and basalt blocks in Bolivia and Peru, and that the megalith builders had to have had advanced methods for moving and stacking gigantic blocks of stone, some weighing over 100 tons. **340 Pages. 6x9 Paperback. Illustrated.. $19.95 Code: ATP**

ORDER FORM

10% Discount When You Orde 3 or More Items

One Adventure Place
P.O. Box 74
Kempton, Illinois 60946
United States of America
Tel.: 815-253-6390 • Fax: 815-253-6300
Email: auphq@frontiernet.net
http://www.adventuresunlimitedpress.com

ORDERING INSTRUCTIONS

✓ Remit by USD$ Check, Money Order or Credit Card

✓ Visa, Master Card, Discover & AmEx Accepted

✓ Paypal Payments Can Be Made To:

   info@wexclub.com

✓ Prices May Change Without Notice

✓ 10% Discount for 3 or More Items

SHIPPING CHARGES

United States

✓ POSTAL BOOK RATE

✓ Postal Book Rate { $5.00 First Item
                     50¢ Each Additional Item

✓ Priority Mail { $8.50 First Item
                  $2.00 Each Additional Item

✓ UPS { $9.00 First Item (Minimum 5 Books)
        $1.50 Each Additional Item

NOTE: UPS Delivery Available to Mainland USA Only

Canada

✓ Postal Air Mail { $19.00 First Item
                    $3.00 Each Additional Item

✓ Personal Checks or Bank Drafts MUST BE

   US$ and Drawn on a US Bank

✓ Canadian Postal Money Orders OK

✓ Payment MUST BE US$

All Other Countries

✓ Sorry, No Surface Delivery!

✓ Postal Air Mail { $29.00 First Item
                    $7.00 Each Additional Item

✓ Checks and Money Orders MUST BE US$
   and Drawn on a US Bank or branch.

✓ Paypal Payments Can Be Made in US$ To:
   info@wexclub.com

SPECIAL NOTES

✓ RETAILERS: Standard Discounts Available

✓ BACKORDERS: We Backorder all Out-of-Stock Items Unless Otherwise Requested

✓ PRO FORMA INVOICES: Available on Request

✓ DVD Return Policy: Replace defective DVDs only

ORDER ONLINE AT: www.adventuresunlimitedpress.com

10% Discount When You Order 3 or More Items!

Please check: ✓

☐ This is my first order   ☐ I have ordered before

Name	
Address	
City	
State/Province	Postal Code
Country	
Phone: Day	Evening
Fax	Email

Item Code	Item Description	Qty	Total

Please check: ✓

	Subtotal ▶
	Less Discount-10% for 3 or more items ▶
☐ Postal-Surface	Balance ▶
☐ Postal-Air Mail (Priority in USA)	Illinois Residents 6.25% Sales Tax ▶
	Previous Credit ▶
☐ UPS	Shipping ▶
(Mainland USA only)	Total (check/MO in USD$ only) ▶

☐ Visa/MasterCard/Discover/American Express

Card Number:

Expiration Date: Security Code:

✓ SEND A CATALOG TO A FRIEND: